ROME IN AFRICA

third edition

Nearly three thousand years ago the Phoenicians set up trading colonies on the coast of North Africa, and ever since successive civilizations have been imposed on the local inhabitants, largely from outside. Carthaginians, Romans, Vandals, Byzantines, Arabs, Turks, French and Italians have all occupied the region in their time.

The Romans governed this part of Africa for six hundred years. Throughout the region their genius for building was readily apparent: there were some six hundred cities, twelve thousand miles of roads and hundreds of aqueducts, some fifty miles long. The remains of many of these structures can be seen today. At the height of its prosperity, during the second and third centuries AD, the area was the granary of Rome, and produced more olive oil than Italy itself.

The broadening horizons of the Roman Empire provided scope for the particular talents of a number of Africa's sons: the writers Terence and Apuleius; the first African Roman Emperor Septimius Severus; famous Christian theologians like Tertullian and Augustine.

Susan Raven recounts the story of this important part of the Roman Empire in North Africa, drawing on a wide variety of historical and archaeological evidence in addition to her own experience of the region, and revivifies the ghosts of the crumbling remains.

Susan Raven is a journalist. She is the co-author, with Alison Weir, of *Women in History.*

ROME IN AFRICA

third edition

Susan Raven

London and New York

First published 1969 by Evans Brothers Limited
Second edition published 1984 by Longman Group

Third edition published 1993
by Routledge
2 Park Square, Milton Park, Abingdon, Oxon, OX14 4RN

Simultaneously published in the USA and Canada
by Routledge
270 Madison Ave, New York NY 10016

Reprinted 1998, 2002

Transferred to Digital Printing 2005

Routledge is an imprint of the Taylor & Francis Group

© 1969, 1984, 1993 Susan Raven

Set in 10/12 pt Palatino by
Selwood Systems, Midsomer Norton

British Library Cataloguing in Publication Data
Raven, Susan
Rome in Africa. – 3rd rev. ed.
1. Africa, North – History – To 647
I. Title
961   DT167

Library of Congress Cataloguing in Publication Data
Raven, Susan.
Rome in Africa.
Bibliography: p.
Includes index.
1. Africa, North – History – To 647. 2. Romans – Africa,
North. I. Title.
DT198.R38   1984   939'.7   84–4423

ISBN 0–415–08261–7
0–415–08150–5 (pbk)

This edition is dedicated
to Professor Colin Wells and his students
at Trinity University, San Antonio, Texas,
who asked for it

Excudent alii spirantia mollius aera,
Credo equidem, vivos ducent de marmore voltus,
Orabunt causas melius, caelique meatus
Describent radio, et surgentia sidera dicent:
Tu regere imperio populos, Romane, memento.
Hae tibi erunt artes, pacique imponere morem,
Parcere subiectis, et debellare superbos.
                    Virgil, *Aeneid VI*, l. 847–53

Let others fashion from bronze more lifelike, breathing images –
For so they shall – and evoke living faces from marble;
Others excel as orators, others track with their instruments
The planets circling in heaven and predict when stars will appear.
But, Romans, never forget that government is your medium!
Be this your art: – to practise men in the habit of peace,
Generosity to the conquered, and firmness against aggressors.
        – Anchises to his son Aeneas, from *The Aeneid of Virgil*
        translated by C. Day Lewis, first published 1952
        (Hogarth Press 1961)

CONTENTS

CONTENTS

ILLUSTRATIONS

Site Plans

PREFACE

I received much kindness and hospitality in North Africa during the autumn of 1965, for which I shall always be grateful. In particular, I owe much to Cecil Hourani, then Director of the Centre Culturel International at Hammamet, Mohammad Bellamine, Governor of Kasserine, and his wife, and, in Algiers, Shelby Dawbarn and Simon Dawbarn, at that time Counsellor at the British Embassy. Moncef Ounaies was kind enough to rescue my car from the Tunis customs, and a number of total strangers on various occasions mended its five punctures, twice patched up its electrical system on the open road, and once pushed it over several hundred yards of mud when I had imprudently embarked on a detour. Collectively they made my first visit to North Africa an extremely happy one.

At the Institut National d'Archéologie et d'Arts in Tunis the Director and his staff allowed me to use the library; the Directors of the Musée National du Bardo in Tunis, the Musée Stéphane Gsell in Algiers, the Archaeological Museum in Tripoli and the museums at Cherchel, Timgad, Sousse and Sfax permitted me to take photographs of exhibits on display; and Khaled Abdul Wahab, of El Djem, lent me stills from his film of the Dominus Julius and other mosaics in the Bardo Museum. I am very grateful to them all.

Professor W.H.C. Frend, of Cambridge University, was kind enough to read the first edition of this book in manuscript, for which I owe him my especial thanks. He did his best to preserve me from error, and if he did not always succeed the fault was never his.

That first edition was published by Evans Bros. in 1969. Since then, there has been much new research both historical and archaeological. For help in updating and revising *Rome in Africa* for its second edition, published by Longman in 1984, I had to thank in particular Mr Charles Daniels, Mr Henry Hurst, Professor Barri Jones, Dr Timothy Potter and Mr C.R. Whittaker, and Professor Barry Cunliffe for pointing me in the right direction. I am still most grateful to them for their advice and encouragement. They kept me from many errors, if not all: those that remained were of course mine and not theirs. I also owed a large debt to Janet Brown and

xiv

Ruins of the two-storey basilica at Leptis Magna, Libya, built by
Septimius Severus and his son Caracalla

Janice Paveley and the designers Ann Samuel and Liz Black at Longman for their care and hard work – now supplemented by that of Sue Bilton and Heather McCallum at Routledge, for which I thank them. This third edition is substantially the 1984 edition, but brought up to date as far as possible with considerable help from Professors Colin Wells, Barri Jones and Graeme Barker, Dr D.J. Mattingly, Dr John Dore and Mr Henry Hurst. I am extremely grateful to them all.

Finally, I owe particular thanks to Richard Stoneman at Routledge for listening when Colin Wells, now at Trinity University, San Antonio, Texas, urged him to reprint this book; and even more to Colin Wells himself, who, when the 1984 edition went out of print, did something about it. Thereafter a stream of comments, corrections, reading lists and invaluable suggestions of all kinds poured out of my fax machine, usually in the middle of the night. Looking forward to reading them made getting up in the morning one of the pleasures of the autumn of 1991.

The author on the steps of the capitol at Volubilis, Morocco

London, January 1992

ACKNOWLEDGEMENTS

We are grateful to the following for permission to reproduce copyright photographs:

Photothèque du Musée du Bardo for pages 22 (left and right), 28 and 114 (upper); Bildarchiv Preussischer Kulturbesitz for page 132; British Museum for pages 8 and 203; C.D. Collison (Priory Productions Limited) for page 99; Professor W.H.C. Frend for pages 157 and 185; Steve Herr for pages xvi, xxxiii and 57; Barri Jones for page 16; Adrian Turner for pages xv, 2 and 120 (lower); Musei Vaticani for page 35; Khaled Abdul Wahab for pages 79, 86, 90, 93, 114 (lower) and 118; Roger Wood for pages 17, 107 (upper), 113, 136 and 155.

The following photographs have been taken from the first edition of *Rome in Africa* by Susan Raven, as we have been unable to trace the copyright holders. We would be grateful for any information that would enable us to do so:

Pages 6, 39, 68 and 69 (*Fossatum Africae* by Jean Baradez, Paris), 75 (Compagnie Aérienne de Photographie), 76 (French Air Force), 97, 153 (*Some Authentic Acts of the Early Martyrs* by E.C.E. Owen, Oxford University Press), 157 (Marcel Bovis), 166 (Images – FRIKHA).

All other photographs by the author.

The publishers are grateful to the following for their kind permission for the use of copyright material as sources for the site plans shown on pages 232–240: to Swan Hellenic Cruises for the plans of Carthage, Dougga, Thuburbo Maius, Sabratha and Leptis Magna; to Pneu Michelin, publishers of the *Michelin Guide to Morocco*, 4th Edition, to North Carolina Press, publishers of *The North African Stones Speak* by Paul MacKendrick, to Philippe Leveau and J.L. Paillet for the site plan of Volubilis; to Librairie Hachette for the site plan of Cherchel (Iol Caesarea). The publishers also acknowledge grateful thanks to I.M. Barton for source material for the maps of the Roman Empire in North Africa at different periods in history, as shown on pages xxviii and xxix.

All maps and plans are drawn by Swanston Graphics, Derby, England.

CHRONOLOGY

c. 1000 BC	Phoenicians from eastern Mediterranean acquire trading concession in Spain and found ports of call in Sicily, North Africa and elsewhere in the western Mediterranean.
c. 814 BC	Traditional date of foundation of Carthage by Phoenicians fleeing from Tyre with Princess Dido. (Earliest finds at Carthage date from a century later.)
Late 8th century BC	Arrival of Greek colonists in the western Mediterranean; gradually Carthage becomes leader and protector of Phoenician colonies in the west.
Mid 6th century BC	Carthage sends an army over to Sicily to help Phoenician colonies there against Greek cities; beginning of intermittent warfare.
510 BC	Carthage expels Greek colony from Tripolitania.
509 BC	Foundation of Roman Republic: first Rome-Carthage trade agreement.
480 BC	Carthaginian fleet and mercenary army defeated by Greeks at battle of Himera; Carthaginians withdraw from Sicily.
Early or mid 5th century BC	Rome becomes leading city of central Italy. Voyage of Hanno down the West African coast; voyage of Himilco up the Atlantic coast of Spain.
5th century BC	Carthage conquers and colonizes her African hinterland.
409 BC	Carthage sends an army to Sicily to fight the Greeks once more: beginning of a century of warfare in Sicily.
4th century BC	Numidian and Moorish kingdoms begin to form beyond Carthaginian frontiers; central Italy under direct control of Rome.
310 BC	Cape Bon, near Carthage, invaded by army under

	Agathocles of Syracuse. Carthaginians sacrifice 500 children to Baal Hammon.
307 BC	Defeat of Agathocles' expedition.
3rd century BC	Rome controls almost all the Italian peninsula south of the River Po.
264–241 BC	First Punic War with Rome, fought mostly in Sicily and at sea.
256 BC	Regulus invades Africa at Clupea (Kelibia, Cape Bon) in 256 BC, but is defeated the following year.
241 BC	Carthaginian fleet destroyed at the battle of the Aegates Islands; Carthage sues for peace, and leaves Sicily.
240–237 BC	The Mercenary War: the revolt of Carthage's army – finally defeated by Hamilcar Barca.
237 BC	Hamilcar – accompanied by son-in-law Hasdrubal and son Hannibal – leaves to conquer new Carthaginian empire in Spain; after 16 years, Carthaginians control whole of southern Spain.
218–202 BC	Second Punic War.
218 BC	Hannibal's crossing of the Alps.
216 BC	Rome defeated at the battle of Cannae; followed by long war of attrition in southern Italy.
209–206 BC	Conquest of Carthaginians in Spain by Roman army under Scipio.
204 BC	Scipio invades Africa.
202 BC	Scipio defeats Hannibal at the battle of Zama.
Early 2nd century BC	Rise of the Numidian kingdoms; King Masinissa (d. 148 BC) begins to encroach on Carthaginian territory.
149–146 BC	Third Punic War, and the final destruction of Punic Carthage by Scipio Aemilianus. Africa Proconsularis founded; rest of Africa divided between native kings.
123–122 BC	Abortive attempt of Gracchi brothers to send colonists to Carthage; beginning of Africa's exploitation by Roman capitalists – the era of the great wheat farms begins.
112–105 BC	Jugurthine War. Masinissa's grandson Jugurtha defies the Romans, and is eventually betrayed by King Bocchus of Mauretania. Veterans of the Roman army given land in Africa.
First half of 1st century BC	Intermittent civil wars in the last years of the Roman Republic. Warfare spreads to Africa in the 80s and again in 49 BC.
46 BC	Caesar conquers his rivals, the followers of the dead

Pompey, and their ally King Juba of Numidia, at the battle of Thapsus. Juba's young son, another Juba, is taken off to Rome. The extent of Roman territory is trebled to include a second province, Africa Nova – most of the old Numidian kingdom. The historian Sallust is appointed Africa Nova's first governor. Caesar founds a number of veterans' colonies.

44 BC   Murder of Caesar, which leads to further struggles for leadership at Rome, and confused fighting in Africa.

36 BC   Octavian becomes uncontested master of Africa; the romanization of Africa begins.

33 BC   Death of King Bocchus of Mauretania; Mauretania taken over by Roman administrators, and Roman colonies founded there.

31 BC   Battle of Actium: Octavian defeats Mark Antony.

29 BC   Official refounding of Carthage. Octavian founds many veterans' colonies in Africa.

27 BC   Octavian becomes Augustus Caesar.

25 BC   Augustus gives Mauretania to Juba II as a client kingdom.

Late 1st century BC   Constant frontier risings until AD 6.

19 BC   Cornelius Balbus conquers Garama (Germa), capital of the Garamantes.

AD 14   Third Augustan Legion completes construction of road from Tacapae to their winter quarters.

AD 17–24   Revolt of Tacfarinas.

AD 23   Death of Juba II; accession of his son Ptolemy.

AD 40   Murder of Ptolemy by Caligula; rising of the Moors under Aedemon leads to annexation of Mauretania to Roman Empire.

AD 42   Suetonius Paulinus crosses the Atlas mountains and penetrates western Sahara.

Mid 1st century   Beginning of prosperity for Roman Africa.

End 1st century   Journeys across the central Sahara by Septimius Flaccus and Julius Maternus.

2nd century   The century of consolidation; spread of olive cultivation and the road network; Africans achieve influence in Rome.

AD 117   Lusius Quietus, a Moorish chieftain, appointed to the senate and senior posts by Trajan.

AD c. 125   Birth of Apuleius at Madauros.

AD 143   Marcus Cornelius Fronto of Cirta, former tutor to Marcus Aurelius, becomes consul.

AD c. 170	Apuleius writes *The Golden Ass*. Birth of Tertullian.
AD 180	First known Christian martyrs of Africa executed.
AD 189	Victor I becomes the first African bishop of Rome.
AD 193	Septimius Severus from Leptis Magna becomes the first African Emperor.
AD 197	Publication of Tertullian's *Apologia*.
AD 202–203	Septimius Severus in Africa. Vast building programme begun at Leptis Magna.
AD 203	Martyrdom of St Perpetua and her companions at Carthage.
AD 211	Death of Septimius Severus; accession of his son Caracalla.
AD 217	Murder of Caracalla; Macrinus, a Moor, becomes Emperor.
AD 218	Deposition of Macrinus; accession of Elagabalus.
AD 222	Murder of Elagabalus; accession of Severus Alexander.
AD 235	Murder of Severus Alexander – and end of the Severan dynasty.
AD 238	Proclamation as Emperor of Gordian I, proconsul of Africa, with his son Gordian II. Death of Gordian II in battle, and suicide of Gordian I. Accession of Gordian III, and disbanding of Third Augustan Legion. Garrison withdrawn from desert outpost of Castellum Dimmidi established by Septimius Severus 40 years earlier.
Mid 3rd century	Olive-tree country in the south continues to flourish and to export massively.
AD 248	St Cyprian becomes bishop of Carthage.
AD 250–1	Decian Persecution of Christians.
AD 253	Serious insurrection on southern frontier; reformation of Third Augustan Legion.
AD 256	Renewal of persecution under Valerian.
AD 258	Martyrdom of St Cyprian near Carthage.
AD 259	Martyrdom of Sts Marian and James at Cirta.
AD 284	Accession of Emperor Diocletian.
Late 280s on	Tribal insurrections; co-Emperor Maximian comes in person to suppress them in AD 298; puts defences of province in order again. Meanwhile Diocletian reorganizes Empire. Spread of Christianity to Numidian countryside. Building of country houses for the rich.
AD 303–5	Persecution of Diocletian.
AD 311	Constantine becomes co-Emperor.

AD 312	Donatist schism begins.
AD 313	Edict of Milan: Christianity becomes official religion of the Roman Empire.
AD 314	Council of Arles.
4th century AD	Increasing strength of Donatism; age of church-building; appearance of the *circumcelliones* in 340s.
AD 354	Birth of St Augustine at Thagaste.
AD 355	Death of Donatus in exile.
AD 363–4	Devastation of city lands of Leptis Magna by Austuriani tribe.
AD 372	Revolt of Firmus in the Kabylie mountains, with support from the Donatists.
AD 375	Firmus defeated by the *comes* Theodosius.
AD 386	Conversion to Christianity of St Augustine.
AD 395	Augustine becomes bishop of Hippo.
AD 397	St Augustine writes his *Confessions*.
AD 397	Revolt of Firmus's brother Gildo, with support of the Donatists.
AD 405	Donatism at last declared a heresy by an Edict of Unity.
AD 406	The barbarians breach the Rhine frontier.
AD 409	The Vandals reach Spain.
AD 410	Alaric the Goth captures and loots Rome for three days.
AD 411	Council of Carthage: Augustine finally discredits the Donatists.
AD 413–427	St Augustine works on *The City of God*.
AD 416	Visigoths make an abortive attempt to invade Africa.
AD 429	Invasion of Africa by the Vandals.
AD 430	Death of St Augustine during the siege of Hippo.
AD 439	Vandals seize Carthage.
AD 455	Gaiseric, king of the Vandals, loots Rome.
AD 468	Vandals defeat imperial fleet.
AD 477	Death of Gaiseric.
AD 490s	*Tablettes Albertini* written.
AD 533	Reconquest of Africa for the Eastern Empire by Count Belisarius; restoration of Catholic supremacy; Solomon undertakes the conquest of the barbarians and the reorganization of the frontier defences.
AD 543	Massacre at Leptis of elders of Louata tribe by Sergius, duke of Tripolitania and nephew of Solomon; general insurrection of the tribes. Death of

	Solomon in battle near Theveste. Period of civil war.
AD 544	Beginning of Three Chapters controversy.
AD 546	John Troglita appointed *comes Africae*; after two years' fighting, peace for 15 years.
AD 563	New governor murders main barbarian ally of the Byzantines. New uprising – warfare intermittent until end of century. Growing strength of the Pope.
AD c. 570	Birth of Muhammad.
Late 6th or early 7th century	Apparent success of Christianity in the oases of the Sahara.
AD 595	Heraclius, leading general of the Emperor Maurice, becomes exarch of Carthage.
AD 602	Emperor Maurice murdered by Phocas. Heraclius leads opposition to the usurper; sends his son Heraclius to Constantinople to avenge the Emperor.
AD 610	Heraclius the younger becomes Emperor.
AD 632	Death of Muhammad at Medina.
AD 641	Death of Emperor Heraclius. By now Palestine and Syria are ruled by Arabs.
AD 641–2	Arabs occupy Egypt.
AD 642	Arabs occupy Cyrenaica.
AD 643	Arabs besiege Tripoli, lay waste Sabratha, and invade eastern Fezzan.
AD 646	Exarch Gregory declares himself Emperor, although he remains in Africa. Moves his capital to Sufetula (Sbeïtla).
AD 647	First Arab invasion of Maghreb; Gregory dies when defeated outside Sufetula.
AD 650s/660s	Series of Arab raids.
AD 669	Campaign of Okba, who seizes Tripolitania and Byzacena. Foundation of Arab city of Kairouan in Tunisia.
AD 683	Okba's expedition to the Atlantic; is defeated near Thabudeos on his return by Koseila, a Berber chieftain. Arabs retreat temporarily from Maghreb.
AD 695	Invasion of Hassan, who captures Carthage; but Arabs are defeated by Al-Kahena, queen of the Aurès.
AD 697	Carthage recaptured by Byzantines; Hassan retreats to Cyrenaica.
AD 698	Carthage conquered by Arabs for good.
AD c. 700	Final defeat of Al-Kahena.

AD 708   Septem (Ceuta), Byzantium's last outpost in Africa, falls to the Arabs. The conquest of Spain follows, and by 711 the Arabs are threatening central Gaul.

A NOTE ON CERTAIN WORDS

Punic – as in Punic Wars – means western-Mediterranean Phoenician, and sometimes simply Carthaginian.

Africa itself meant nothing to the Greeks, who regularly used the word Libya for all African territory west of Egypt; the Romans used 'African' indiscriminately of the people, but confined the noun to Africa Proconsularis – roughly Tunisia. Only in the late third century did the 'diocese' of Africa cover all the north-west African provinces except the area round Tingis (Tangiers). In Byzantine times, the north-west African provinces retrieved by Justinian became the exarchy of Africa. The original Afri were probably one tribal group in one small part of Tunisia. Later, north-west Africa was called *Ifriqiya* by the Arabs.

Libyan was used by the ancient Greeks of all non-Punic Africans living west of the Egyptian border. It was the name the Egyptians themselves gave to a desert people living beyond their western frontier. From the time of the Punic Wars both Greeks and Romans use 'Libyan' solely of Africans living on Carthaginian territory.

Numidian and **Mauretanian,** or Moorish, were used of tribal Africans *outside* Carthaginian territory, but not living as far south as the Sahara desert. (Those tribes living in the western desert were called Gaetules, those living in the desert south of Tripolitania were Garamantes.) Numidia and Mauretania acquired territorial meaning only under the Romans. For example, Masinissa started his career as *rex Massylorum*, king of the Massyli – a people – but died *rex Numidiae*, king of Numidia – a territory. Masinissa's Numidia included much of southern Tunisia and western Algeria. Numidia disappeared under the early Empire, and when it returned it was soon restricted to a triangle with its apex on the coast north of Cirta, and its base along the southern frontier between the Chott El Hodna and the Chott Djerid. For a brief time it included the hinterland (but not the coast) of Tripolitania. Mauretania, which was variously divided at different periods, was all of north-west Africa north of the desert and west of Numidia. Mauri – Moors – eventually came to mean all the non-romanized inhabitants, including those in Numidia and even the former Africa Proconsularis. It was probably a contraction of a Punic word for 'westerners'. The Arabs divided the Maghreb's entire population into 'Roms' and Moors.

Berber Although both Greeks and Romans referred to barbarians, meaning – in the case of the Greeks – all who were not Greek, and – in the case of the Romans – all who lived beyond their frontiers, the use of the word 'Berber' to describe the indigenous inhabitants of north-west Africa only came in with the Arabs in the eighth century. I have, however, used it in the later chapters of this book, even though its use is strictly speaking anachronistic. The word may have been a corruption of the Roman *barbari* (barbarians, from the Greek *barbaroi*), but some scholars now think it derives from an indigenous tribal name.

Maghreb also came in with the Arabs: it means 'far west', and stands for north-west Africa.

Magna Graecia ('Greater Greece') was the whole area of Greek settlement in southern Italy and eastern Sicily. It had no political meaning.

Byzantium was the name of the original settlement where the city of Constantinople was founded in the fourth century, and which eventually gave its name to the Eastern Roman Empire.

Oued, wadi Both these words mean stream or river – *wadi* is commonly used in modern Libya, and *oued* in the rest of north-west Africa.

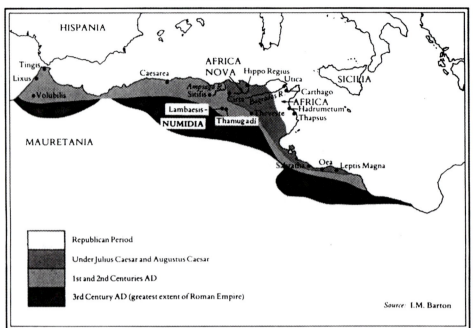

Roman Africa from the Republican period to third century AD

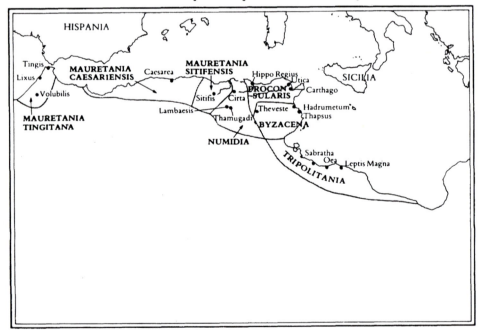

North Africa in the fourth century

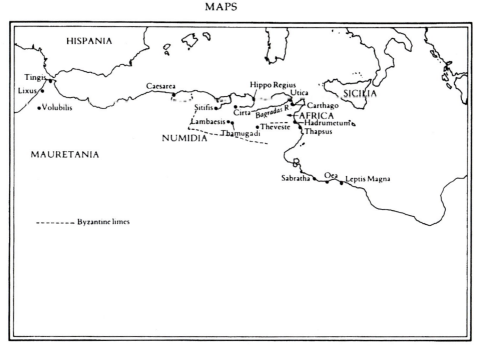

Byzantine Provinces in North Africa (seventh century AD)

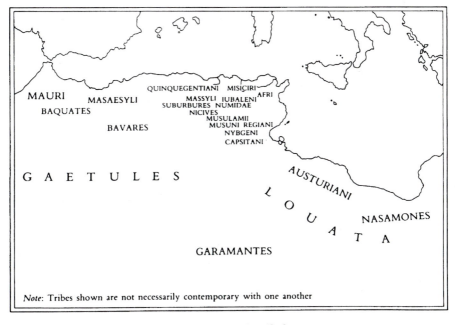

North Africa showing main tribal areas

INTRODUCTION

North Africa is wonderfully rich in Roman remains. There is nothing as monumentally impressive, perhaps, as the temples at Baalbek in the Lebanon, or as well preserved as the Pantheon in Rome; nothing as historic as the Forum of the Caesars, or as haunting as the ruins of Pompeii. But the sight of Timgad in Algeria, its acres of half-demolished buildings and flagged streets stretching for what seems like miles on the edge of a baked plain, or Djemila, perched on its tilted spur among hills now wrinkled with erosion, is unforgettable. The great amphitheatre which still stands at El Djem in Tunisia is almost as big as the Colosseum in Rome – and, towering as it does over the one-storey Arab dwellings clustering round it, even more overwhelming. In Libya, Leptis Magna and Sabratha survive to bear striking witness to the one-time prosperity and grandeur of the great seaports of Roman Tripolitania. And there are many smaller cities which were, like them (and unlike Carthage and most of the cities of the coast), never overlaid by overbuilding and which have therefore been less complicated to excavate: Mactar, Dougga and Thuburbo Maius in Tunisia, for example, or Khémissa and Tipasa in Algeria.

None of the cities of North Africa is more than a ghost town. Monuments have survived, but not – with rare exceptions – shops and houses, except for walls a few feet high. Even the monuments, when the Romans departed, eventually fell into disuse and decay, and most were pillaged and used as quarries by succeeding generations. This was to be expected in the cities of the coast, from which transport was easy; indeed, in the Middle Ages, boatloads of the columns of Roman Carthage found their way to Spain and Italy, as well as to mosques all over North Africa; and in later centuries columns from Leptis Magna were supplied, through the agency of enterprising European consuls, for the palace of Versailles, for the church of St Germain des Prés, and even for George III's improvements at Virginia Water in Surrey. The cities of the interior fared scarcely any better: by and large they were less rich to begin with, and they bore the brunt of the invasion of the Hillalian Arabs in the eleventh century – an occurrence which finally destroyed the last vestiges of the Roman inheritance in North Africa.

A good deal remained, however, to amaze the French when they invaded Algeria in 1830. But the nation which, under Napoleon, had founded Egyptology, and whose scholars were later to pursue the study of archaeology both in North Africa and elsewhere, was in the early years of its rule responsible for nearly as much damage as its predecessors. At Philippeville (ancient Rusicade), the army commander ordered the destruction of the Roman theatre and amphitheatre, the forum, a basilica, a temple and a water tower. At Tipasa the most accessible ruins were removed in 1847 to build a cholera hospital. Two huge temples were pulled down at Constantine, and the Roman bridge over the Rummel was allowed to fall down. Just south of Bône (ancient Hippo Regius, now Annaba) a beautiful hump-backed bridge was pulled down and replaced. At Tazoult (Lambaesis), near Batna, Roman remains were used to build a penitentiary over a large part of the former garrison of the Third Augustan Legion, undoubtedly one of the best preserved legionary fortresses of the Roman world.

Within the last half-century, too, the conquering armies of Europe have much to answer for, quite apart from the damage to be expected during fighting. The Italians, after taking over Libya earlier this century, used stone from Leptis Magna to build military forts, and demolished the gateways of Bu Ngem. They were also in the habit of collecting Roman milestones from the surrounding desert to embellish their barracks at Mizda, and, since no record was kept of where their trophies had been found, archaeologists trying to work out the network of Roman roads in Tripolitania have been deprived of valuable evidence. During the Second World War, British and American soldiers sheltering in the underground houses at Bulla Regia lit cooking fires against the walls, and mutilated mosaics.

The study of Roman North Africa does, however, owe something to the military. Already in the 1830s the French army was undertaking scientific expeditions of exploration, and the names of Capitaine X and Lieutenant Y virtually monopolize subsequent reports and maps of Roman hydraulic works. In 1851, French officers and their prisoners were embarking on the excavation of Lambaesis, and it soon became fashionable for young French officers to spend their leave and their spare time investigating Roman remains. In the First World War, German prisoners were set to work excavating at Volubilis, and soon afterwards the French and Italian air forces were taking the aerial photographs which have unlocked some of the secrets of Roman exploitation.

By the end of the nineteenth century, French archaeologists – and pre-eminently Stéphane Gsell, whose eight-volume *Histoire Ancienne de l'Afrique du Nord* was to appear between 1913 and 1928 – were laying bare both outline and details of the pre-Islamic past of north-west Africa, and the great civilian work of rehabilitating as much as could be uncovered or restored had begun. It was work to which other nationalities – the Italians, the British, the Americans and the modern inhabitants – subsequently contributed. The excavation of ancient Carthage since the 1970s, originally under the auspices of UNESCO, has been a notable example of international enterprise.

The finest, most important or extensive remains have by now, one must suppose, been rescued – Leptis Magna from the sand dunes of Libya, Carthage from its encroaching suburban gardens – or at least identified; but much, clearly, remains underground. There are frequent uncoverings of a minor sort: cisterns or Christian tombs are exposed when a new road is cut through a hillside, or mosaics are revealed under the sand when a modern theatre auditorium is carved out of the seashore. British archaeologists have done sterling work at the invitation of the Libyan government in surveying the interior in the last four decades; they have found remarkable evidence of the efficiency of desert farming during the Roman period, made possible by scrupulous management of intermittent rainfall; and there are hopes that such evidence will show how modern agriculture can thrive in a terrain that is now comparatively unproductive.

There must also be innumerable inscriptions, statues and artefacts still awaiting discovery; and perhaps some stone-strewn acres where once a city of the Tunisian steppe flourished will yield an excavation as interesting as neighbouring Mactar. But there will not be another capitol like that at Sbeïtla, or an aqueduct like that near Cherchel. Even so, much survives – not least the fifty thousand inscriptions from which so much of the political, social and economic history has been pieced together.

The charm of the ancient sites of inland north-west Africa is their unselfconscious informality, the unpretentiousness of their setting and display. At least until a few years ago, although the boys seemed to spring out of the cracks in the paving with coins for sale or guidebook information, there was a refreshing absence of the paraphernalia of tourism which can make visits to some of the major classical sites of the Tunisian and Moroccan coast a dubious pleasure.

There is a healthy, sometimes too healthy, lack of reverence. The furrows run almost up to the crumbling walls of ancient Lambaesis, in and among the ruins wherever soil has settled. Uncounted Corinthian capitals are used as stands for flowers or garden seats in every self-respecting hotel or private house in Carthage and Tunis. At Tébessa, a Roman house which was once, perhaps, a governor's residence is part of a row of shops. At Mactar, the old amphitheatre, where wild beasts tore their victims to death, housed until recently in the remnants of its galleries the *gourbis* of the poor; near Tunis the vast pillars of an aqueduct only lately offered shelter for lean-to huts huddled into a hamlet. The great bridge over the Medjerda at

Chemtou, where the much-prized rosy-red Numidian marble used to be hewn from the quarries of ancient Simitthu, lies in ruins and has never been replaced: one must cross the river by a watersplash. A fine Roman bridge near Béja, which once carried the traffic from Carthage to Bulla Regia and the west, now carries men and donkeys from one ploughed field to another; of the highway which it served there is no sign. It is all a long way from the harsh, rich, orderly world in which these Roman monuments were originally constructed, and in which the people who created them were born and lived and died.

Remains of early third-century basilica at Volubilis, Morocco. It originally had two storeys, and was probably modelled on the one at Leptis Magna

1

BETWEEN THE DESERT
AND THE SEA

Much of the history of north-west Africa is the history of foreigners. Its civilizations have been imposed on its indigenous people largely from outside, and it was usually conquered from outside. Yet they have endured with considerable vigour. The Arabs, for instance, have dominated North Africa and its people since the seventh century AD; their religion and language survive to this day. The Phoenicians arrived at the beginning of the first millennium BC and remained its most powerful inhabitants – although a tiny minority – until the second century BC. Their maritime empire under the Carthaginians lasted nearly four centuries – longer than the land empire of Alexander the Great. Their influence, like that of the Arabs after them, survived for centuries afterwards, even when their power had been completely destroyed, and Carthage itself had been obliterated by the Romans.

The achievement of the Romans, too, was remarkable. They ruled north-west Africa for more than five hundred years, and the country which they had almost inadvertently conquered became, by the time of the Antonine Emperors of the second century AD, their most profitable acquisition and the one which demonstrated most strikingly their gift for government. Though its natural resources were greatly inferior to those of Gaul, for instance, and though the Romans controlled less than one hundred and forty thousand square miles, the territory they exploited in north-west Africa contributed far more to the agricultural wealth of the Roman Empire. Its cities numbered nearly six hundred to Gaul's sixty, and one of them, Leptis Magna, provided an imperial dynasty, that of the Severi. It was the birthplace of Terence and Apuleius, of Tertullian and St Augustine – native Africans all. Its volatile inhabitants adopted Christianity with an exuberance equalled only by the enthusiasm with which they adopted its heresies and, later, welcomed Islam. It was in some ways the most romanized of all Rome's subject territories, and in its turn it influenced the destiny of the Empire.

The social and political forms of Rome outlasted the extraordinary interregnum of the Vandals, who set sail with wives and children from their

1

Gorgon's head from the forum at Leptis Magna

base in Spain and seized north-west Africa in AD 429; those forms lingered on, weakened but still recognizable, when the Byzantines reconquered Africa a century later for the Eastern Empire. The first Arab invasions swept through north-west Africa in the seventh century, though it was only with the second wave, in the eleventh century, that the last vestige of Roman influence finally vanished. But by then North Africa had become once more part of Africa and the East. Her brilliant Mediterranean past had been forgotten. The lessons of Punic and Roman agriculture were ignored, harbours silted up, most of the twelve thousand miles of Roman road sank under either a tide of sand blown in from the desert or soil

2

washed down from the mountains. Cities fell under the hammer of the quarrier or were engulfed by the dunes. The all-devouring goat supplanted the ox, the camel supplanted the horse; and in the towns of the coast the merchant made way for the pirate, whose predatory activities warded off the European until the nineteenth century.

In the eighteenth century, less generally was known about the northern half of Africa than had been known in the days of the Romans.[1] Maps were non-existent or worthless. The most accurate was still that of Ptolemy, who lived in the second century and whose map of the world, in a twelfth-century Byzantine copy, was the only one known to have survived from antiquity. European knowledge of the interior still depended on classical writers. There were one or two European explorers in the seventeenth and eighteenth centuries, but it was only in the nineteenth that the northern Mediterranean seriously rediscovered the southern. Napoleon's campaign in Egypt in 1798 led directly to the discovery of the temples of the Nile and the beginnings of Egyptology, and the French annexation of Algeria in 1830 (an interregnum which fared hardly better than that of the Vandals) at last revealed to the modern world the wealth of Roman remains in North Africa. Of all Rome's provinces those in Africa are richest, at least in quantity, in the monuments of her might. She built to last, and neither the Arabs nor the encroaching desert were able to extinguish entirely the marks of her rule.

A LAND OF DROUGHT

Most of the continent of Africa north of the 15° parallel is desert. The Sahara forms the western end of the vast belt of virtually rainless land which stretches diagonally across Arabia, Syria and Jordan, Turkestan and north of the Himalayas to the Gobi desert in northern China. On either side of the Tropic of Cancer, crossing from Rio de Oro on the Atlantic to the Red Sea, three thousand miles to the east, lie the Saharan, Libyan and Nubian deserts – nearly four million square miles of sand, gravel, bare rock and mountain ranges. They cut off the equatorial forest of the Congo and the Niger from the Mediterranean coast as effectively as an ocean. Rain is not unknown; without it there would be no oases. But it is nowhere more than five inches a year, and only its irregularity can be relied on. One oasis has recorded a drought lasting twelve years and, although torrential rain occasionally falls for as much as two or three days together in mountainous regions of the central Sahara, causing flash floods, there are huge tracts where rain never falls at all.

Such rainfall as there is mostly evaporates under the Saharan sun; but

---

1 The Carthaginians had explored the coast of West Africa in the fifth century BC; it was two thousand years before the Portuguese followed in their wake.

enough finds its way underground to supply a certain number of oases – some large, like Ghadames, Germa, Kufra or Tamanrasset, which all support palm groves and other crops; others hardly more than wells. Oases may be close together or as many as one hundred and fifty or two hundred miles apart. The water is often brackish, but its existence has meant that the North African desert belt has never been entirely uninhabited. In historic times there have always been nomadic tribes moving from oasis to oasis and feeding their animals on such long-rooted scrub as somehow survives years of drought, or on the plant life that springs up on the most barren land after a sudden shower of rain. Even in its driest period there have been caravan routes between the Mediterranean and the Niger.

Quite distinct, however, from the deserts of North Africa are four areas which can support a settled population because they have a regular supply of water: Egypt, to which the Nile brings the rainfall of the highlands of Ethiopia and Uganda; Cyrenaica, six hundred miles across the desert from the Nile delta, on the Libyan coast; the tiny coastal belt of Tripolitania, a further eight hundred miles to the west; and finally, separated from Tripolitania by a comparatively brief stretch of desert, the whole much larger region of north-west Africa which the Arabs call the Maghreb and which corresponds roughly to the Atlas mountains and their coastal plain. This is a region some two or three hundred miles deep from the Mediterranean to the northern edge of the Sahara, stretching 1,400 miles from the Atlantic to the Gulf of Gabès opposite Sicily. It comprises Morocco (Mauretania to the ancient world), northern Algeria (east Mauretania and Numidia) and Tunisia (Africa Proconsularis).

The Maghreb's source of water is not, as in Egypt, a river, but rain, brought in on the west winds of winter from the Atlantic and falling on the flanks of its many mountain ranges. Further east, Tripolitania and Cyrenaica have ranges of hills which attract rainfall, though the highest, only some two or three thousand feet high, do not compare with the 13,500 of Mount Atlas in Morocco, and both regions are in fact a good deal drier. But they are all part of the general geological structure of the Mediterranean basin. They have the same steep-sided mountains of porous limestone that ring the north Mediterranean coast from the Pyrenees through the Alpes Maritimes and the Dolomites to Greece and Asia Minor; they share the same tendency to earthquakes; and they enjoy the same general climatic conditions – rain in winter, drought in summer. Indeed the Maghreb, which has some rain in spring and autumn as well, is wetter than parts of Spain.

FLORA AND FAUNA

As well as sharing the typical climate, north-west Africa has had for thousands of years a plant life which is also more Mediterranean than

4

African. The mountains are still partly, and were once wholly, covered in forests of conifers and evergreens such as holm oak and wild olive. Like other Mediterranean lands the country took readily to the vine, the olive and the fig and, in the most fertile regions, to cereals when they were introduced long before the Romans. But the fauna is nearly all of African origin. The poisonous snakes of Tripolitania and Tunisia are not found in Europe; the scorpions are tropical varieties. The so-called Barbary sheep, which is neither sheep nor goat, is an African species. Ostrich, gnu, several varieties of antelope and gazelle were once, or still are, found in north-west Africa, and one Roman mosaic in the Bardo museum in Tunis shows a hartebeest.

As late as the first century AD, and probably later, elephant inhabited the Maghreb, and the wild beasts – panthers and leopards, lions and bears – which Africa shipped to Rome for the games and circuses were captured north of the Sahara.

These animals reached the Mediterranean coast at a period when the interior of the continent was much wetter than it has been for the last three thousand years. Our own era is possibly the driest phase, in an alternation of wet and dry, that it has ever known. There was once greater rainfall, more rivers, and even vast lakes. There is still an enormous water-table under the eastern desert, laid down hundreds of thousands of years ago, which supplies the oases in low-level depressions like Siwa and Kufra. In the western desert, it seems likely that the Niger, which runs north-east from the mountains of French Guinea to Timbuctoo, where it turns sharply to the southeast and flows out into the Bight of Benin, as recently as five thousand years ago continued north from Timbuctoo into the vast flats of the El Juf depression. There it evaporated from a shifting series of marshes and shallow lakes some 60,000 square miles in extent. A watercourse from Timbuctoo has been traced far to the north of the present Niger bend, and fossil remains of fish, hippopotamus, reed-rat and a variety of mollusc have been found. There are also signs of past habitation of giraffe and elephant, which suggests that what is now desert was once open steppe. The whole western Sahara is seamed with dried-up watercourses, too long and too well-defined to be accounted for by the run-off from rainfall as intermittent as it is today; the most famous runs from the Hoggar massif in the central Sahara to the Touggourt Depression, and possibly as far as the Chott Melrhir just south of the Aurès mountains in northern Algeria – a distance of some seven hundred miles. As far north as Biskra a central African mud-fish has been found, and in the Hoggar there have been reports of central African crocodiles whose ancestors can have established themselves there only in a much wetter period. All these species must have crossed what is now desert tens of thousands rather than thousands of years ago; elephants, for instance, probably arrived early rather than late, for the North African variety is known to have shown distinct signs of

Evidence that giraffes once lived in the heart of the Sahara desert:
prehistoric rock painting in the Tassili n'Ajjer

dwarfing in Roman times, a change which must have evolved over a long
period. But a wetter climate made possible not only the spread of animals
but also large-scale migrations of peoples.

THE FIRST NORTH AFRICANS

By the end of the Ice Ages, c. 10,000 BC, most of the Mediterranean region
was occupied by bands of hunter-gatherers, of broadly Mediterranean
stock. As the climate gradually became warmer, sea levels rose and the
land became more forested. The inhabitants adapted to the new environment, and fishing became more important.

Between about 6000 and 3000 BC farming – the growing of cereals and
pulses, the herding of animals – spread gradually across the Mediterranean
basin. Its arrival used to be regarded as the result of the westward spread
of a new people, but it now seems more likely to be primarily the result of

the adoption of the new resources, and the methods of exploiting them, by the indigenous populations of hunter-fisher-gatherers.

These early North Africans have left records of themselves and their environment in countless rock engravings. The southern foothills of the Atlas range are rich in engravings of the extinct giant buffalo, elephant and panther; the sides of desiccated watercourses in the Libyan Fezzan show giraffe, elephant, rhinoceros and hippopotamus, as well as sheep and domestic cattle. The engravings cannot be dated with any certainty, but they reveal a past age when large mammals, which are today seen only south of the Sahara, were a commonplace sight in areas which now scarcely support the occasional hyena or wild boar, and bear witness to the survival of many of them in the Africa known to the ancient world.

With the eventual drying up of the desert around 2000 BC the people who occupied the plains and mountains of north-west Africa were, like the animals, virtually isolated. They remained at a Stone Age level of development, hunting wild animals, raising cattle and horses, or settling to a simple form of agriculture in the more fertile parts. It was with them and their descendants that the Phoenicians and the Romans came in contact, the people whom the Greeks called Libyans (adopting the name from the Lebu tribe on the border of Egypt), the Romans called Africans, Numidians and Moors, and the Arabs were to call Berbers (probably from the Latin *barbari*, barbarians). This is the stock from which many of today's North Africans – Berber tribesmen and town dwellers alike – and tribes of the desert like the Tuareg are descended, for neither Carthaginians nor Romans, Vandals nor even Arabs invaded in sufficient numbers to alter greatly this ancient ethnic inheritance.

COLONISTS FROM THE SEA

Meanwhile the Minoans, the Greeks and the Phoenicians, at the other end of the Mediterranean, were taking to the sea, to commerce and to conquest. All three peoples had penetrated the western Mediterranean by the early first millennium BC. The Minoans, who were trading by sea with Egypt at least two thousand years before Christ, must have obtained the block of liparite found by Sir Arthur Evans in the palace of King Minos at Knossos on Crete from the Aeolian islands north of Sicily; they may even have sailed beyond the straits of Gibraltar (the pillars of Hercules of Greek legend) in the second millennium BC. The Old Testament 'ships of Tarshish' were probably Phoenician ships sailing to Tartessus, on the Atlantic coast of Spain, around 1000 BC. And although it is not possible to chart any coherent route for the voyages of Odysseus, the *Odyssey* shows that by 800 BC, when Homer lived, the Greeks also had accurate knowledge of the countries of the west: the lotus plant, for instance, which features in the story of Odysseus's travels, does grow on the coast of Tripoli, and the land

Seventh-century BC Assyrian bas-relief from Nineveh of a ship thought
to be Phoenician, now in the British Museum

of the Lotophagi has been confidently identified with the island of Djerba,
in the Gulf of Gabès.

From the eighth century BC onwards the North African coast was colonized first by the Phoenicians and then by the Greeks. That is fact, though
the details are largely lost in legend, for the western Phoenicians left no
written records. However, a third-century BC Greek historian in Sicily,
Timaeus, who very probably derived his information direct from Carthaginian sources, recorded that Carthage was founded thirty-eight years
before the first Olympiad (i.e. 814 BC) by the Phoenician Princess Elissa, or
Dido, who fled from Tyre when her husband was murdered by her brother,
King Pygmalion. The date is plausible, give or take a hundred years;[1] the
princess's great-aunt Jezebel had married King Ahab of Israel some forty
or fifty years earlier. But Dido, if she existed at all, was simply following
the example of others of her countrymen: Utica, a few miles along the coast
to the north-west, and Gades (Cadiz) in Spain were already Phoenician
settlements.

As for the Greeks, they were reputed, according to Herodotus, to have

---

1 Virgil, writing after the destruction of Carthage, antedated the legend by some centuries
to the time of the Trojan War, so that Dido could welcome Aeneas, the founder of Rome,
on his way to Italy after the sack of Troy.

founded fishing colonies in Cyrenaica at the prompting of the Delphic oracle. But it was at a time, a century or so after the Phoenicians, when the Greeks too were colonizing all round the western Mediterranean – part of a general movement dictated by the desire for trade, and later by pressure of population at home. Delphic oracle notwithstanding, the founding of Cyrene in 640 BC fitted naturally into this pattern.

The Phoenicians, however, were the people who first opened up a regular trade route to the far west and monopolized the coast of north-west Africa. It was not the land itself which drew them. Apart from the beds of *murex*, the shellfish from which the Phoenicians extracted their celebrated purple dye and which was to be found in quantity both at Mogador (Essaouira) on the Atlantic and in the Gulf of Gabès, Africa held few attractions – rather the reverse, in the shape of dangerous wild animals and potentially hostile tribes. Its metals – iron, zinc and lead – were unsuspected by the new settlers. In any case, access to the interior was always difficult: what rivers there are run off the mountains in torrents after the winter rains, down steep ravines, and, except in Morocco, nearly all dry up or run very low in summer, like many other Mediterranean rivers. None are navigable for any appreciable distance inland. The mountain ranges lie parallel to the coast, with few valleys reaching back into the interior, and although they afforded some protection against sudden raids by the indigenous tribes, they also cut off the coastal settlements, not only from their hinterland but from each other. Even the possibilities of anchorage were poor. Ancient ships, being made of wood, were better beached than anchored or tied up at a jetty all night, since constant immersion soon fouled the hulls; but shelving beaches were few, and such natural harbours as had been eroded in the rocky limestone cliffs were exposed, if not to the west wind, then to the north. 'No other part of the earth,' reported Pliny in his *Natural History*, 'has fewer bays or inlets in its coast.'

But North Africa lay along one of the two sea routes to Spain, where the ships of Tarshish bartered for silver and tin with the Tartessians, at prices extremely favourable to themselves. The developing civilizations of the eastern Mediterranean were hungry for metals, and it was on this trade that the prosperity of the Phoenicians was based. They needed watering places for their ships, for even with a following wind the vessels of the ancient world could sail only thirty-odd miles a day. The two thousand-mile journey from Tyre to Tartessus can rarely have taken less than nine or ten weeks. The Phoenicians, therefore, soon established a chain of settlements, to serve not only as victualling points but also as refuges from the sudden storms typical of the Mediterranean, occasionally as winter quarters (for the months from November to March were a close season for sailing in the Mediterranean), and later as bases from which to protect their sea-routes from the encroaching Greeks. With Utica in Tunisia and then Motya off western Sicily, two of their earliest foundations which were more than landfalls, they commanded the straits of Sicily. They soon added Gades (Cadiz), Carthage, Malta and Nora in Sardinia, amongst many others.

Unlike those of the Greeks, which were from the start independent city states, the early Phoenician settlements were not intended even then to be much more than rest and repair stations or places of temporary exile from troubles at home in Phoenicia. They were established on off-shore islands like Motya off Sicily, or on peninsulas like Utica[1] and Carthage, or on coasts virtually inaccessible from inland like Hippo Diarrhytus (Bizerta): all of them sites which could be defended by a small population. They remained under the direct suzerainty of the Phoenician kings; even Carthage, long after all genuine dependence had disappeared, continued to pay some tribute to her mother city of Tyre in Phoenicia.

Yet the name of Carthage – Kart Hadasht to the Phoenicians (Carthago was the Roman corruption) – meant 'new capital' as well as 'new town'. It may well have been planned from the first as a possible alternative capital in the west, for at that time Tyre itself was being seriously harried by the Assyrians. The Phoenicians who came west during the next couple of centuries were as much refugees as colonists, exactly as Dido herself had been. Phoenicia never had population to spare as the Greeks had; it was only after the conquest of Tyre by Nebuchadnezzar, King of Babylon, in the sixth century that settlements like Mogador on the Atlantic, Tipasa in Algeria and Hadrumetum in eastern Tunisia became fair-sized towns, and that Carthage itself became the leading Phoenician city of the west.

Throughout the history of Carthage, in fact, shortage of manpower put a brake on both her colonial and her military activities; it meant that, ultimately, she was no match for Rome. It also made her achievements the more remarkable.

THE THREAT FROM THE GREEKS

By the sixth century BC, the Greeks, too, were colonizing in the western Mediterranean – in southern Italy, eastern Sicily, southern France and south-east Spain. The newcomers showed every sign of seizing control of the sea from the Phoenicians (who were established in western Sicily, north-western Africa and other parts of Spain) and – worse – were prising away a significant share of the Spanish metal trade. They may even have been diverting direct through Gaul some of the north European tin which had, until then, been brought by ship to the Phoenician colony of Tartessus in Spain by the sea-going inhabitants of Europe's Atlantic seaboard. Finally, around 580 BC, the Greek city states in Sicily tried to push the Phoenician

---

1 Utica is now, because of silting, seven or eight miles inland.

settlements in western Sicily at Motya (Mozia), Panormus (Palermo) and Solus out of the island.

Until this point Carthage is scarcely mentioned in the surviving records. But now she emerges as leader and protector of the Phoenicians of the west. She was already the largest of the Phoenician colonies, and had begun to found daughter colonies (Ibiza had been the first, in 654 BC); and when Tyre fell to Nebuchadnezzar in 574 BC she became at last the 'new capital' of the west. But she depended for her security on her command of the straits of Sicily; a wholly Greek Sicily was therefore unthinkable. She put a standing army into the island and looked round for allies.

The struggle between Greeks and Phoenicians, led by Carthage, went on for a hundred years, and not only in Sicily. Carthage had long had trading relations with the Etruscans,[1] who were at that time, the Greek colonies apart, the most powerful people in the Italian peninsula. Now, in alliance with the Etruscans, Carthage drove the Greeks out of Corsica. In 510 BC, she expelled a Greek colony from Tripolitania, on her doorstep. She probably also managed to restore her monopoly of the Spanish metal trade, and with it her maritime supremacy. But her allies the Etruscans were in decline; they were shortly, in 474 BC, to be resoundingly defeated at Cumae, near Naples, by the Greeks who had settled on the Italian mainland. Meanwhile the Greeks were stronger than ever: the Athenians won a decisive victory over their most dangerous enemies, the Persians, at the naval battle of Salamis in 480 BC. In the same year, the Carthaginians had to sue the Greek cities in Sicily for peace after they lost an army, and, more disastrously, most of their fleet at the battle of Himera. They withdrew from the island, and their fellow Phoenicians were left to manage as best they could.

The Carthaginians themselves were not cut off from the source of their wealth in the west, and they were still able to buy foodstuffs from Sicily. All the same, the loss of Sicily and Sardinia was a severe blow, especially when the rise of Athens made the eastern Mediterranean a Greek lake. The latter deprived the Carthaginians of a ready outlet for their wares in the east, and immobilized most of their gold, silver and tin in their own treasuries. During the rest of the fifth century – the great age of the Athenian democracy – the Carthaginians had to learn, quite literally, to cultivate their own back garden. They were to do this so successfully that, in the words of the first-century AD Greek historian Dio Chrysostom, they turned 'from Tyrians into Africans'.

---

1 That Carthage had long had trading relations with the Etruscans is eloquently illustrated by the discovery at Pyrgi in Italy in 1964 of a shrine to Astarte, one of the most popular Phoenician deities.

THE NEIGHBOURS OF CARTHAGE

The tribal society which the Carthaginians found when they turned their attention to their hinterland might well have been recognizable to their modern descendants. But until after the Roman conquest in the second century BC, unfortunately, the early historians and geographers who mention the indigenous inhabitants of north-west Africa, like Herodotus and Scylax, plainly knew very little about them.

Almost all our sources mention stock-raising, however, and it is clear that the ancient world thought of the Africans as pastoralists. Recent archaeology has been confirming that picture, from Morocco to Tripolitania; and the fact that so much of the terrain is admirable pasture, and that thousands of their descendants still gain their livelihood from rearing sheep and other animals, makes it a convincing one. By Roman times, the interior of north-west Africa was famous for its animal husbandry. Polybius, who visited the country in the mid-second century BC, mentions seeing horses, cows, sheep and goats 'in greater quantity than elsewhere'.

But the use by both Greeks and Romans of the word 'Numidians' to describe the peoples nearest Carthaginian territory gives a misleading impression. For it is by no means certain that the word is derived from the Greek for nomad. There was certainly some agriculture also – and in just those regions said to be occupied by Numidians. The early sources do not offer much in the way of positive evidence, but several refer to the country's fertility, sometimes specifically mentioning crops; and none of them explicitly deny the existence of farming.

That so little was known by the ancient Greeks and Romans about the interior of north-west Africa suggests that the inhabitants kept themselves to themselves, practising a subsistence economy which provided them with everything they needed – a mixed economy, with the emphasis on crops where crops might be easily grown, and on animals where they could not.

The sources mention the names of several peoples, or tribes, and also a substantial number of places in the interior. Plainly these were not townships like the Phoenician ports, but they seem none the less to have been permanent settlements. The tribes with which the Carthaginians were to come in contact already had centres from which their 'kings' ruled. Apart from Iol (later Caesarea, modern Cherchel), which was on the coast, Volubilis, Cirta (later Constantine), Siga, Zama and Thugga (Dougga) were all inland tribal centres before the Punic wars, and no doubt were already beginning to derive some prosperity from exchanging goods with a Carthage newly interested in her African neighbours. It is not without significance that so many of the cities in the interior which became rich under the Romans had Libyan names.[1]

---

1 A common example is the T – T formation, as in Theveste, Tubusuptu, Tiaret, Thagaste.

Classical texts also frequently mention hilltop settlements – *castella* and *oppida* – and the ruins of such fortified promontory settlements can still be seen in mountainous and hilly country all over north-west Africa, from western Morocco right across to the Fezzan, four hundred miles south of Tripoli. In addition there are many mentions of *pyrgoi* and *turres* which were probably built by semi-farming communities to protect or conceal granaries and silos.

But the key fact about any pastoral or semi-pastoral society in a region like north-west Africa, particularly in a mountainous region with marked variations in climate and in summer and winter temperatures, is the practice of transhumance: that is, the movement of flocks and herds between winter and summer pastures. In some areas, that may mean merely moving sheep and cattle to fresh grazing in the uplands for the summer, and bringing them down to the nearby plains and valleys for the winter when the lowland grass has grown again. In other cases, immense journeys may have to be undertaken – for instance, if the extension of settled agriculture means that flocks and herds are displaced from the most convenient pastures. In recent times, winter and summer pastures have sometimes been two hundred miles or more apart. The tribes, or some members of them, winter with their flocks in the warmer south; and in summer, when the fierce sun begins to burn off the sparse winter and spring grass and the desert oueds (or wadis further east in Libya) are running dry, they retreat to the cooler, more fertile steppes and valleys further north, returning once more to their southern pastures as the cold weather approaches.[1]

It is highly likely that such long journeys were undertaken in ancient times also, for a need for vast areas of land would help explain the apparently extraordinary territorial size of the early North African kingdoms, and their extreme amorphousness. It would also help explain many of the revolts, uprisings and rebellions which punctuated Roman North African history. They are part of the perennial friction between 'the desert and the sown', between shepherds and farmers competing for the same land, or squabbling because the settled try to block the transhumants' immemorial routes between summer and winter grazing grounds, since livestock may eat or trample the farmers' crops before they are harvested.

At the same time the relationship is necessary to both. The shepherd needs the produce of the farmer, grain above all. The farmer needs the produce of the shepherd – milk, meat, wool, leather, perhaps dates from the oases in the south – and his labour: cereals need intensive work for a short period every summer (or autumn for olives) and the tribes come north with their livestock in the months of harvest, just in time to help the farming community at the busiest time of the year.

In modern times, this interdependency has often meant that the same

---

1 There is snow every winter in the mountains and on the High Plains.

tribal group includes both shepherds and farmers. It is possible (though not proven) that in pre-Roman times, too, many Numidian and Moorish tribes included both pastoralists and farmers – or that a pastoral tribe was allied to a farming tribe.

No one can be sure what was the pattern in North Africa except that it must have varied. No doubt sometimes livestock were raised and crops grown side by side in one area by the same tribe. By and large, however, transhumance would have been essential to keep the animals alive. And it is possible that the kind of noble-and-client clans observed in modern times among the nomadic Tuareg and the settled populations of the Sahara oases[1] had a precedent in the tribal structure in north-west Africa in Carthaginian and Roman times. Herodotus (IV, 172) appears to be describing such an arrangement in the fifth century BC when he writes of the relationship between the nomadic Nasamones and the inhabitants of the oasis of Augila.

Such combinations could help explain the volatility of the tribal structure. Sometimes the alliances – or federations – were huge; they must have involved many tribes. It is striking that few names seem to survive in the historical sources for more than a century or so, and that new tribes, or at least new names, constantly emerge, apparently from nowhere, into the limelight of history.

This theory also offers a better idea of the nature of tribal leadership. The 'kings' who were to play such a key role in the fall of Carthage and the early centuries of Roman rule were much more like El Glaoui, the famous twentieth-century Lord of the Atlas, than feudal kings as Europeans understand the term. To talk of kingdoms, meaning territories, is confusing, for the reality comprised peoples, flocks and herds, winter and summer grazing rights and rights of passage between the two, with a comparatively small proportion of agricultural land and permanent settlements for only some members of the tribe or tribal grouping.

Very few sites are known with certainty to have been occupied in pre-Punic or pre-Roman times, chiefly no doubt for lack of excavation, and only a few pre-Roman field systems, with dry-stone walls, have been identified outside Carthaginian territory. Those that are known, and the many possible sites which have retained Libyan names, are mostly at the junction of two types of terrain, land suitable for arable farming, and land suitable for pasture, for instance towards the foot of a mountain range – where, too, springs would be likely to be more plentiful. That certainly suggests the possibility of a mixed economy of animals and crops. Early on, there was probably no deliberate cultivation of fruit or olive trees – that would be a lesson learned from the Carthaginians – but nearness to

---

1 Before the arrival of the French in Algeria certain nomads, led by their sheikhs and caids, helped protect their farming fellow-tribesmen against their enemies.

forests would mean the presence of wild animals and game.

Not much is known of the culture of these tribal peoples. They spoke a language ancestral to modern Berber – their word for king, for instance, which was based on the consonants GLD, is related to *aguellid*, the modern Berber word for chieftain. They were to borrow the idea of writing from contact with the Carthaginians, though the evidence amounts to no more than a handful of inscriptions, none of which have been adequately deciphered. This script is encountered later as *ti-finagh*, the written language of the Tuareg of the Sahara, and other Berber dialects.

They had great respect for the dead, which gave rise to their most notable artefacts: stone tombs. It has not yet proved possible to date many, but so far they have mostly been found in cemeteries, sometimes thousands strong. There are many different types according to the region: tumuli, cairns, rock-cut chamber tombs, dolmens. Tumuli are found west of the Ampsaga river, and dolmens to the east; the former similar to Iberian burial customs, the latter apparently linked to Sicily. Their numbers and their location suggest a widespread population.

The most impressive are the astonishing royal tombs. At Medracen, a drum-like construction a good eighty feet in height and nearly 200 in diameter stands in hilly country some twenty miles north of Lambaesis – well outside the territory of Carthage although it shows signs of Mediterranean stylistic influence. It was built of enormous blocks of sandstone, and held together by clamps of lead (nearly all robbed). Now believed to date from the first half of the second century BC, its existence presupposes a ruler rich and powerful enough to organize the necessary labour, including that needed for the mining of the lead, which must have been considerable. It suggests a grand alliance of tribes, at least. It may have been the tomb of the Numidian king Masinissa, or even of his father Gaia. A very similar mausoleum, the so-called Tomb of the Christian Woman, was built near Iol Caesarea something over a century later, possibly for King Bocchus II of Mauretania, or for Cleopatra Selene, wife of Juba II. By the first century BC, however, such an ambitious undertaking is less surprising.

There are other princely mausolea from the period of the native kingdoms. The most famous is at Dougga, Tunisia. Another at Le Khroub, ten miles south of Cirta, also has claims to be the last resting place of Masinissa (or possibly of his son Micipsa, who died in 118 BC). It is a substantially-built square, stepped structure which dates from 140 BC or later.

Such royal tombs were of course heavily influenced by a combination of Hellenistic and Punic styles. But they developed out of a powerful native tradition, and it was the society which was capable of building their forerunners with which the Carthaginians now had to learn to live.

So-called Tomb of the Christian Woman, which overlooks the coast road
some thirty-five miles west of Algiers

2

THE RISE OF CARTHAGE

Punic mask of sixth or seventh century BC. Such masks, less than life-size, were placed in tombs to ward off evil spirits. Now in the Bardo Museum

Almost nothing is known of the early development of Carthage, except what can be deduced from the archaeological evidence. Though her inhabitants' ancestors in Phoenicia invented the alphabet, by an irony of fate only the most fragmentary written records of the Carthaginians of any period have survived. When Carthage was destroyed, her libraries were given to the kingdoms of Numidia; their contents vanished as the Punic language gradually fell into disuse by the literate, Latin-speaking upper classes in the later centuries of Roman rule and the scrolls could no longer be understood. Even for the centuries when her power and prosperity were greatest, therefore, the history of Carthage that has come down to us was written by her Greek or Roman enemies. Any historian of the ancient world is working with painfully incomplete information, with fragmentary data that have escaped destruction more or less by accident; some names, some incidents, and those not always the most important, are far better documented than others. In the case of Carthage, the accidents of time have been compounded with bias.

Yet the Roman period cannot be understood without some knowledge of the pre-Roman. Punic Carthage was to be destroyed utterly; but she was the greatest city of the western Mediterranean for several hundred years, and she left behind her not only a legend that has haunted the European imagination ever since but customs, language and habits of mind which interacted with those of her African neighbours. The earliest Phoenicians colonized a Stone Age, the Romans a Liby-Phoenician Maghreb. The recovery of Carthage had a transforming effect on the hinterland of Africa.

THE GHOST OF ANCIENT CARTHAGE

The Lake of Tunis forms a vast land-locked harbour, protected on the seaward side by a narrow spit of land which has been breached to enable ships to enter the man-made deep-water channel which cuts across the seven miles of shallow water to Tunis. Alongside this channel a dyke carries a road and a little local railway out from Tunis towards the sea. On the far side of the lake, where they reach land again, they turn north. Three miles further on, road and railway reach Carthage.

It is impossible to visualize one of the great cities of the ancient world in the string of suburban railway stations and the rows of seaside villas which have inherited that legendary name. In spite of the energetic excavations and restoration undertaken in the city's remains during the past twenty years, there are few spectacular traces of the Carthage which rose again, under the Romans, to become second only to Rome itself. The Romans built streets and aqueducts, baths and houses, a theatre and an amphitheatre; the Christians built basilicas, as they built them in dozens of cities all over North Africa; but in Carthage little enough remains. Streets and the foundations of houses have been uncovered, but the amphitheatre, originally almost the size of Rome's Colosseum, now hardly rises above ground level; it has been hideously restored with concrete. The theatre, also restored, though more tactfully, is nowhere near as well-preserved as the comparatively modest theatre at Kasserine (Cillium), for instance, where the stones are as sharp-edged as if they were cut yesterday; and the odeon, the only one built in Africa, is hardly more than a site. The Baths of Antoninus, which once rivalled the Baths of Caracalla at Rome for magnificence, have long since been robbed of their marble facings; the upper storeys have vanished, and although the vast brick and rubble piers indicate their former immensity it is still hard to imagine that the surviving four-ton Corinthian capital now re-erected on a column there was once one of eight, each on a grey granite column six feet in circumference, in the main hall on the first floor. Down on the shore, the rubble cores of outlying pillars are battered by the sea; half the pebbles on the beach are smoothed remains of Roman brick or concrete. The best statues and mosaics have long since been removed to museums, to the Louvre or to the Bardo in Tunis; weeds push their way through many of the everyday

Fallen Corinthian capital in the ruins of the Baths of Antoninus at
Carthage. It has recently been re-erected

paved floors that have been left behind. The great cisterns which stored water for Roman Carthage long ago declined into outdoor cellars for the hamlet of La Malga, used as rubbish tips and hen-runs and stables; the 90-kilometre-long aqueduct which supplied them with some 8.5 million gallons a day from distant Zaghouan is almost crumbled away. An occasional misshapen lump of rubble betrays its route through the fields towards Tunis, although beyond, nearer Zaghouan, there are still fine stretches.

Without its once-impregnable fortifications, Carthage was too vulnerable, too accessible by land and sea. Throughout the centuries of the Arab occupation its buildings served as quarries for its new conquerors. The ruins of Roman Carthage were plundered to build mosques and palaces all over North Africa and Spain. There are dozens of corinthian columns in the prayer room of the Great Mosque of Tunis, their capitals now painted red and green, and even more in the Great Mosque of Kairouan. The Arabs also exported marble columns to the Christian world, some of which may be seen in the cathedral at Pisa; there were enough

Remains of cisterns in the hamlet of La Malga which once stored water for Roman Carthage

and more to spare. But there are not many left at Carthage.

Of Punic Carthage, even less remains: so little, that until this century its site had not been established by modern scholars with any certainty. Rival theories disputed the claims of half a dozen places along the ten miles of coast north of the Lake of Tunis. Several ancient writers describe its topography in considerable detail but, since the Romans razed the Punic city to the ground in 146 BC, and during the next two thousand years parts of the coastline silted up and identifying landmarks disappeared, judgement between these rival theories had to await the development of archaeology. In the last hundred years Punic tombs and foundations of houses have been excavated round the hill dominated by the former French cathedral (erected in honour of Louis IX, who died in Tunis in 1270). This hill is now known to be the Byrsa, or citadel, of Punic Carthage, and French archaeologists have shown that the houses were originally two storeys or more, were built round a courtyard beneath which water was stored in cisterns, and had excellent drainage. The streets were stepped (as they are

The northernmost of the two Le Kram lagoons, once the circular port.
The central island is in the background, the former cathedral on the
Byrsa in the distance

today in nearby Sidi Bou Said). Meanwhile German excavations have proved that the earliest settlement, in the eighth century, was down by the shore, between the Byrsa and the sea.

Half a mile to the south, on the coast towards Tunis, the once mysterious Le Kram lagoons have been identified with the rectangular and circular ports which are described in ancient texts. They are bordered now, not with warehouses and docks, but with three or four dozen pleasant suburban villas; but the foundations of the Carthaginians' second-century BC ship-sheds and admiralty buildings were uncovered by British archaeologists in the 1970s on the artificial mound that reaches towards the centre of the circular lagoon. Visitors can see models of what the buildings must once have looked like in a small site museum.

Nearby, inland, excavation had already uncovered the sinister precinct of the Punic goddess Tanit, with thousands of urns containing the remains of little children burnt alive as offerings in the hideous ceremony described with such verve by Gustave Flaubert in *Salammbô*: horrible proof that the infant sacrifice for which the other peoples of the ancient world so detested the Phoenicians was practised throughout the history of Carthage, and merely increased in vigour in times of crisis like the last days of independence. No ghosts walk: the sanctuary has been tamed into a sunken garden, with pelargoniums planted beside the neatly ranged votive tablets under the cypress trees. Like the rest of Carthage, it has been suburbanized.

For the first three or four hundred years of the city's existence, the Carthaginians occupied barely twenty square miles round their Byrsa. Dido herself, it was said, had paid a sum to the Libyan tribe of the Maxitani for as much land as would be covered by an ox-hide (Greek *byrsa*); then, by cutting the ox-hide into narrow strips and laying them end to end in a vast semi-circle, had secured not only a beaching point for her party but

Left: priest preparing to sacrifice a child. Part of a fourth-century BC stele found in the precinct of the goddess Tanit, Carthage. Right: terracotta mask, probably of Tanit, dating from the fifth or sixth century BC. Both now in the Bardo Museum, Tunis

also the hill. In succeeding centuries, the suburbs, with their cemeteries and market gardens and summer villas of the rich, had crept outwards round the citadel; for the land on the fringes the Carthaginians continued to pay tribute in rent to the Libyans, except for a brief period when their power was at its height in the sixth century. The isthmus they lived on, between the Lake of Tunis and the Sebkhet er Riana, a bay (now land-locked, then open to the sea) some three miles north-west of the Byrsa, was enough for a city which can hardly have numbered much more than a hundred thousand souls, a merchant people who had not thought of earning their living except by the sea and commerce.

Not, that is, until their defeat at the hands of the Greeks in 480 BC. Now they had lost control of half their sea routes, and with them half their livelihood. Protected by cliffs towards the open sea, a bay and a lake on either side, Carthage was admirably placed for defence, but it was a tiny, and an insecure, base for a trading power to which commerce was vital. Carthage responded to the challenge.

THE RECOVERY OF GREATNESS

Throughout the fifth century, at a time when Greek civilization both in Greece and in Sicily was entering its golden age, brilliant, prosperous and powerful, and when Rome was taking a leading role in Italy, the Carthaginians turned in a new direction. It was a time of revolution and reform. A brutal and inflexible oligarchy set about the task of restoring the city's fortunes with energy and ruthlessness. There was a fierce reaction against all foreign, especially Greek, influence, which had become strong during the Sicilian wars. The power of the priesthood, which had been reinforced by refugees from Tyre,[1] became a stranglehold. The genius of the Carthaginians was concentrated in the elaboration of their hideous rituals, and in the creation of their national character: superstitious, philistine, harsh, conservative, and by turns obsequious and obstinate, and yet, *in extremis*, capable both as a people and as individuals of great courage and nobility.

But the most important factor in the regeneration of Carthage was expansion into her Tunisian hinterland. Until the fifth century, much of her food had been imported from Phoenician allies in Sicily and Sardinia, or bought from Libyan cultivators. But with the temporary setback in Sicily she had to depend more on local supplies.

Almost nothing is known of how the Carthaginians did it, but there is no doubt that the intelligent development of agriculture in Tunisia enabled them to make the most of their potentially fertile corner of Africa. The only Carthaginian work which is known to have been translated into Latin was a treatise on agriculture by one Mago, who was recognized as a considerable expert by the ancient world. Both original and translation have been lost, but Mago was constantly quoted by later Latin authors. He probably lived in the third century BC, at the time of Hannibal, but he must have drawn on a considerable body of experience: his immediate predecessors had put their talents and the traditions of their Middle Eastern ancestors to work to some effect.

Cape Bon, to the east of the Lake of Tunis, must have been one of the first areas to be organized. Writing in the first century AD, but drawing on a much earlier source, Diodorus Siculus described its fertility in the late fourth century BC in these words:

---

1 The city of Tyre was conquered by Nebuchadnezzar in 574 BC.

'It was divided into market gardens and orchards of all sorts of fruit trees, with many streams of water flowing in channels irrigating every part. There were country houses everywhere, lavishly built and covered with stucco, which testified to the wealth of their owners. The barns were filled with all that was needed to maintain a luxurious standard of living, as the inhabitants had been able to store up an abundance of everything in a long period of peace. Part of the land was planted with vines, part with olives and other productive trees. Beyond these, cattle and sheep were pastured on the plains, and there were meadows filled with grazing horses. Such were the signs of the prosperity of these regions where leading Carthaginians had their estates.'

By the fourth century BC the Carthaginians had turned themselves into farmers. They also showed what could be done in north-west Africa by methodical exploitation. Before the final destruction of Carthage by Rome two centuries later, records Plutarch, 'it is said that Cato, the famous Roman orator, shook out the folds of his toga and contrived to drop some Libyan figs on the floor of the senate house, and when the senators admired their size and beauty he remarked that the country which produced them was only three days' sail from Rome', hoping to inspire his fellow senators with greed for – and also perhaps fear of – the wealth of Carthage. It was not virgin soil which the Romans later turned into a granary.

The Carthaginians probably farmed directly only Cape Bon and the fertile land immediately to the south-west of Carthage. But they established their control as far as Thugga (Dougga) and, eventually, most of Tunisia and Tripolitania. By the late third century their empire was to stretch along the coast west to the Atlantic, and they may also have gained authority over tribes outside their territory.

They bred poultry and domestic animals on scientific principles. They introduced the proper cultivation of olives – essential in ancient times not only for cooking but for lighting and bathing (though the poet Juvenal complained in the second century AD that African oil smelt disgusting) – either grafting them on to the native wild mastic or planting new trees. Mago directed that they should be planted seventy-five feet apart; that is how they are grown in the olive groves of eastern Tunisia today. Vines were grown, and date palms (the symbol of Carthage) and fruit trees: not citrus fruits, which were introduced only in Arab times, but almonds, figs and pomegranates, which the Romans called *mala punica*. They raised bees for honey, which was the ancient world's only form of sugar; and Punic beeswax, used not only in industry but for medicinal purposes, was later much sought after by discriminating Romans.

Most of the native African farmers and pastoralists in the most fertile parts of Tunisia must have been impressed into working the new estates.

- an ancient city in Tunisia.

It is possible that some Libyan smallholdings remained more or less inde- *North Africa*
pendent alongside their new masters, in Cape Bon for instance *in Tunisia*; and the
upper valleys of the rivers Bagradas and Miliana, and the plains of central
Tunisia, which were more suited to the growing of cereals (which the
Carthaginians seem not to have cultivated themselves), were left in the
possession of Libyan farmers. But the Carthaginians exacted a tithe *tax* of the
crop to feed the city of Carthage – a tithe which at times was raised to a
quarter or even a third; and recruited from these client populations for
their army.

The Carthaginians were not popular with their new subjects. The dispossessed hovered outside Carthaginian territory, casting hungry eyes on
the fertile land they had been driven out of, ready to stir up disaffection
among those of their kinsmen who were now in servitude.

THE THREAT FROM THE LIBYANS

The Carthaginians, who were short of manpower, had always depended
to a large extent on their African subjects and neighbours for the mercenaries of which their armies were composed. They recruited their soldiers all round the western Mediterranean, but the core of their fighting
strength consisted of their Libyan infantry, who stood up to hot weather
better than Greeks or Romans, and the famous Numidian cavalry[1] for
which they recruited tribesmen from the mountains further west.

It was a serious source of weakness that these subjects and neighbours,
professionally trained for war as many of them were, were so readily
provoked or tempted to turn against the Carthaginians. Once Carthage
had turned herself into a landed power, she found she had to be ready to
defend herself as much against Africans as against Greeks and Romans.
The discord *disagreement* between conqueror and conquered was complicated in this
case by the likelihood of discord between Africans who were primarily
semi-nomadic pastoralists, and Carthaginians – and Africans – who were
settled farmers. It was a problem the Romans were to inherit.

For the moment, however, Carthage could feed herself; she was not
dependent on imports. But her ambitions remained those of a maritime
trading nation, and she also tightened her hold on the whole north-west
African littoral, from the Gulf of Syrte to the Atlantic. Daughter colonies
settled the trading posts of Tripolitania at Oea (Tripoli), Sabratha and
Leptis Magna, perhaps to keep an eye on the trade from the interior which
was controlled by the powerful tribe of the Garamantes. But here, too, the
Carthaginians introduced agriculture, in particular the growing of olive
trees – so successfully that the export of olive oil alone would have been

---

1 The only battle Hannibal was to lose was the one in which he was not supported by
  Numidian cavalry.

enough to explain Tripolitania's prosperity. In the east, their territory stretched to the border of the powerful Greek city of Cyrene in Cyrenaica – a border settled, it was said, by two Carthaginian brothers who ran from Leptis to meet envoys who had left Cyrene at the same time, and then, when accused by the Greeks of cheating, volunteered to be buried alive in defence of their victory. Arae Philaenorum (or altars of the Philaeni) was so-called after their supposed burial mounds.

Ruins of Kerkouane, Cape Bon – the only Phoenician town so far discovered in Africa not subsequently built over

In the west, it was an age of great expeditions. The Phoenicians were never able fully to overcome the problem of returning from maritime expeditions down the Atlantic coast of Africa against the prevailing north wind, and the inspiring voyage of the fifth-century BC admiral Hanno, the first individual Carthaginian of whom a record survives, who sailed down the west coast of Africa apparently as far as the Bight of Benin, seems not to have been repeated. All the same, Phoenician seafarers certainly traded down the Moroccan coast as far as Mogador, and perhaps further. At the same time, another Carthaginian, Himilco, was exploring the sources of the Tartessian tin trade along the Atlantic coast of Gaul; he may have crossed to Britain and Ireland. Madeira and the Canary Islands were also known to the Phoenicians by this time, but here, too, no permanent posts were established, and visits were probably extremely rare: there was no good commercial reason for them.

However, the voyages of fifth-century merchant adventurers such as Hanno had restored the metal trade to its former lucrative level. It was thanks to him, Dio Chrysostom claimed only a little extravagantly, that the Carthaginians 'lived in Africa rather than Phoenicia, became very wealthy, acquired many markets, ports and ships, and ruled on land and sea'.

WAR AGAINST THE GREEKS

The Carthaginians celebrated their revived prosperity by returning to the attack in Sicily, where the warring tyrants of the rival Greek city states, besides threatening the remaining Phoenician settlements in the island, offered plenty of tempting opportunities for meddling. The war which broke out in 410 BC went on with scarcely a pause for over a century, and led directly to the first great war with Rome. During that time the armies of Carthage managed to sack, on one occasion or another, all the Greek cities of Sicily except Syracuse: to this day the ruins of Selinunte and Agrigento bear eloquent witness to the ferocity of the fighting. The struggle was marked on both sides by unspeakable atrocities. A Carthaginian general had three thousand prisoners of war tortured and sacrificed in revenge for the death of his grandfather at Himera seventy years before; in 398 BC the Greeks massacred the entire civilian population of Motya.

Neither side ever succeeded in conquering the whole island. The war was vastly complicated for the Greeks by the internecine rivalries of the various city tyrants: Greek fought Greek in alliance with the Carthaginians. The Carthaginians were severely hampered by desertions and revolts in their armies and by risings at home among the African population (who on one occasion seized the town of Tunis). Twice Syracuse was saved from capture only by an outbreak of disease in the ranks of the Carthaginian army. Twice Carthage had to sue for peace, twice she was obliged to pay a heavy indemnity. Yet she still did not give up, and not only because control of the far side of the straits of Sicily had for centuries been the cornerstone of her foreign policy.

For this savage warfare paid off. It was, for Carthage, a source of revenue; almost an arm of trade. The booty sent back to Carthage from captured Greek cities more than compensated for her military and naval expenses, and even for the indemnities that were demanded. Further, the war was fought on foreign soil, and with mercenary troops. They were not Carthaginian farms and cities that were razed to the ground, nor Carthaginian crops that were laid waste, nor – on the whole – Carthaginian families who lost sons and brothers. Although the generals were always Carthaginian citizens (rather than the soldiers of fortune to whom the Greeks tended to entrust their armies), and although it was a point of pride among the nobility to volunteer, their corps d'élite was a tiny minority beside the hired mercenaries: cavalry from the tribes of Numidia, slingers from the Balearic Islands, javelin-throwers from Spain, Libyans from their own territory, Celts, Ligurians, even Greeks and Italians.

But this immunity did not last. Between 310 and 307 BC, towards the end of the long struggle, Carthage itself was threatened. Agathocles, the reigning tyrant of Syracuse, unable to raise the siege of his city, boldly set sail for Africa with fourteen thousand men to make a counter-attack. He

First-century AD terracotta statuette of Baal Hammon from Cape Bon,
now in the Bardo Museum

landed on Cape Bon, burnt his boats behind him because he could not
spare the men to guard them, and for three years lived off the countryside –
at one point, with help from the Greeks of Cyrenaica, capturing both Utica
and Hippo Diarrhytus (Bizerta), where he was able to build shipyards and
then ships to re-establish his communications with Sicily.

For the rulers of Carthage, the pillage of their estates was a novel
experience. But they did not attempt to treat with Agathocles by yielding
in Sicily; they were not open to blackmail – especially since they still had
control of the sea. Instead, two hundred children from the leading families
were sacrificed to the god Baal Hammon – children known to have been
improperly saved on previous occasions by the substitution of slave children. For Agathocles was seen as the instrument of the cheated god's
revenge. Three hundred more children were voluntarily sacrificed by other
parents who were suspected of similar impiety.

The fearful holocaust was shortly rewarded by the departure of Agathocles (who spent the last years of his life planning to re-invade Africa).
Temporarily, though she was obliged to return to her old boundaries in
Sicily and to pay an indemnity, Carthage had been spared. Yet an example
had been set, a lesson learned. Africa was not impregnable and, moreover,
she was worth having: it was through the eyes of Agathocles' troops
that Diodorus Siculus was describing the countryside of Cape Bon in
the passage quoted earlier. Where they had led, others could follow. For
Carthage, it was the most serious consequence of the many decades of
warfare against the Sicilian Greeks.

THE GREEKS 'CONQUER' CARTHAGE

The other main result of the war was that Carthage was drawn back into
the mainstream of Mediterranean civilization. Greek prisoners of war in
Sicily were shipped back as slaves to Carthage, where they re-introduced
Greek skills in the plastic arts – a field in which Semitic peoples like
the Phoenicians, with their distrust of the graven image, were notably
deficient. Greek luxury objects reappear in the graves of the period, and
Greek plumbing was installed in rich men's houses. At Kerkouane on Cape
Bon, where the only known Carthaginian township not later overlaid by
Roman building has been uncovered, one can see the smart bathroom
floors of the period: a pink or blue cement inlaid with chips of white
marble, which the Romans called *pavimenta punica*. In Carthage itself,
which was vastly increasing in size at this period, 'New Carthage' was
built alongside 'Old Carthage', on a Greek town plan and borrowing Greek
architecture. The Punic ports also belong to the fourth century. All these
improvements were paid for not only in Sicilian booty, but perhaps also
in the wheat Carthage was now able to export. The Greek goddesses
Demeter and Persephone became a cult at Carthage – to expiate, it is
thought, the destruction of their sanctuary outside Syracuse during the
Sicilian wars (an act to which the superstitious Carthaginians had attri-
buted a subsequent reversal of fortune) and because harvest goddesses
might answer the prayers of a people now dependent on their own farmlands. Dionysius was also worshipped at Carthage; and Hellenistic
religion, perhaps because it offered a more cheerful after-life than their
own, became so popular that the Greek funeral custom of incineration
replaced burial. The Carthaginians, though loyal to the end to their own
relentless gods, were like magpies in their adoption of those of other
people. They had early imported various Egyptian gods and goddesses;
Egyptian amulets are among the commonest finds from the Punic period,
and in the third century BC the influence of Hellenistic Egypt remained
strong.

Shifting alliances in Sicily also led to some intermarriage between Greeks and Carthaginians: the mother of the great Hannibal himself was a Greek. Both Hannibal and his father, the general Hamilcar, modelled their strategy on that of Alexander the Great. The use of elephants in war was also adopted from the Greeks; so was the minting of money.

Yet the hellenization of Carthage, though in some ways real enough, remained superficial, even among the rich. Education was either severely practical, or in the hands of the priesthood: boys who learnt Greek mostly learnt it because they were going to be merchants in their fathers' businesses. It is possible that girls, who did not need vocational training of this kind, were actually better educated than their brothers. Although some Carthaginians did go to Greece to study, and one of them later became head of the Academy at Athens, there is no sign in Carthage of the humanism of the Greek world. The elaborate religious ceremonies were the only public festivities; theatres were unknown. The dulcimer and the zither were frequently represented on sacred statues, and music was played at religious ceremonies or to accompany ritual dances, but in general the arts were neglected.

However, this nation of merchants took a great interest in clothes and hair, in cleanliness and, like the modern Arabs, in perfume and jewellery, in food and creature comforts; but none in their bodies. Their textiles, their pastry-cooks and their confectionery were famous, but there were no games in Carthage, no athletes, and their gods, like those of all Oriental peoples and unlike those of the Greeks, were always represented clothed. Although the women adopted female Greek costume (its elegance spoilt, perhaps, by over-abundant jewellery), the men remained faithful to the beards, the skullcaps and the long-sleeved robes of their ancestors, which were less appropriate to physical exercise than to impressing others with the wearers' dignity. They tended to overweight and self-importance. 'The Carthaginians,' wrote Plutarch in the second century AD but quoting an earlier opinion, 'are a hard and gloomy people, submissive to their rulers and harsh to their subjects ... they keep obstinately to their decisions, are austere, and care little for amusement or the graces of life.' This judgement might be modified if their literature had survived, and if we knew more about their domestic life; they were, for instance, exceptionally for that time, monogamous. It serves to show, however, how alien they always seemed to the Greeks and Romans.

The half-century that followed the failure of Agathocles' expedition to Africa was an extremely prosperous period in the history of Carthage. She resumed trading relations with the eastern Mediterranean. She was growing enough wheat to export; her textiles were much in demand; and a falling-off in the supply of Spanish tin (due possibly to insurrections among Iberian tribes) now mattered less than in the days when her only other exports were the indifferent pottery and metal artefacts which, though they satisfied her barbarian customers, were despised by those

30

who could choose the marvellous ceramics and *objets d'art* being manufactured by the Greeks of this period.

By this time, too, Carthage had become the overlord of the other Phoenician settlements along the Algerian and Moroccan coasts. She proved hardly more popular with them than with the native Africans, for in return for her offer to defend them she greatly restricted their right to trade. There was much grumbling, and one or other of them, in despair at the harshness of her rule, was constantly defecting to her enemies. This was to contribute to Carthage's eventual downfall. Hannibal, in Italy, could never persuade Rome's allies to desert her; but the Romans had little difficulty, once they landed in Africa, in persuading Phoenician cities, as well as Libyan tribes, to turn against Carthage.

THE NEW AFRICAN KINGDOMS

If Carthage herself was now to a certain extent open to outside influences, by virtue of being rich, powerful and landed, she was also beginning to have a significant effect on her immediate neighbours. Her African mercenaries returned home to their tribes with at least a smattering of civilization, and a taste for more. Their chieftains sought to emulate in their own territories the successes of Punic agriculture, borrowing Carthaginian experts to help them, and to embellish their own settlements with some of the symbols of city wealth. They soon realized that turning more of their pastoral tribesmen into settled farmers made possible an increase in the productivity of the land, and also added to their own power: farmers were easier to control – and to tax – than shepherds. It added to their prestige, too. Where Dido had refused to marry a Libyan chieftain, preferring to throw herself on a funeral pyre, now the daughters of Carthage were given away in marriage to African princelings. Africans gave Carthaginian names to their children and adopted both Carthaginian gods and, in part, the Punic language. In turn, the Carthaginians adopted African fertility gods – necessary to them, like the Greek goddesses Demeter and Persephone, now that they were farmers themselves – and certain African funeral customs. It was a trend which operated like a kind of crystallizing process during the final century and a half of Carthage's existence. More than Hanno in the fifth century BC, it was the Libyans in the third who finally transformed 'Tyrians into Africans' and, in turn, became the upholders of neo-Punic language and traditions for centuries under the Romans.

The earliest of the indigenous kingdoms to emerge into history was, however, the one furthest from Carthage. The Moors of Mauretania had formed themselves into a tribal federation by the fourth century BC.[1]

---

1 They were pastoralists, but were also growing wheat by the time the Romans colonized their country.

Then, by the third century BC, northern Algeria was shared between two particularly powerful tribes. The kingdom of the Masaesyli stretched more than five hundred miles to the west of Cape Bougaroun, north of Constantine. It was loosely based on two widely-separated capitals, Siga and, later, Cirta (Constantine). The kingdom of the Massyli further east was more modest in extent, but bordered Carthaginian territory; it may at one time have included Cirta, and perhaps extended much nearer Carthage itself. Nothing is known of the inter-tribal warfare by which they must have established their supremacy over other tribes. Both were to play a leading part in the downfall and destruction of Carthage.

Further south, the region nearest the desert, from the Atlantic to southern Tunisia, was inhabited by peoples whom the ancient historians called Gaetules, who remained, not least because their territory was much less amenable to cultivation, comparatively untouched by Mediterranean influences.[1] To the east, south of Tripolitania, were the Garamantes, who occupied the oases and wadi-beds of the Fezzan. Their horse-drawn chariots, probably adopted from the Greeks of Cyrenaica, are mentioned by Herodotus in the fifth century BC, and are represented in rock engravings in the dry wadi valleys of the central Sahara.[2] There were other desert tribes, such as the Nasamones; but these arid regions can have supported only small numbers of people. Yet they, too, were to be a constant anxiety to the future masters of north-west Africa.

---

1 It is possible that the Gaetules were the builders of the great native tomb near Lambaesis known as Le Medracen, which, although indigenous in form, shows Mediterranean influence in its decoration. Others think it was built by the Massyli.

2 These chariots were not used for transport. They can only have been for ceremony and prestige – like the chariots used by the Greeks in the Trojan War. But it was the Garamantes who first invented harness for four-horse chariots.

3

THE WARS BETWEEN ROME AND CARTHAGE

Meanwhile another rival had risen to power across the Mediterranean: Rome. By the middle of the fifth century BC, when Carthage had temporarily withdrawn from the Mediterranean, Rome had become the leading city of central Italy. In the fourth, when Carthage was once more at war in Sicily, many other towns of central Italy yielded to Rome the right to control their foreign policy and call on them for military help; this was in return for protection against the Gauls to the north, or other enemies, and for the right of their people to Roman citizenship if they chose to live in Rome – and in some cases even if they did not. Liberal treatment of defeated neighbours was something quite new in Mediterranean history; the Romans were to be rewarded for it. The rest of Italy soon joined their confederacy, or was brought under the Roman yoke, and by the third century they controlled almost the whole of the Italian peninsula south of the Po valley, including all but one of the Greek city states of southern Italy. It was to give them a commanding advantage in manpower during the wars with Carthage.

Not that Rome's armies were conspicuously well led: rather the reverse, since her political constitution gave military command to two elected leaders for a year at a time only. Such a custom preserved her from tyranny, but too often proved a recipe for incompetent generalship; or, if by good fortune the assembly elected as one of its chief magistrates a man who had both military experience and a talent for command, his victories were liable to be undone either by his fellow consul or by their successors when their year in office was up. The Romans did not destroy the Punic empire until they entrusted command to a general who was a match for Hannibal – and allowed that general to remain in command until Hannibal had been defeated.

According to the historian Polybius, writing in the second century BC, the earliest record of dealings between Rome and Carthage was a treaty which must have been signed in 510 or 509 BC. The Romans were at that time under the protection of Carthage's allies, the Etruscans, and the treaty merely defined their respective fields of interest: the Romans were to have limited rights to trade in African and Sardinian ports, and Carthage recognized Rome's territorial rights in Latium (central Italy). It was a treaty neither side would be tempted to break. In 348 BC, another treaty was signed: Carthage still recognized Rome's rights in central Italy, but Rome was now allowed to trade only in Sicily and in Carthage itself. The balance of power remained with Carthage; but the terms implied that she was conscious of Rome's growing strength, and that their respective spheres of interest might one day collide.

Forty years later, Rome was agreeing not to interfere in Sicily, in return for Carthage not interfering in Italy. In 278 BC, they came to their last agreement: this time it was a modified alliance against the Greek King Pyrrhus of Epirus, who had come west to carve out a new kingdom for himself at the expense of Rome in Italy, and then of Carthage in Sicily; or so he intended. When he failed, and returned to the East, he is said to have remarked: 'What a field we are now leaving for Carthaginian and Roman to fight in.'

Fourteen years later, Rome and Carthage were fighting for Sicily.

The causes of the First Punic War seem trivial, almost accidental. A group of Italian colonists in Sicily, technically Roman citizens, appealed to the Romans for help against the Greeks of Syracuse. They had also appealed to the Carthaginians. The Romans were afraid that the Carthaginians would use this local quarrel as an excuse to defeat Syracuse and make Sicily at last a Phoenician island; the Carthaginians were afraid the Romans would make it a pretext to drive the Phoenicians out of Sicily. In any event, the local quarrel was soon forgotten in the war which broke out in 264 BC, and which lasted, with intervals for recuperation, more than twenty years. It was Rome's first military venture outside Italy.

The Romans soon realized that they would never conquer the Carthaginians in Sicily without defeating them at sea. Their own maritime strength at that time amounted to fewer than fifty ships manned by Greek or Italian allies. Yet they refused to be intimidated by the reputation of the Carthaginian navy for invincibility; and in spite of horrifying reverses they never gave up their aim of destroying the enemy's sea power.

Construction of their first fleet of a hundred quinqueremes and twenty triremes was begun in 261 BC. The quinqueremes were modelled on a Carthaginian ship which had been wrecked on the Italian coast, and the whole fleet, according to Polybius, was built in the incredibly short time of two months. Most historians have, in fact, chosen not to believe it – but the discovery and raising from the seabed off western Sicily of a sunken Punic warship (the only warship of classical times so far found), and part of the bows of another, complete with underwater ram, during the 1970s has yielded dramatic circumstantial evidence in support of Polybius's account. Carpenters' marks found in the planking strongly suggest that the parts were prefabricated before assembly – which would have made any production line much speedier.

Detail from bas-relief of Roman warship, in the Egizio Museum in the Vatican, Rome

The Romans also armed each ship with a boarding device known as a crow, which could be swung outwards and attached by spikes to enemy ships and was intended to turn a sea battle into something more like a land battle. They then trained their rowers on dry land. Such optimism was fortified by unexpected successes during the next couple of years, which did much for their morale and dissipated the legend of the unconquerable Carthaginian navy. However, the Romans did not shake the Carthaginian hold on Sicily.

The Romans began building another, larger, fleet in 257 BC and boldly set sail for Africa the following year. But the fate of Agathocles half a century before was repeated in spite of initial successes. The first Roman invasion of Africa came to an ignominious end: seventeen thousand of their twenty-thousand strong army under Regulus were killed or captured in 255 BC by the Spartan Xanthippus, to whom the Carthaginians had appealed for help. This was immediately followed by a disaster for the Romans at sea. Their fleet, returning to Sicily from Africa with the remnant of Regulus's army and with a large number of captured Carthaginian ships, some two hundred and sixty-four ships in all, was hit by a southerly gale. All but eighty were driven on to the rocks off Sicily and destroyed –

with a loss of life, including rowers and soldiers, which may have approached one hundred thousand men. Polybius considered that it was the greatest disaster ever to have happened at sea.

Yet the Romans were not deterred: they built another fleet, and when one hundred and fifty ships were destroyed in another storm, they prepared to replace them once more. And their policy was justified: sea power was to win the war, in spite of the successes of the Carthaginian general Hamilcar Barca (father of Hannibal) in Sicily some years later. For the Roman losses lulled their enemies into a false sense of security, and the Carthaginians laid up their own war fleet.

Throughout the Punic wars the Carthaginians reckoned without Roman resolve, that blind determination to win no matter what the cost. A census of 247 BC suggests that the war had already cost the Romans seventeen in every hundred of their adult males – a higher loss than that of Germany in the First World War – and it is likely that their allies had suffered similarly. Yet, short of money and manpower though they were, in 243 BC the Romans built another two hundred quinqueremes on a more recent Carthaginian model. This time they found they had the sea to themselves. It was eight months before Carthage got a fleet to sea again. When she did, she was defeated. Her rowers were out of practice, and the battle of the Aegates Islands was at last a decisive victory for Rome. Carthage sued for peace. She had to give up Sicily, the Aegates Islands and Lipara, and pay an indemnity of 3,200 talents spread over ten years. It was a triumph for Rome.

THE MERCENARY WAR

There now occurred one of the most horrifying episodes in the entire history of Carthage. Hamilcar's mercenaries had been sent back from Sicily to Carthage, where they were to be paid what was owing to them. But the rulers of Carthage, thinking of the losses they had sustained and the enormous indemnity they would have to pay, hoped to avoid paying as much as had been promised. The mercenaries (more than half of whom were Libyan and not best disposed towards their Carthaginian overlords) were sent with their families to Sicca (El Kef), a hundred miles off, with a gold coin apiece, to await the balance. But the money did not arrive, and the mercenaries grew tired of waiting. They left Sicca, and returned to threaten Carthage from the neighbourhood of Tunis. The Carthaginians, terrified, at last paid the money – too late. The mercenaries had tasted opportunity, and stepped up their demands. These were not met, and a slave of Italian origin, Spendius, and a Libyan called Matho stirred up a mutiny not only among the mercenaries (and opponents of their plan were stoned to death) but among the Libyan peasantry, who, profoundly oppressed by the heavy taxes levied during the war, willingly swelled their ranks by twenty thousand men. Meanwhile the Carthaginians raised a citizen army and recruited fresh mercenaries.

What followed was the fearsome 'truceless war' described by Polybius.[1] Atrocities were committed by both sides. Carthaginians captured by the mercenaries had their hands and parts cut off and legs broken before being flung into ditches and buried alive. Hamilcar had his prisoners trampled to death by elephants. At one point the starving mercenaries were reduced to eating their prisoners and slaves; at another, Hamilcar crucified a peace party of ten men, among them Spendius. The war lasted more than three years. It ended, though only after the Numidian tribe of the Massyli had joined the Carthaginians, in the virtual annihilation of the mercenaries.

During the crisis, Rome sympathetically returned to Carthage her unransomed prisoners and forbade the Italians to help the rebels; but at the end of the Mercenary War she took advantage of Carthage's weakness herself to seize Sardinia and demand a further 1,200 talents, which Carthage was in no position to refuse. This was one action in Rome's history that her most patriotic apologists could not justify as 'self-defence' – even Livy admitted that it was adding insult to injury. It certainly made impossible a genuine peace between Rome and Carthage. The vengeful hatred it inspired in the hearts of the Carthaginians had more than a little to do with the support they gave a generation later to the Barcid family (of which Hannibal was a member) in the Barcids' long-laid plans to destroy Rome.

THE MOVE TO SPAIN

Sicily had been the guiding principle of Carthage's foreign policy for three hundred years. For Sicily she had embarked on wars, first against the Greeks and then against the Romans, which were among the bloodiest known to the ancient world. But where the Greeks had failed, the upstart Romans had succeeded. Sicily was lost to Carthage for ever. It was the first Roman province outside Italy.

Its loss did not ruin Carthage. But she now had to look for new sources of money and manpower to raise the indemnity and to restore her fortunes. She turned to Spain, rightly divining that the iron, silver and copper mines of the interior had by no means been exhausted. In 237 BC Hamilcar Barca left Carthage to conquer a new empire, taking with him his son-in-law Hasdrubal and his nine-year-old son Hannibal, who, according to Livy, 'begged with all the childish arts he could muster, to be allowed to accompany him; whereupon Hamilcar, who was preparing to offer sacrifice for a successful outcome, led the boy to the altar and made him solemnly swear, with his hand upon the sacred victim, that as soon as he

---

1 Otherwise known as the Mercenary War, it provided Flaubert with the subject of his novel *Salammbô*.

was old enough he would be the enemy of the Roman people'.

In the next sixteen years, the whole of southern Spain fell into the hands of Hamilcar and, after his death, into those of his son-in-law, either by military conquest or by diplomatic alliances. Indeed Hasdrubal, after his first wife's death, married an Iberian woman, as Hannibal himself did later. The Barcids modelled themselves on Alexander the Great, who a century earlier had conquered the whole of the Persian Empire in ten years with a comparatively small but loyal army. They never tried to break the link with Carthage, but the regime they established in Spain did resemble, at least superficially, a Hellenistic kingdom. The coins they minted show them wearing the royal wreath, and the capital Hasdrubal founded on the site of modern Cartagena was named Kart Hadasht – 'new capital' – like Carthage before it, and perhaps with the same end in view, that it should be the cornerstone of a new Phoenician empire. But, like the Hellenistic kingdoms, the conquest did not strike roots; the Romans had no difficulty later, using the same opportunist methods, in seducing the Iberian tribes from the Carthaginian cause.

Meanwhile, however, New Carthage provided a base, and Spain provided the manpower and the wealth, for the extraordinary enterprise which the young Hannibal, now twenty-eight, undertook in the year 218 BC, three years after he had taken command on the death of his brother-in-law.

HANNIBAL'S GREAT ENTERPRISE

Hannibal's famous crossing of the Alps, accompanied by thirty-seven elephants, was embarked upon in the hope of conquering Italy. It took the Romans almost completely by surprise and astonished the whole of the ancient world; it remains astonishing today. There were no proper paths; guides proved incompetent; local tribes, hoping for loot, harried Hannibal's army as it struggled through steep ravines, and caused many casualties; rock barring the way is said to have been cracked apart by picks after being heated by bonfires and made friable with water; men and animals slid down ice-bound slopes, or fell off precipices. For a fortnight, in the late autumn, animals and men together, most of them used to a warmer climate, were above the snowline. The crossing cost Hannibal half his troops by death or desertion, many of his horses and almost all his celebrated elephants. Yet he remained in Italy for the next seventeen years, and during those years he did not lose a single battle.

That first autumn, in 218 BC, Hannibal defeated a Roman army led by the consul Publius Cornelius Scipio in one of his most audacious battles. The following spring, in spite of losing the sight of one eye from a chill caught while crossing the marshes of the middle Arno, he annihilated another Roman army of twenty-five thousand in an ambush on the shores

Terracotta of war elephant, found at Pompeii

of Lake Trasimene. For a year, while Rome recovered from the shock of being outclassed by a general of genius, Quintus Fabius Maximus was able to employ his famous 'Fabian tactics' of harrying the Carthaginians without ever giving Hannibal the opportunity of battle; but the consuls who succeeded him, one a great deal less prudent and the other less firm-minded, attacked Hannibal at Cannae in the August of 216 BC. This was Rome's greatest military disaster. Polybius put the Roman losses at seventy thousand, Livy at fifty thousand; they were certainly thirty-five thousand, the bulk of their army. Hannibal's casualties were fewer than six thousand. It was no wonder that the cry of *Hannibal ad portas!* (Hannibal at the gates!) – which the Romans expected virtually on the morrow – became for centuries the catchphrase with which Roman mothers alarmed their children.

No one has put more clearly than Livy the situation which faced the Romans when the first news of the disaster reached the capital:

'Never, without an enemy actually within the gates, had there been such terror and confusion in the city ... Rome left without a force in the field, without a commander, without a single soldier, Apulia and Samnium in Hannibal's hands, and now nearly the whole of Italy overrun. No other nation could have suffered so tremendous a series of disasters, and not been overwhelmed ... Nobody doubted that Hannibal, now that the armies were destroyed, would attack Rome ... the streets were loud with the wailing and weeping of women, and nothing yet being clearly known, living and dead alike were being mourned in nearly every house in the city.'

The Carthaginians had brought the war home with a vengeance. Yet the Romans did not ask Hannibal for peace terms. Livy's pride was justified: they really were like 'no other nation in the world'. They even, it was said, gave a sympathetic welcome to the surviving consul after his escape from the field of battle.[1] No energy was wasted on recrimination. The Romans had some extra edge of pride, tenacity and that belief in eventual victory which had enabled them to win the First Punic War a generation before. This was the spirit which was to conquer the known world. It was given a voice by a survivor of Cannae, the young son of the Scipio whose army had been defeated two years earlier: 'I swear, with all the passion of my heart, that I shall never desert our country, or permit any other citizen of Rome to leave her in the lurch.' This younger Scipio was destined to conquer Hannibal fourteen years later. Cannae was a great battle, but not a decisive one. What was decisive for the history of the ancient world was Rome's refusal to surrender.

Two Vestal Virgins who were discovered to have broken their vows of chastity were, of course, condemned to death, and the populace demanded that two Gauls and two Greeks should be buried alive; human sacrifice was not unknown outside Carthage in times of stress. This offering to the gods was rewarded, so it seemed, just as the sacrifice of five hundred Carthaginian children had been a century before: Hannibal did not, or could not, follow up his victory.

For Hannibal had not, in spite of his lenient treatment of their captured soldiers, persuaded any of the allied cities of central Italy to give him more than the most trivial help in his fight against Rome. There had been no rising of the Italians against their masters. Although in Sicily the Syracusans revolted, the Romans eventually retook the city after a long and arduous siege,[2] and defeated a Carthaginian fleet at the same time. Nor, without a fleet, was Hannibal able to make the most of a personal alliance he had formed with Philip V of Macedon.

Most crucial of all, his army was simply too small to follow up his dazzling victories. Living from hand to mouth in southern Italy as best he

---

1 The normal Carthaginian practice was to crucify unsuccessful generals.
2 The defence was directed by the great inventor and mathematician Archimedes, whose machines of war proved a serious obstacle to the attackers; he was killed by a Roman soldier when the victors sacked the city.

could during the years that followed, he and his army were bound to be increasingly dependent on reinforcements. But they never came, neither from his base in Spain nor from Carthage itself. Carthage had no fleet; Spain was having serious troubles of its own. For the Roman army which, right at the beginning of the war, had been sent to cut Hannibal's lines of communication, had gone on to Spain and, in spite of initial reverses, had eventually seized New Carthage. Hannibal's brother, another Hasdrubal, whom he had left in charge, was pinned down; Carthaginian troops which had been intended for Hannibal had to be diverted to help Hasdrubal. In vain: when Hasdrubal at last followed his brother to Italy in 207 BC, nine years after Cannae, it was because the Romans, now under the command of young Scipio, virtually pushed him out of Spain. Hasdrubal and his troops had no more luck in Italy. Cannae was revenged by the Romans at the battle of the River Metaurus: Hasdrubal was killed, and his head, so it was said, was sent to Hannibal. It was the first and last time in more than ten years that he saw the brother for whose help he had waited so long.

Hannibal now had no prospect of defeating Rome. The most he could hope for was a decent peace. This was thwarted by Scipio, who followed up the advantage he had at last secured in Spain by finally driving out the remaining Carthaginians in the year after the battle of the River Metaurus. That done, he was free to return to Rome to urge that he should be allowed to attack, not Hannibal, but Carthage itself. However enfeebled, Hannibal's magical gifts could not be discounted: he had pulled off too many incredible victories out of the most unpropitious situations. The Sibylline Books were consulted: they counselled seeking the support of the Great Goddess Cybele. Her symbol, the Black Stone, was brought from Pessinus in Anatolia in 204 BC and installed in a splendid new temple (remains of which can still be seen on the Palatine Hill).

Meanwhile the tough, single-minded Scipio recognized that to strike straight at Carthage would cut off any further help for Hannibal at source and would also draw him out of Italy. Better to risk defeat at Hannibal's hands in Africa than dangerously near Rome. But Scipio did not expect defeat. He had already come to an arrangement, if not an alliance, with Syphax of the Masaesyli, king of the most powerful of the African kingdoms at that time, which controlled western Numidia. The Roman senate agreed to his plan.

SOPHONISBA: A HEROINE FOR CARTHAGE

The position of Carthage was by now extremely vulnerable. Too late, she made two attempts to get help to Hannibal. Both failed, and their failure left her even more exposed. But it happened that Hasdrubal (not one of the Barcid family), the general who had been in command latterly in Spain and was now in charge of the defence of Carthage, had a daughter,

41

Sophonisba, and the ageing Syphax was persuaded to desert the Roman cause – for love. According to Livy, Syphax fell passionately in love with Sophonisba. Hasdrubal gave him her hand in marriage, and Syphax was quite won over to the cause of his new in-laws.

Carthage was not out of danger, but Scipio had lost his major ally. He had to make do with the problematical support of Masinissa of the Massyli (the other major kingdom of Numidia), son of the king who had been Carthage's ally at the time of the Mercenary War half a century before. The tortuous succession arrangements which operated in the African kingdoms had led to such confusion on the death of this king that Syphax had been able to steal the territory of the Massyli, in eastern Numidia, and the young Masinissa was little better than an outlaw, constantly on the run from Syphax's troops. But it was this unpromising ally who – in spite of a dramatic temporary defection – helped Rome defeat Carthage.

Hasdrubal, who knew Masinissa's quality of old, recognized that he 'was a man of far loftier spirit and far greater ability than had ever been seen in anyone of his nation'. He might yet offer a serious threat to Carthage. The Carthaginian general urged Syphax, his new son-in-law, to destroy him if he possibly could. Masinissa and his tiny band of followers were therefore hounded by Syphax and, it was thought, exterminated. But three men survived, and one of them was Masinissa. His reappearance among his own people, after he had been given up for dead, created such an upsurge of loyalty that large numbers flocked to his standard; and, although Syphax conquered him in battle, Masinissa was able to retreat to southern Tunisia, to await the arrival of the Roman invasion and his chance to avenge himself on Syphax.

Scipio landed on Cape Farina with some 30,000 men in 204 BC and set up his headquarters near Utica – ever Carthage's rival, and willing enough to be Rome's ally when prompted by Roman troops on the doorstep. In the first year Scipio had little more success than the Greek Agathocles and the Roman Regulus before him. However, under cover of peace negotiations he was able to discover the disposition of the Carthaginian and Numidian camps and succeeded in setting fire to them, killing a large number of the opposing armies. Soon after, he scored a victory over Hasdrubal himself, and seized Tunis. He also captured Syphax. Masinissa, seeing his opportunity, invaded the territory of his old enemy and captured Cirta, Syphax's capital.

But on the threshold of the royal palace the Numidian conqueror was met by Sophonisba, who 'was in the full flower of her youthful beauty; as she clung to Masinissa's knees or clasped his hand, begging him to promise never to give her up to a Roman, her words grew little by little more like the blandishments of a lover than the supplication of a captive, and at this the conqueror's heart not only melted into pity but – with the characteristic inflammability of the Numidian race – was itself vanquished and led into captive love'. So went the legend recounted by Livy; and Masinissa married Sophonisba that very day.

Scipio was understandably alarmed on hearing the news. He had lost one ally, Syphax, to Sophonisba; now he had lost the other – just as he was beginning to be useful. The captive Syphax added fuel to the flames, by declaring that it was some comfort to him that Sophonisba had now 'transferred her corrupting influence to the house and home of his bitterest enemy'. Scipio sent word at once to Masinissa, pointing out that his bride, as the wife of Syphax, belonged to the Roman people, and must be given up. Masinissa, after much groaning and sighing, yielded to the thinly veiled threat; but, remembering his promise to her that she should not fall into the hands of the Romans, he sent her a cup of poison. She drank it, saying to the slave who brought it: 'I accept this bridal gift – a gift not unwelcome if my husband has been unable to offer a greater one to his wife.' Livy adds that she showed no sign of perturbation. Thus, it was said, died Hasdrubal's daughter.[1]

Meanwhile the bridegroom was welcomed back into the Roman fold, and rewarded with the official title of king and a Roman triumph: the first foreigner to be so honoured. King Masinissa's reign was to be long and glorious.

SCIPIO'S REVENGE

With Syphax defeated and Masinissa once more an ally of Rome, the Carthaginian leaders had to sue for peace. But negotiations broke down when a Roman fleet bringing food to Scipio's army was shipwrecked near Carthage and the citizens, famished after a year cut off from their farmlands, salvaged what they could for themselves. News had also reached Carthage that Hannibal had disembarked at Leptis Minor (Lemta, on Tunisia's east coast), and with it came new hope. Hannibal was resting his army and raising reinforcements among the African tribes.

The final confrontation was not long delayed. The armies of Hannibal and Scipio met near Zama in central Tunisia. The two generals are reputed to have met before the battle; and indeed, how curious they must have been to see each other, the elder who had been uncrowned king of Spain and seen his kingdom wrested from him by the younger, the younger who remembered the shame of Cannae. But if, as Livy suggests, Hannibal proposed peace terms, Scipio refused to grant them. The battle took place in October 202 BC. Masinissa was there to support Scipio; but Syphax's son Vermina, with the remnants of his father's army, arrived too late to help Hannibal. It was Hannibal's first defeat in the field, and Scipio's final revenge. The Second Punic War was over.

---

1 Appropriately, her story is the subject of nearly a score of eighteenth-century Italian operas.

Carthage was not yet destroyed: that fate was still half a century distant. But she gave up all her foreign territories, and her African land was limited by a 150-mile ditch which Scipio ordered to be dug from Thabraca (Tabarka) on the north coast to Thaenae near Sfax; beyond, Masinissa was left the ruler of the whole of Numidia, which included much of the region that later became Tripolitania. Carthage gave up all her war booty and all the riches she had brought back from Sicily, and had to pay a crippling indemnity of ten thousand talents. She gave up all her warships bar ten triremes, and all her elephants – so deadly an instrument of war did these tanks of the ancient world seem to the Roman legionaries, even if their effectiveness was mostly limited to inspiring terror.[1]

She still had her greatest son; after a life-time's absence from his native city, Hannibal by the strength of his personality pushed through financial and agricultural reforms which enabled her to pay off the indemnity within a few years; and she took up once more her old maritime trade. But Carthage was not allowed to wage war, even in self-defence.

Of this fact, Masinissa of Numidia took full advantage. When Carthage protested to Rome about his annexations the senate chose not to intervene. For reasons that remain obscure, Hannibal fled into exile in 195 BC and spent the remaining dozen years of his life as a soldier of fortune in the pay of Rome's enemies in Asia Minor; but if he had remained, it is doubtful whether even his genius could have forestalled the ambition of Masinissa to create, out of North Africa, a genuine African kingdom.

Hitherto, the African kingdoms had been temporary tribal coalitions; Masinissa did not wish to be a tribal chieftain, but a true king, with settled subjects, with a proper army and a fleet financed by taxes rather than by irregular and erratic tribal contributions. And indeed the tribal chieftain who began his rule as king of the Massyli ended it as king of Numidia – a territory.

The Punic example had inspired some agricultural advance in Numidia and there was already an increasing number of towns and villages; but Masinissa was determined that there should be yet more settlement in Numidia. 'This was the greatest and most remarkable thing he did', wrote Polybius. 'Before him, the whole of Numidia was useless, and thought to be by its very nature incapable of cultivation. He was the first, he alone' – Polybius was certainly exaggerating – 'to show that she could yield everything, as much as any other country, for he put to the fullest use enormous areas.' These were mostly in the east of Numidia, but the king himself owned large estates – so many, according to Diodorus Siculus, that he was able to leave each of his ten surviving sons (he had had around fifty) a property of more than two thousand acres. Punic administration was adopted for the towns, and the worship of the Greek harvest goddess was

---

1 The elephants tended to be almost as dangerous to their own side as to the enemy.

introduced, as it had been to Carthage when the Carthaginians took to agriculture two hundred years earlier. Masinissa built himself a new palace at his capital, Cirta, struck his own coinage, and gave his huge family a Greek education. He intended Africa to become part of the Hellenistic world.

Yet the richest farmlands still belonged to Carthage. Masinissa had his eye on them: was he an ally of Rome for nothing? They may once, also, have been part of the Massylian kingdom. Over the next decades he seized first one piece of Carthaginian territory, then another, including part of the coast of the Gulf of Syrte in 174 BC; and was encouraged in this rape on his old enemy because the Romans turned a deaf ear to the complaints of Carthage. Masinissa announced that Africa belonged to the Africans.

Rome was content, for the moment, to allow Masinissa to harass Carthage on her behalf. But Carthage remained wealthy. Her merchants were still familiar in the ports of the eastern Mediterranean,[1] she was able to volunteer to build a fleet for her conquerors for their war against Antioch (the offer was refused), and when the elder Cato visited Africa in 153 BC he was struck by the threat which the prosperity of Carthaginian agriculture posed to the sadly declining fortunes of his fellow landowners in Italy. That was the occasion when he showed the Carthaginian figs in the Roman senate, and said that Carthage must be destroyed.

The city's fate drew nearer. A year earlier, in 154 BC, Masinissa had annexed the fertile region around Souk El Khemis, less than a hundred miles from Carthage. This last was too much: Carthage, illicitly, prepared to defend herself, and sought allies in Mauretania and Libya. Masinissa, now eighty-eight, led the Numidians to victory in 150 BC; he hoped to conquer Carthage himself, which he must have looked on as a suitable crown for his life's work.

THE THIRD PUNIC WAR

Rome was by this time alive to the possible dangers of Masinissa's ambitions: a new and prosperous kingdom, based on Carthage, on the other side of the straits of Sicily. Carthage's action now provided Rome with the perfect excuse to thwart Masinissa – by now a friend of fifty years' standing – without actually fighting him. She would destroy Carthage and annex her territory as a Roman province. Yet fear of Masinissa, whose kingdom was still poor and backward, was certainly not the uppermost motive. Carthage had been the most feared enemy for so long that the Third Punic War was undertaken in a spirit of very real hate, with all the force of ancestral tradition behind it.

---

1 One of these Carthaginian merchants figures in *Poenulus*, a comedy by the Roman playwright Plautus.

The story of Carthage's three-year struggle for survival between 149 and 146 BC is haunting and horrifying. It was marked on the Roman side by duplicity and cruelty, and on that of Carthage by all the contradictions of the Punic character: folly and humiliating self-abasement, heroism and self-sacrifice.

The Carthaginians realized they could not hope to win when a Roman army some 84,000 strong landed at Utica, which had joined Rome in 149 BC. Six Phoenician cities on the east coast also took Rome's part, including Hadrumetum, Leptis Minor, Thapsus and Acholla. The peace party in Carthage, ready to accede to Roman demands, executed those who counselled resistance, and gave up to the Romans all their armaments, their ships, and three hundred noble children as hostages, even before they knew what the Roman terms would be. But these were cruelly, impossibly severe: Carthage was to be abandoned, and its inhabitants, dependent on maritime trade though they were, only allowed to rebuild at least twelve miles from the sea.

It was too much, and Carthage, in her extremity, sold herself dear. 'They no longer fought for their interests,' in the words of the French historian Charles-André Julien, 'but for an idea.' They restocked their arsenals: every

Stone catapult balls used during the siege of Carthage in 146 BC, piled in the gardens of the Antonine Baths

day, hundreds of swords and lances were manufactured. The women cut off their hair to make ropes for the catapults, for which thousands of large stone missiles were fashioned, some scratched with letters and symbols: great piles of them can be seen today in the garden of the National Museum at Carthage and in the Antonine Baths down by the shore.

For three years the Carthaginians resisted behind their enormous ramparts, half starving but with no further thought of yielding to anything except death. The city was finally conquered by assault in 146 BC by the Roman commander, Scipio Aemilianus, adopted grandson of the Scipio who had defeated Hannibal at Zama in 202 BC; even then, when the Romans had breached the defences, the carnage went on for six days and six nights. The second-century AD historian Appian has left an unforgettable account, based on a lost chapter of Polybius, who actually witnessed the siege:

'Three streets leading from the market place to the citadel were lined on both sides with six-storey houses, from which the Romans were pelted. They seized the first houses and used them as a base for attacking the next. From their roofs they made bridges of planks and beams to cross over to the next. While one battle was in progress on the roofs, another was fought, against all comers, in the street below. Everywhere there was groaning and wailing and shouting and agony of every description. Some were killed out of hand, some flung down alive from the roofs to the pavement, and of these some were caught on upright spears or sabres or swords. Fires ... spread devastation far and wide ... Those told to remove the debris with axes, crowbars and boathooks and smooth a way for the infantry shoved the dead and those still living into holes in the ground, using their axes and crowbars and shoving and turning them with their tools like blocks of wood or stone. Human beings filled up the gullies. Some were thrown in head down, and their legs protruding from the ground writhed for a considerable while. Some fell feet down and their heads were above the surface. Their faces and skulls were trampled by the galloping horses, not through the riders' design but because of haste.

'Nor had the sweepers done their deed of design: there was the tension of battle, the expectation of quick victory, the excitement of the soldiery, the shouts of the criers and blasts of the trumpets, the commands of officers to advance or retire – all of which created a kind of madness and an indifference to what their eyes saw. Six days were spent on this effort ...'

House by house, street by street, the city was taken. The wife of the Carthaginian commander sent a message to Scipio, begging that her two children might be spared; the request was granted. But when she saw her husband finally give himself up to the Romans, she turned on him for not fighting to the death, and threw herself with her children into the flames of the dying city: a true compatriot of Dido and Sophonisba.

Even at that moment, Scipio saw the poignancy of the city's fate, and thought of Rome: Polybius noticed him weeping and heard him quoting

Homer's lines, 'One day holy Troy will perish also, and Priam, and the people of Priam ...'

The survivors – some 50,000 starving men, women and children had been permitted by Scipio to leave the dying city a few days before the end – were sold into slavery; the ground was formally cursed; the first Roman governor took up residence at Utica.

4

NEW MASTERS FOR AFRICA

The fertility of North Africa had certainly not been lost on Cato, brandishing figs in the Roman senate as he reiterated *'Delenda est Carthago'*,[1] nor on his hearers; but the new masters of Africa did not at once set about exploiting the province which was to become, with Egypt, the most valuable as a source of food, at least cost in men and money. For a hundred years, their policy was dictated by their resolve that no power should again arise on the far side of the straits of Sicily which could threaten either their hold on Sicily or their sea routes across the Mediterranean. Not that their acquisition of Africa can be regarded as entirely accidental: during the next century and a half they established their rule round the whole of the Mediterranean basin, and north-west Africa could scarcely have escaped the common fate for long.

The Roman Republic was not equipped, however, and never adapted itself to run an empire. It was as if 'Marylebone Borough Council suddenly found itself with Ireland, France, and half Spain,' to use J.C. Stobart's apt simile. Rome had acquired Sicily in 241 BC, after the First Punic War, Corsica and Sardinia in 237 BC, after Carthage's Mercenary War, Spain thirty years later after the Second Punic War, Carthage's old territory in Africa after the Third, in 146 BC, and Macedonia in the same year – five provinces in the space of a century, and the Romans still had no coherent provincial administration. Senators were sent out to govern for one year; they had absolute authority, military, executive and judicial, and there was no bureaucracy either to help them or to keep a check on them. The right to collect taxes was farmed out to contractors. The traditional honesty of the Roman aristocracy which had so amazed Polybius when he first went to Rome soon deserted its representatives abroad, surrounded by the temptations offered by rich provincial cities; speculation and the worst forms of usury and tax-farming were to become so commonplace that even a man like Cicero did not hesitate to line his pockets with a fortune.

---

1 'Carthage must be destroyed!'

Street in Djemila (ancient Cuicul), Algeria

Carthage having been laid waste, her corner of Africa was not immediately ripe for this kind of wholesale exploitation. A watching brief limited to peace-keeping and the exaction of war tribute was, to begin with, the extent of official Roman policy. The territory enclosed by the ditch which the earlier Scipio had had dug after Hannibal's defeat in 202 BC, from Thabraca on the north coast south-east to the Gulf of Gabès, was surveyed and divided amongst the deserving. Some of it was given, free of tax, to the seven Phoenician cities which had sided with Rome and had therefore become *civitates liberae et immunes*.[1] They continued to govern themselves. Some of the land was allotted to two thousand Carthaginian soldiers who had deserted to the Roman side during the war; some was given to Libyans who had surrendered, in return for a fixed tax; much was sold to rich men

---

1 Free and exempt city states.

in Italy – the beginning of the vast *latifundia* which were later to arouse the cupidity of Nero. The Libyans who had worked the land for the Carthaginians continued to work the land, but for new masters.

There was room enough for extortion and repression but for the moment the Romans left the provincials to manage their own lives. Although towns and villages which had been loyal to Carthage were sacked and their occupants sold into slavery – or 'sold' with the land itself – the remainder, even in Carthaginian territory, continued to govern themselves in the Punic manner. Punic was still generally spoken and many Africans now learnt it for the first time. Enterprising Italian traders came to settle in the coastal towns and at Cirta (Constantine), and a few impoverished Italian farmers immigrated under their own steam. A quarter of a century after the sack of Carthage the Gracchi brothers, recognizing the new province's potential, tried to settle several thousand Italians in holdings in northern Tunisia as part of their agricultural reforms in Italy; but this project failed.

The native kingdoms were left to themselves.

THE JUGURTHINE WAR

The neglect of the native kingdoms proved a mistake. Carthage as a military threat may have been destroyed for ever, but the Africans could be counted on to quarrel among themselves, largely because the problem of the succession to African kingdoms, which was not based on primogeniture but on the eldest-of-the-family principle or a division between brothers, was never resolved. The old native habit of handing sovereignty to the most competent ruler, whether son or brother or nephew, accorded ill with Masinissa's family's ambitions. The Romans themselves were dragged against their will into dynastic squabbles. Worse, during the civil wars of the last decades of the Roman Republic, rival candidates to the throne of Numidia took opposite sides in the struggle for power in Rome. But it was one thing to make trouble for each other, quite another to interfere in the internal affairs of Rome itself, to side with one Roman general against another. From that moment, even nominal independence was doomed.

Masinissa, who had died during the siege of Carthage, had eventually been succeeded as king of Numidia by his son Micipsa; he, like his father, was a loyal ally of Rome and a competent ruler. But the succession problem which had bedevilled Masinissa's own rise to power was masked, not ended; for at first Micipsa had had to share kingship with two of his brothers, who both died soon afterwards, leaving him sole heir. One of these brothers, however, had left a bastard son, Jugurtha, who was older than Micipsa's two sons, and an ambitious and capable young man.

Jugurtha took after his grandfather Masinissa. He was outstandingly handsome and brave, a great huntsman and soldier, and very popular with his uncle's subjects. According to Sallust, whose *Jugurthine War* provides the principal account of the dramatic feud which was to follow, Micipsa realized that his nephew would be a dangerous rival to his own sons and for this reason sent him in 134 BC as commander of Numidian troops to fight for the Romans against the rebellious Iberian tribes, hoping that he would be killed. The plan, such as it was, failed. Jugurtha – who was then about twenty years old – distinguished himself during the campaign, made many friends among the young Roman noblemen who were fighting alongside him, and returned to Numidia more popular than ever with his troops, and with an enthusiastic letter of recommendation to Micipsa from the Roman commander, Scipio. Micipsa took the hint: he made Jugurtha joint heir with his two sons, Hiempsal and Adherbal.

It was disastrous. When Micipsa died in 118 BC, the cousins were unable to keep up any pretence of friendship. Micipsa's sons were jealous, and Jugurtha, believing himself the better man, was impetuous and greedy. After murdering Hiempsal and defeating Adherbal in battle, he seized the throne for himself and set about bribing his friends in the Roman senate to turn a blind eye to his action.

The Romans were in some difficulty. By their lights Jugurtha was in the wrong, and it was difficult to resist the appeals of Adherbal, who had fled to Rome to canvass for support. They could hardly ignore the situation, since Numidia was a client kingdom; but they delayed. Jugurtha visited Rome to distribute more bribes, to encourage further delay. Then, when the Romans finally decreed that half Numidia should go to Adherbal, they did not back up the decision with force. Jugurtha was soon showing further contempt for the imperial power, and the cousins were once more at war. Still the Romans showed no signs of intervening.

In 112 BC, however, Jugurtha brought them down on his head. He committed the error, while sacking Cirta as a punishment for sheltering Adherbal, of killing indiscriminately all the adult male inhabitants, a certain number of whom were Italian settlers. The Romans felt obliged to avenge this atrocity. The war which then broke out, during the latter stages of which the Roman generals Marius and Sulla made their names, lasted for six years, and ended only when Jugurtha's father-in-law, King Bocchus of Mauretania, was induced to betray him and deliver him in chains to Sulla. Jugurtha died in prison in Rome, no doubt leaving behind him a legendary reputation as a heroic defender of Africa against Rome, just as his grandfather Masinissa had been the symbol of the African struggle against Carthage. He was not the last hero in this cause.

THE END OF NUMIDIAN INDEPENDENCE

For the moment Rome made no move to annex the heartland of Numidia, which was given to a half-brother of Jugurtha called Gauda, from whom the Romans felt they had nothing to fear. Their new ally, Bocchus of Mauretania, was rewarded with the western part of Numidia for his treachery to his son-in-law. Some of Marius's veterans, following what was beginning to be standard Roman practice in Italy with retired soldiers, were given, at the end of their army service, land on the border between the province of Africa and Numidia. But even though it was becoming clear that the native kings could not be relied on to rule their client kingdoms in peace or without involving Rome in tiresome and expensive punitive expeditions, the Republic made no attempt to extend its authority.

The next wars on African soil stemmed directly from the civil wars in Italy. Two sons of Gauda, Hiempsal and Hierbas, shared the throne of eastern Numidia after his death in 88 BC, and each used the rivalry between Marius and Sulla to advance his own cause: Hiempsal took the part of Sulla, Hierbas that of Marius. When Marius was defeated, and with him Hierbas, Hierbas was put to death in 81 BC by Sulla's troops under their commander Pompey, and Hiempsal was left as sole ruler of eastern Numidia. Once more the succession problem had been resolved by force. But the wheel of fortune turned: thirty-five years later Hiempsal and his son Juba I chose the wrong side during the civil war of the Triumvirate. When the Three Men, Caesar, Pompey and Crassus, had divided the Roman provinces between them, Pompey received Africa; and when war broke out between Caesar and Pompey, the Numidian king quite properly sided with Pompey, who was not only governor of Africa but had rid him, years before, of his brother Hierbas. After Pompey's death at Pharsalus, the Pompeian party continued to hold Africa and wage war against Caesar from there; for it was not then by any means a foregone conclusion that Julius Caesar would become the master of the Roman world.

The outcome was no more certain when Caesar finally landed in Africa to do battle with his adversaries; his troops were fewer, and his principal ally was an Italian soldier of fortune called Sittius who had fled to Mauretania after a spectacular bankruptcy, and had made a career for himself in Africa as a freelance military officer. Although Caesar could also count on the two kings of Mauretania, well to the west, the Pompeian strength was considerably greater, not counting Juba I's large forces. However, in 46 BC Caesar defeated the Pompeian army at Thapsus, on the east coast a few miles north of Mahdia. It was one of the decisive battles of the ancient world. Caesar lost fifty men; his enemies lost ten thousand.

At almost the same moment, Sittius annihilated Juba's army, which was guarding Numidia, and both Juba's kingdom and Pompey's province fell to Caesar. The leading Pompeians committed suicide; for Juba, too, there was only one way out, and he engaged in a fight to the death with a Roman legionary. A slave dispatched the survivor; no one knows which of the two it was. Juba's young son was taken to Rome in Caesar's train to be shown off in his triumph, and to be brought up a Roman in Caesar's household.

THE ROMAN OCCUPATION

It was Julius Caesar who at last extended direct Roman rule well beyond Scipio's *fossa regia*,[1] which had for a hundred years marked the boundary of Roman Africa. At one stroke, Roman territory in Africa was trebled to include most of the Numidian kingdom. The original African province was now called Africa Vetus to distinguish it from Africa Nova, as the new annexation was called, and the historian Sallust was appointed Africa Nova's first governor. His governorship gave him the opportunity to gather material for his book *The Jugurthine War*, which had been fought nearly seventy years earlier, but at the time it was principally remarkable for a rapacity which shocked even Sallust's contemporaries.

Caesar had learned the lesson of his campaign in Africa: that from the Roman point of view the native kingdoms were better abolished. True, King Bocchus of Mauretania was rewarded for his support in the Thapsus campaign by being given the western part of Numidia; but after his death in 33 BC his kingdom was ruled directly by the Romans, and then handed over in 25 BC to Juba II, the romanized son of Juba I.

Caesar was also responsible for the first major Roman settlements in Africa. His ally Sittius installed himself with his veterans on the western frontier of Africa Nova in a semi-autonomous fief based on Cirta, which formed a useful buffer state between the Roman territory and Mauretania and which, when Sittius died, could be readily absorbed into the province. Caesar also settled in Africa others of his veterans and – following the example of the Gracchi brothers – some of the dispossessed Italian peasants who were by now creating serious population problems in Rome itself. Carthage, Thysdrus (El Djem), Hippo Diarrhytus (Bizerta) and a handful of places in the Cape Bon peninsula were among the townships which seem to have received Julian colonies during Caesar's brief reign.

Caesar's principal African project was the refounding of Carthage, which had been deserted for a hundred years. Before he could make it a reality he was murdered, in 44 BC, and the struggle for the control of the Roman world which followed led once more to a period of confused fighting in Africa. The two provinces passed to Caesar's great-nephew Octavian, then to Lepidus; Africa Vetus fought Africa Nova; and it was only in 36 BC that Octavian became their uncontested master. Elsewhere in the Roman world the war lasted until Octavian defeated Mark Antony and Cleopatra at Actium in 31 BC. Two years later Octavian, shortly to assume the title of Augustus, or Emperor, officially refounded on the site of the Punic capital the city which, under the Empire, was to become once again a great metropolis of the Mediterranean world.

Carthage was just one, if the most important, of a number of Augustan

---

1 Demarcation ditch.

colonies in Africa. Huge armies had been involved in the civil wars, and the new Emperor was faced with the problem of reducing the immense number of soldiers who had been recruited. In his *Res Gestae*, a summary of his activities which he composed late in life to be inscribed on his tomb (the main copy of which was found in Ankara), Augustus claimed that during his reign he either sent back to their own towns or settled in colonies more than three hundred thousand men. Some of those veterans, like those of his great-uncle Julius Caesar, were settled in Africa: inland from Carthage at places like Sicca Veneria (El Kef), Thuburbo Minus (Tébourba) and Uthina (Oudna); and also – a new departure – on the Atlantic coast of Mauretania, far to the west. There were also half a dozen Augustan colonies on the coast between Igilgili (Jijil) and Cartennas (Ténès); and another three were founded inland to help bolster up the authority of the new man whom Augustus now put in to rule Mauretania. The romanization of Africa was about to begin in earnest.

JUBA, KING OF MAURETANIA

Augustus gave the whole of Mauretania in 25 BC to Juba II of Numidia, then twenty-six or twenty-seven years old. Julius Caesar, cheated of the chance of displaying the elder Juba in his triumph, had taken his young son, also Juba, to Rome in his stead; and when Caesar was murdered the prince was brought up in the household of Caesar's heir Octavian. Like other sons of the Roman nobility of the day, Juba was given an education more Greek than Latin. He proved a willing pupil. He grew up with a passion for the arts, for literature and for science, and wrote books himself – all in Greek – on subjects as various as the history of Rome, Arabia, the Assyrians, African geography, painting, the theatre and even a medicinal herb. All these books are lost; their contents are known only through what was repeated or plagiarized by other writers. King Juba seems, for all his encyclopaedic knowledge, to have been more credulous than critical. Yet in one sphere at least he was exceptional: he had a genuine and discriminating appreciation of art.

Juba married Cleopatra Selene, the daughter of Mark Antony and Cleopatra. She, too, had been taken to Rome after the defeat and death of her parents and brought up in Augustus's household by Augustus's sister Octavia, Mark Antony's generous and forgiving widow. Together these two children of Rome's enemies were to create at Iol Caesarea (Cherchel), King Bocchus's old capital now renamed by Juba in honour of Augustus, what must have seemed to them, in their exile from all they had known in their youth, an oasis of civilization. A temple, a palace, a theatre and an amphitheatre were built in classical style; there was probably a Roman-style forum and a royal palace (not yet located). Celebrated actors were imported, a fine library was founded, statues were commissioned from

Greek ateliers. It is to this royal art patron, wholly African by blood, that the museums of Algiers and Cherchel owe the finest works of Greco-Roman art found in Africa. Juba had a second capital far to the west, at Volubilis in modern Morocco; here, too, many of the beautiful bronzes in the museum at Rabat are almost certainly a testimony to his taste. It has even been claimed, with perhaps less justification, that the splendid cargo of first-century BC Greek bronzes and statues found in 1907 in a sunken Roman merchantman off Mahdia, on the eastern coast of Tunisia, and now in the Bardo Museum in Tunis, was on its way not to Rome but to Juba in Caesarea.

Although his tastes were Greek and his lineage African, Juba's loyalty was to Rome and to his protector Augustus. It never wavered during his fifty-year reign. From that point of view at least, the Emperor had chosen his agent of civilization with his customary prudence. Juba's kingdom was, however, enormous, mountainous and extremely vulnerable to attack from tribes which did not welcome subservience to Rome as much as he did. If Augustus had hopes that Juba would be able to suppress risings with his own troops without calling on the help of Roman legionaries, they were not fulfilled. When there was trouble, Rome had to go to the rescue. For the most important factor in the romanization of Africa and the development of its immense prosperity was not one client king or a few thousand Italian settlers. It was peace.

Roman rule was a mixed blessing, but the *pax Romana* was not an idle phrase. The Greek city states had declined not least because throughout their history, both at home in Greece and abroad in Magna Graecia (Sicily and southern Italy), they had been unable to avoid fighting each other. Peace was Rome's great gift to the decaying Hellenistic world and to the new provinces carved out of Europe and North Africa. She acted as foster mother to the old cities of the east and the new cities of the west, so that they lived amicably side by side. For the next four hundred years serious warfare was by and large confined to the frontiers of the Empire.

The remarkable prosperity of the lands bordering the Mediterranean was made possible by peace. And peace, if not always easily kept, was made possible by the Roman legions under the command of the Roman Emperor.

THE THIRD AUGUSTAN LEGION

In 27 BC Augustus had divided government of the Empire between himself and the senate. The frontier provinces, where fighting was still going on and which needed legions for peace-keeping, he kept under his own direct control, ruling them through legates, while the pacified provinces, which needed soldiers only for civilian policing purposes or as a token guard for the proconsul who governed in the name of the Roman people, went to

Arch of Caracalla of AD 216–17 at Volubilis. It originally had on top a
bronze statue, probably of Caracalla, in a six-horse chariot

the senate. To this rule, however, Africa was an exception. Although it was
a frontier province and needed a legion to guard it, Augustus ceded it to
the senate. This may have been a diplomatic concession. So it was the
proconsul, the representative of the senate, now in residence in the newly-
founded *colonia* of Carthage, who was commander-in-chief of the Third
Augustan Legion which the Emperor seconded to the province.

The Third Augustan Legion's first identifiable base in Africa was at
Ammaedara (Haïdra) in the steppe country some one hundred and fifty
miles south-west of Carthage. This was a strategic position from which the
Legion could police the movements of the tribes between the southern
steppes and the Tunisian plateau and keep an eye on any incursions from
the Aurès mountains to the south-west.

The Legion was recruited at this time largely from Rome's western
provinces, in particular from Gaul;[1] for it was Augustus's policy to guard
the provinces with legions raised in other parts of the Empire. This policy
was to change; but for the moment the Third Augustan Legion was a
body of some five or six thousand foreigners. However, they were Latin-
speaking and Roman-trained and even when, a century or so later, the
army raised legionaries in Africa itself, those recruits all had to learn the

---

1 The soldiers of General Bugeaud who conquered Algeria in 1830 were not the first Gallic
troops to set foot there.

Hexagonal mausoleum at Haïdra (ancient Ammaedara) in Tunisia, once
the Third Augustan Legion's headquarters

Latin language and Roman discipline, and were trained in Roman skills
of all kinds.

For four hundred years (with one thirty-year interval) the Third Augustan was the only Roman legion permanently garrisoned in north-west
Africa.[1] It was assisted by auxiliary units of non-Roman citizens and the
total effective strength of Rome's African army was probably between
20,000 and 25,000 men – certainly no more. It was responsible for the
keeping of internal peace and for defence from outside attack. A region
some fifteen hundred miles wide, which stretched from the Atlantic to the
Libyan desert, was policed, if sometimes with difficulty, by these 25,000
men. In times of crisis, reinforcements were drafted in from other parts of
the Empire, from Pannonia, for instance, or Spain, as we know from
inscriptions and gravestones; the nature of the army changed over time,
but it was essentially the Third Augustan Legion and its auxiliaries which
bore the brunt. They were to be kept busy.

---

1 Compare tiny Britain, with four legions tied up there during almost the whole Roman
period.

Portico of Petronius Felix and his sons at Thuburbo Maius, near Pont du
Fahs in Tunisia, built in AD 225

THE REVOLT OF TACFARINAS

In 21 BC, within a year or two of the Legion's arrival, the proconsul of Africa
was awarded a triumph for a military campaign about which nothing is
known except that it was fierce enough to deserve a triumph.

Very little can now be reconstructed of the native opposition to the
Romans. The big set pieces – the rebellion of Jugurtha, the revolt of Tacfarinas – are reported by Roman historians, but there were certainly others.
A succession of triumphs awarded to his generals for campaigns in Africa,
otherwise unrecorded, in 34, 33, 28 and 21 BC testify to constant dis-
turbances during the early part of Augustus's reign. In 19 BC yet another
triumph was awarded to the new proconsul, L. Cornelius Balbus (who
had been born in Phoenician Spain), for a victory over the Garamantes of
the Fezzan, in the desert south of Tripolitania. In a notable expedition into
the Sahara four hundred miles south of the coastal cities, he reached the
oases of Garama (Germa) and Cydamae (Ghadames); but the Roman
presence was not permanent, and further campaigns had to be waged
against the Garamantes later. In Juba's Mauretania fighting seems to have
been endemic for a quarter of a century, until the western tribes were

defeated, with, of course, Roman help, in AD 6, but again only for a short period.

In AD 17 the most serious of north-west Africa's early wars broke out. This was the revolt of the Musulamii under Tacfarinas. In AD 14, the last year of Augustus's reign, the Third Augustan Legion had constructed their first military road in Africa. It ran north-west from the port of Tacapae (Gabès) in southern Tunisia towards Ammaedara (Haïdra) – perhaps across the Musulamians' traditional routes between their summer and winter grazing grounds – and the new road may have seemed a provocation. The first rising was swiftly put down, but the next, under their new leader Tacfarinas, was another matter.

Tacfarinas, like Jugurtha before him and many another of the Empire's most dangerous enemies, had learnt the art of war from the Romans themselves; he added gifts of his own. The Roman historian Tacitus tells us in his *Annals* that Tacfarinas 'had deserted from service as a Roman auxiliary. His first followers were vagabonds and marauders who came for loot. Then he organized them into army units and formations, both infantry and cavalry, and was finally recognized as the chief, no longer of an undisciplined gang, but of the Musulamian people – a powerful tribe on the edge of the desert.[1] Taking up arms, they brought in the neighbouring Mauretanians, under their leader Mazippa ... Tacfarinas retained in camp an élite force equipped in Roman fashion, which he instructed in discipline and obedience; while Mazippa's light-armed troops burnt, killed, and intimidated.'

It was a model guerrilla campaign, with Tacfarinas, according to Tacitus, 'giving way under pressure and then attacking from the rear'. Conventional Roman victories had little meaning in such a war; the survivors simply retreated to the desert to re-form and then returned to make lightning raids where they were least expected, constantly harrying the static Roman positions.

The Romans soon learnt that guerrilla attacks must be parried by guerrilla tactics. But Tacfarinas was not easily defeated. Despite frequent setbacks, he 'raised reinforcements in the interior and had the insolence to send representatives to Tiberius [who had succeeded Augustus as Emperor] demanding land for himself and his army. As the alternative, he offered endless war. No personal or national slur, it is said, ever provoked the Emperor more than the sight of this deserter and brigand behaving like a hostile sovereign ... With Roman power at its height, was this bandit Tacfarinas to be bought off by a treaty granting lands?'

Tiberius was enraged. He ordered an amnesty in the hope that many rebels would lay down their arms; meanwhile the Romans hurriedly

---

1 The Musulamians in fact occupied the region between Theveste (Tébessa) and Sicca Veneria (El Kef).

taught themselves new methods of war, mobile, light-armed, fast striking, the very antithesis of the solid legionary formations. They even, most unusually, continued fighting in winter. In spite of some success, however, including the capture of Tacfarinas's brother, 'enough of the enemy was left to revive hostilities'; and Tacfarinas was still at large.

The fighting flared up with renewed vigour shortly after Juba II died in AD 23, and left Mauretania to his son Ptolemy – 'too young for responsibility', reported Tacitus with unusual mildness. The Moors revolted almost immediately against the tyrannical rule of the new king's favourites. Tacfarinas seized his chance: he appealed to all who preferred freedom to slavery to make a united effort to get rid of the Romans altogether, and soon had a new army composed not only of Musulamians and Moors but also of disaffected or dispossessed peasants from Africa Proconsularis itself, and troops sent by the Garamantes. The Roman governor of the year, however, was a man of energy and military gifts called Dolabella; and within a few months, having induced the unwilling Ptolemy to join the fight, his troops surprised the enemy in their encampment at Auzia (Souk El Ghoziane), some fifty miles south-east of Caesarea, in a dawn attack: they 'were dragged to death or captivity like sheep', and Tacfarinas himself was killed. With his death, the heart went out of the rebellion. It had lasted seven years.

The revolt of Tacfarinas was by no means the last of the uprisings. There were plenty of others – scarcely a decade went by without trouble somewhere. But they were better contained; the Romans now knew the kind of warfare they could expect, and had learnt that mobility was more important than brute strength.

A NEW *MODUS VIVENDI*

The following reign, that of Caligula, brought important military and political changes. In AD 37 the Emperor took the Third Augustan Legion out of the control of the proconsul, who could not provide continuity of command (nor, necessarily, military experience), and entrusted it instead to a legate chosen by himself for his professional capacities as a soldier, who commanded the whole region where Roman troops were garrisoned.

A year or two later Mauretania was annexed to the Empire. Juba's son Ptolemy, who had no heir, was the last king. He had been officially recognized as *socius et amicus*[1] of Rome for his part in the war against Tacfarinas; but he made the mistake of appearing at an imperial function in Rome in a style even more ostentatiously luxurious than that of Caligula, who was his cousin (they were both descended from Mark Antony). The Emperor, his jealousy inflamed by greed, had Ptolemy put to death and

---

1 Friend and ally.

seized Mauretania, though not without trouble. Aedemon, a freedman loyal to Ptolemy, raised a rebellion in protest, which took Caligula's successor Claudius some three or four years to put down, even though certain Moors supported the Romans. Volubilis, an ancient Moorish township and second capital of Juba II, was rewarded for her loyalty to Rome with special status.

But the rising is principally of note as the occasion of another Roman expedition to the far south. In AD 41, in pursuit of the Moors retreating to the desert, C. Suetonius Paulinus[1] crossed the Mount Atlas range and led his troops into the typical *reg* of the Sahara, all bare rocks and red gravel. Though it was midwinter, his troops suffered from heatstroke and thirst, and he had to turn back after ten days' march. His colleague, Cn. Hosidius Geta, also reached the desert, while pursuing another Moorish chieftain. Only prayers to the local gods, and a providential shower of rain, saved the troops from dying of thirst. Henceforth the western desert was left to its own people.

Leptis Magna, Libya: the Arch of Trajan seen through the Arch of Tiberius. The market is immediately to the right

There were also expeditions across the central Sahara towards the end of the first century AD, reported by Ptolemy of Alexandria in his *Geography*. The first was a disciplinary foray in AD 70, after the Garamantes from the

1 Suetonius Paulinus was later sent to Britain, where he conquered Boudica (Boadicea).

Fezzan pillaged the territory of Leptis Magna. Later, the Romans mounted two exploratory campaigns: one, a decade later, under Septimius Flaccus, was a march of some three or four months into 'the midst of the Aethiopians' (perhaps as far as the Tibesti mountains), the other, at the turn of the century, under Julius Maternus, reached the land of Agisymba (unidentified), 'where the rhinoceroses foregather' – probably Lake Chad.

But the only evidence yet found of any contact between the Romans and the people on the southern edge of the Sahara are the Roman coins found in the fourth-century tomb of Tin Hinan, so-called queen of the Tuareg, at Abelessa in the Hoggar mountains in southern Algeria.

There appear to have been close ties, however, between the people of the Fezzan and the Romans from the first century onward. At Germa, their capital, four hundred and thirty miles south of Leptis Magna, is the most southerly Roman-style monument in Africa west of the Nile Valley, first noted by an English traveller in 1826, a magnificent mausoleum probably dating from the late first century A D. Even more interesting is the complex of *foggaras*, or subterranean water channels, constructed to tap water from underground water levels sometimes many miles away, which was discovered in the 1930s by an Italian archaeological expedition. There are other Roman remains which suggest links with Rome – in the shape not of rulers or administrators, but of traders and technical experts, no doubt sent to advise the inhabitants. The Romans certainly made no attempt to conquer the Fezzan and rule it directly.

*   *   *

From now on Roman Africa consists of Mauretania as far south as Volubilis (divided for administrative convenience into Mauretania Tingitana and Mauretania Caesariensis); Numidia as far south as the Aurès mountains; and Africa Proconsularis with the narrow coastal strip of Tripolitania. Between the first and third centuries of our era these regions were fundamentally peaceful, especially the fertile north-east: the unwalled cities, the vast olive groves of the second century, the vulnerable aqueducts – all are silent witnesses to the tranquillity of the countryside.

The desert tribes outside the borders probably numbered no more than a hundred thousand, at the most: during the course of centuries, many must have been drawn to live inside the Roman provinces themselves. In the interior, some precautions had to be taken against sudden raids from isolated mountain communities. The cities of the west, civilian as well as military, were walled: at Volubilis, the territory of the Baquates tribe reached almost to the gates, and others were occasionally besieged. But many of these tribes too were gradually drawn under the Roman influence.

5

THE CONQUEST OF A COUNTRY

There is a legend that a Roman soldier fell in love with a native princess, who, as proud as Dido, would have nothing to do with him; she would never marry him, she said, until the waters of Zaghouan flowed to Carthage. The impossible condition was fulfilled, the fifty-mile aqueduct which still strides across the plain of the River Miliana was built; the Roman claimed his bride, who threw herself in despair from the aqueduct's summit. The story perfectly illustrates that the Roman genius for the art of the possible extended to the improbable. The Romans saw possibilities where none had seen them before. Where others had seen them but had been overwhelmed by difficulty, they saw only a job to be done, and did it. Carthage needed more water.

Remains of the aqueduct crossing the valley of the Oued Miliana, some twenty miles south of Tunis

Of course great roads and aqueducts and irrigation systems had been constructed before; pyramids had been built, fifty-ton blocks of stone quarried, transported, dressed and carved and set on end for palaces and temples. And the Romans, too, built for display and prestige. But they were the first to realize that such techniques could be applied on a vast scale, and extended to the remotest corners of the Empire and the smallest needs of everyday life. The sheer size of the Roman conception required an imaginative leap which took civil engineering right beyond the dictates of immediate necessity or religious awe, beyond palaces and temples and royal tombs and processional ways. Magnificence had been hitherto the prerogative of kings and priests; the Romans made it secular. Their genius was firmly grounded in an infinite capacity for taking pains, but it was more than that. They applied their minds and skills to mastering their environment to an unprecedented degree. If something was necessary, or even desirable, and if it was possible, then they did it, however difficult; and took the doing for granted.

So-called Bridge of Trajan, near Béja, probably built in AD 29 to carry the road from Carthage to Bulla Regia and Hippo

The surveyors and civil engineers of the Roman world were the legions. The Roman army was not only an army of soldiers, but an army of sappers. For in order to conduct war properly, they needed communications; above all roads and harbours. In order to prevent war breaking out, they needed camps and fortifications; and these needed a proper water supply. In order to keep some track of their conquered territories, and to organize the redistribution and taxation of property and to make the collection of corn tribute possible, they needed to survey them.

Nothing reveals the Romans' methodical thoroughness better than the great survey of the new province of Africa which was put in hand by Scipio immediately after the sack of Carthage in 146 BC. It was more than a survey, for at the same time the land was divided into basic agricultural units by means of ditches or roads. In Africa, this unit was about eight hundred yards square, so that there were four to the Roman square mile. Traces of this vast digging operation can be seen from the air over the greater part of Tunisia; it extended right to the edge of the desert and the borders of the Chott Djerid (Lake Triton) south of Gafsa, inland from the Gulf of Gabès. Only mountains, forests and marshes were ignored: the Romans did not attempt to turn into agricultural land what was uncultivable or not needed. What is astonishing, however, is the inclusion in their land survey of large areas, particularly in the south, which look today as if they have never known cultivation; but the Romans must have found them worthwhile or they would not have been included.

This survey and division of the land was the work of the army surveyors, and so was much of the hard labour. It took more than a century and a half in Africa Proconsularis alone, a good deal longer for all north-west Africa's farmlands. But once the bulk of the province was covered, the work must have kept pace with the gradual penetration of the military to the south and west.

ROADS

The roads were closely linked with the survey, often serving as boundaries of newly-mapped territories, and guidelines for further division. They, too, followed the army. The Carthaginians had left behind them roads linking their capital with its neighbours: there were a number of roads in Tripolitania, and others between the larger towns. To begin with, the Romans must have made use of these, patching them up as need arose. But their view of the function of roads was more systematic than that of any people before them. They saw that a road linking two minor towns was itself of minor importance, unless it also formed part of a logical network of roads covering a whole province. That logic was in the first place military, in the second administrative – for the collection of corn and taxes – and only a very poor third, however useful, for the benefit of the inhabitants.

The two hundred-mile Tacapae-Ammaedara military road which the Third Augustan Legion had constructed by AD 14 was the first road to be recorded in inscriptions. It was the start of the network of roads in Africa which, by the middle of the third century, totalled some twelve thousand miles. Few traces of this network remain. Away from the cities, only one road was paved with flagstones, the main route from Carthage through

Ammaedara and south-west to Theveste (Tébessa), a garrison which became the Legion's new headquarters some time in the first century. The rest – though properly constructed of three or four well-drained layers of large stones, smaller stones and gravel, one or more bound with mortar, laid out in a trench perhaps two or three feet deep – had to make do with a surface of packed earth and large pebbles. Like most monuments of man exposed to the weather, roads, even the best, require upkeep. The modern metalled roads of the Algerian mountains subside under the winter rains often enough; it is scarcely surprising that more than fifteen hundred winters have washed away the roads of the Romans. Aerial photography has picked out a number, but nearly all are in the dry semi-desert country of the south, or show up as cuttings in hilly terrain.

Yet the network has been worked out in considerable detail, thanks to the orderly Roman habit of marking their roads with milestones. More than two thousand have been discovered in Africa; others must still lie under the surface. Nearly all, especially those of the early Empire, are neatly and legibly engraved with the name of the Emperor in whose reign the road was built and the number of miles from the nearest military garrison, important crossroads or major city. This was done as much for propaganda purposes, to impress the name of their ruler on the travellers who used the roads, as for the record: but the practice has incidentally enabled scholars to date them.

There is another valuable source of information. A people which brought surveying to a fine art certainly had accurate maps for official use. The Elder Pliny reports that a great map of the Roman world was put up in Rome in Augustus's day, and at the beginning of the third century Caracalla put on show a vast map of Roman roads. Unhappily, the only surviving account, Ptolemy's celebrated *Geography*, is no help at all for roads. However, two Roman itineraries have come down to us, both of which offer clues to Roman roads and settlements in North Africa. The Antonine itinerary has no map; it is simply a list of mileages, possibly made for administrative rather than military use. The Peutinger Table, named after the man who discovered it at Worms at the end of the fifteenth century, is a twelfth- or thirteenth-century copy of an enormous third-century scroll which showed the main roads of the Roman Empire from Great Britain to the frontiers of India. The scale is too small to be very useful, and roads and rivers are only indicated schematically and quite out of scale, but the Table does give the distances between cities. Most of Mauretania is missing, but the rest of North Africa, in spite of what seems the eccentric omission of major cities like Thugga (Dougga), Mactar, Cillium (Kasserine) and Sufetula (Sbeïtla), which may be the copyist's fault, has proved in most respects very accurate.

Inscriptions help too. In the middle of the nineteenth century, a French general, struggling with a detachment of soldiers through the narrow

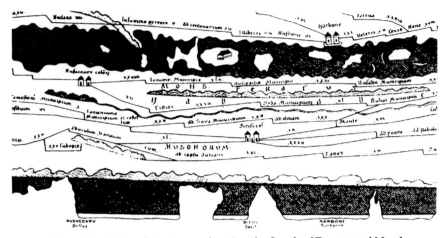

Part of the Table of Peutinger, showing the South of France and North
Africa. Clearly visible are Rusuccuru, Sitifis, Cuicul, Saldae, Calama and

Tighanimine gorge in the Aurès mountains south of Lambaesis on a
journey of exploration, was astonished to find a Roman inscription cut
into the side of the cliff: so little was then known about the history of North
Africa that he had assumed that they were the first Europeans to penetrate
so far. The inscription, clearly visible at the side of the modern road, records
that a road from Lambaesis to Vescera (Biskra) was constructed in AD 145
by a detachment of the Sixth Ferrata Legion as the Romans pushed the
frontier further towards the desert.

The network took more than two hundred years to construct. But by the
end of the first century AD Theveste (Tébessa), where the Legion had been
quartered since the 70s, was the centre of a spider's web of roads connecting
the garrison not only with Carthage and Capsa (Gafsa) and the coast, but
with Hippo Regius (Annaba) on the coast due north and, to the west, with
military posts on the mountainous frontier leading to Mauretania. There
was already a garrison at Auzia (Souk El Ghoziane), south-east of Algiers,
where Tacfarinas had been killed; now it was linked, through a string of
forts along the line of the mountains north of the Chott El Hodna, with the
Legion's headquarters. Under Trajan, when the Empire as a whole reached
its greatest extent, the frontier was pushed well south of the old frontier
road which ran from Theveste to the gulf of Syrte; a new military road was
built, on the Emperor's orders, along the edge of the Sahara south of the
Nementcha and Aurès mountains. The tribes were now closely supervised
even in this semi-barren region. Other roads linked the southern shores of
Chott Djerid with the interior of Tripolitania.

Trajan – or his successor, Hadrian, who first visited Africa in AD 128 –

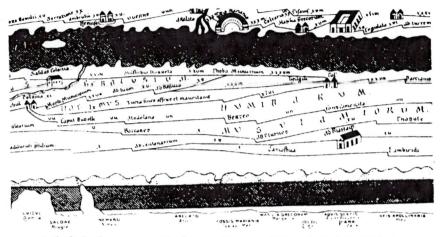

Igilgili. In France, note Narbonne, Nemuso (Nîmes), Arelato (Arles),
Masilia Grecorum (Marseilles of the Greeks) and the Rhône estuary

had the Legion's headquarters moved westwards again, to Lambaesis, so
that it was better placed to police the whole length of the frontier. The
military road inched on. Other roads were constructed to connect it with
the old frontier road: the map was filled in. The Vescera-Lambaesis road
built by the Sixth Ferrata Legion led on northwards to the coast by way of
Cirta (Constantine), where one of the Romans' finest bridges spanned the
deep rift which surrounds the city on three sides. A road ran the full length
of the coast, and there were other major arteries inland leading west
through Sitifis (Sétif) towards western Mauretania; these, too, were connected by minor roads, mostly the responsibility of the local townships.

In Africa as elsewhere the Romans built their roads as straight as possible. They were designed primarily for marching men; the shortest way,
even up slopes, was best. Up the steepest hillsides, they did build in loops;
but they preferred not to, for their carts, having fixed axles, could turn
sharp corners only if the road was heavily cambered or special ruts were
cut into the surface to guide the wheels. Straight roads were best, in spite
of the fact that the hard horse-collar, which was generally introduced some
centuries later, was probably unknown, and hauling a heavy load uphill
made the yoke worn by draught animals press heavily against their wind-
pipes, reducing their efficiency by half.[1] If necessary, cuttings and embank-
ments were made to smooth out curves or keep the road as level as possible.

Where they had the choice, the military engineers preferred their roads
to run along the crests or sides of mountains rather than in the valley. A
low road was vulnerable to sudden raids from the surrounding hills; a

---

1 A load hauled today by one animal had to be hauled then by two.

The Sixth Ferrata Legion marked their passage through the Tighanimine gorge in the Aurès in AD 145 with an inscription in the rockface (to the right of the cutting)

high road offered a better view. When, in the mountainous country of Numidia, the Romans did have to build a road through a gorge or along a valley floor, modest forts were built well above it to keep a look-out, within sight of each other so that they could signal in case of trouble. There seems to have been a certain amount of brigandage on the roads of Numidia and Mauretania. In Tunisia, which was safer, some gorge roads were left unprotected, but elsewhere the Romans left nothing to chance.

PORTS AND AQUEDUCTS

The Romans also turned their attention to improving those ports which were most useful to them. Even in Africa, all roads led to Rome; harbours were simply staging posts on that one journey. They concentrated on ports with good access to the interior, which were also near the main centres of production. Carthage itself was the major outlet for the corn tribute of the north-east; the three cities of Tripolitania were the ports used for the export of olive oil and goods traded from the interior – possibly Gigthis (Bou Grara) also; there were half a dozen more on the east coast of Tunisia. In the north and west, the marble of Simitthu (Chemtou) was exported through Thabraca (Tabarka); the Legion at Lambaesis used Rusicade (Philippeville); Tingis (Tangiers) communicated with Spain; Caesarea was the naval base in the war against pirates; and half a dozen others were improved for the export of horses, wild beasts and the timber and cereals of Mauretania. No rivers were navigable for any distance, and road transport through mountain country was still difficult, so sea journeys from point to point along the coast were standard practice. The fishing fleets which farmed

Part of the great quay at Leptis Magna. The harbour, to the left, is now silted up

the sea also needed harbours; but when they were for local use only the Romans left responsibility for maintaining them to the inhabitants.

The Phoenicians had probably built moles and jetties – they are difficult to date – and at Carthage and Hadrumetum (Sousse), where the coast was comparatively unprotected, built a *cothon* or inland basin, with a narrow access to the sea, round which their ships were put in dry dock. Caesarea (Cherchel), too, had a proper Punic harbour. The Romans, whose ships were larger than those of the Phoenicians, brought energetic improvements of their own. At Leptis Magna, they re-routed the wadi to prevent the silting up of the harbour, and rocky islets were linked to the coast by huge moles carrying warehouses, a lighthouse and other buildings – the ruins of which survive – in order to make a proper deep-sea port. At Caesarea and Acholla (Ras Botria) the remains of Roman jetties still break the surface a short distance from the shore. A lighthouse was built at Sullectum (Salakta), and an artificial basin at Tipasa. At Carthage, the old *cothon* was large enough for the Romans, but they rebuilt the naval harbour for use by cargo ships and added, seawards, a complex of breakwaters and a promenade. Hippo Diarrhytus (Bizerta) was ignored; it was ill-placed for inland transport – an advantage in early Punic times when the mountains cut it off from tribal raids, a disadvantage for Roman purposes. The *cothon* at Hadrumetum (Sousse) was one of many which eventually silted up; while the progressive silting up of the estuary at Utica was already severe by the third century.

---

1 Coping with silting was a major and sometimes insoluble engineering problem. Utica is now several miles from the sea.

71

The Romans also constructed causeways across the sea. The Phoenicians may already have built one linking Djerba to the mainland, but the Romans rebuilt it (the modern road runs on their foundations); they also joined the two Kerkenna islands.

Aqueducts, too, were designed by army architects, and not only for military camps and colonies. The Third Augustan Legion lent their engineers to the cities to supervise the organization of their water supply. A famous inscription describes how an engineer from Lambaesis was called on to direct the building of a tunnel for the aqueduct bringing water to the city of Saldae (Bougie); how, having directed the workmen to start tunnelling from both sides of the mountain, as was usual, he left them to it, but had to be summoned back when it became clear that the tunnellers had missed each other in the depths of the earth. The existence of the inscription suggests that mistakes of this kind were a rarity.

'With so many indispensable structures for all these waters you are welcome to compare, if you will, the idle pyramids or all the useless, though famous, works of the Greeks,' wrote the pragmatic Roman who was in charge of the city of Rome's eleven aqueducts. Nothing constructed in Africa compared in scale with the capital's water supply, nor in size with the aqueduct of Segovia in Spain and the Pont du Gard which carried water to Nîmes in southern France. But the same spirit inspired the building of aqueducts twenty, thirty, even fifty miles long. Cherchel's main aqueduct was twenty-eight miles long. Although Roman hydraulic skill enabled them to use siphons for alterations in level, because of the necessary lead they were expensive to build and most aqueducts were built with a continuous gradual slope the whole immense distance. Their design called for – although it has to be said it did not always get – great precision from both architects and masons; the fall of water had to be regular, and neither too sluggish nor too rapid. No doubt a certain variation was tolerated, but if a nearby source was too high the aqueduct had to take a longer roundabout path in order to reduce the incline and lower the pressure. They could also be built with impressive speed. The twenty-five-mile long Lambaesis aqueduct was constructed in eight months.

THE NEW MODEL TOWNS

Wherever the Legion set up a permanent headquarters it was built to last. Not that it always has lasted: Ammaedara (Haïdra), which was their base for less than a century, was soon overlaid with civilian dwellings and later Byzantine fortifications, and now lies in ruins. But the rigid rectangular grid which the military planners imposed on Roman Theveste can still be clearly traced on the street map of modern Tébessa, though the Legion itself was quartered there for only a few decades before the town was left to civilians. Roman legionary fortresses were model towns: the streets ran

Roman bath at the oasis of Gafsa (ancient Capsa) in southern Tunisia

at right angles, living quarters, stores, temples alike were built of stone, all was orderly, precise, squared-off. One of the best-preserved buildings of Roman Africa is the third-century headquarters forehall at Lambaesis, where the Legion had an outpost from AD 81 – replaced by a fortress by the late 120s. The forehall is roofless but the walls stand to the second storey. Round it can be plainly seen the rectangular grid of streets, the barracks and other buildings.

The most famous of the Legion's towns was not strictly military, however: for Thamugadi (Timgad) was built c. AD 100 not as a fortress but as a colony for its veterans and their families. Yet more perfectly than any other, Timgad reveals the military mind at work: the aerial view is justly famous for it shows, within the walls, the typical geometric pattern following the logic of set-square and ruler. At ground level severity is relieved by the tilt of the site: the streets march straight up it and over the crest regardless, but the eye is deceived into a pleasant impression of variety.

The Legion usually built forts, fortresses, camps and veterans' towns on rising ground, choosing a spur overlooking the plain. It is difficult to believe that this was only for prudent reasons, or that the Romans were

Forehall of praetorian headquarters at Lambaesis, for centuries the main
garrison of the Third Augustan Legion

wholly indifferent to the wide horizons so many of their settlements enjoy.
But even the veterans' towns did, after all, have a paramilitary purpose; a
soldier who had served his twenty-year term was an experienced man still
in the prime of life, and if now he turned to family life and farming his
own land, it was sensible that he should do so where his military experience
would not come amiss if the need arose. Timgad was founded on the
southern frontier (though within a few years the Romans had built a
military road yet further south); Diana Veteranorum, much smaller, was
founded to the north-west in the heart of the old tribal country of Numidia;
other veterans were settled in *canabae* alongside legionary fortresses or in
other towns. Old soldiers never die: the veterans of the Legion remained,
in a very real sense, *en poste* until the end of their lives. Even if they had
retired to be masters of their own farmland, and their role was inactive,
their mere presence contributed much to the *pax Romana* which was technically the responsibility of their former brothers-in-arms.

The Emperors themselves recognized the value of these settlements, and
continued the granting of land to veterans, often under the eye of the

Timgad from the air. The theatre and the forum can be clearly seen; so
can the erosion of the surrounding hills

Legion. Veterans were soon being encouraged to live in *vici* and take
leaseholds on the imperial estates (which one authority puts at one third
of the land near the Aurès mountains) so that the Emperor's property
could be efficiently farmed, the army supplied with food, and the native
inhabitants romanized. Timgad and Diana Veteranorum, purpose-built by
the Legion for the veterans and granted freehold land, were not repeated.
Imperial policy had changed.

Yet soon these veterans were not Romans from other parts of the Empire.
Soldiers were not allowed to marry during their military service; but by
the time they retired they had usually contracted a common-law marriage
with a local woman, and settled down with her and their children. From
the beginning of the third century soldiers were permitted to marry and
live with their families outside the camps. Their children grew up in
townships beside the camps, or in colonies of veterans: what more natural
than that the Romans should have looked for recruits to the sons of old
soldiers, already half Roman by language and adoption? After the first
generation or so, it was an African army which romanized the frontier
provinces of Africa.

---

1 Settlements next to forts.

THE *LIMES*

In the middle and late 1930s aerial photography – both civilian and military – was undertaken in the semi-desert country south-west of the Aurès mountains. What those photographs revealed led to two archaeological expeditions just before the Second World War; their work was continued in the late 1940s by Colonel J. Baradez, and his discoveries were published in his book *Fossatum Africae*.

The empty country was crammed with the faint remains of forts, roads, farms, villages, canals and waterworks of all kinds, and substantial ditch-and-dyke earthworks. They were part of a great complex of frontier settlements in southern Numidia in an area on the fringe of the desert which is now almost uninhabited. These discoveries caused great excitement at the

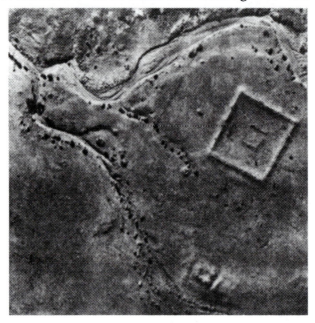

Fort of Zebaret, south of the Chott El Hodna – one of hundreds of photographs in Jean Baradez' *Fossatum Africae* showing military and hydraulic works in what is now desert

time, and have been the source of much controversy since.

The *fossatum* or ditch was constructed not continuously but only in certain areas: across south-western points of entry into the Aurès massif, encircling the eastern end of the Hodna mountains, and along the Oued Djedi just south of Hadrian's outpost fort at Gemellae (El Kasbat). Traces of similar *fossatum* have been found near Rabat in Morocco, and in southern Tunisia.

It is not certain when the sections of the *fossatum* were constructed; but in southern Numidia at least it was probably in the 120s, on Hadrian's orders. There are many similarities to the major military undertaking of his reign, at the northernmost extremity of the Empire – Hadrian's Wall in Northumberland. But the purpose of Africa's *fossatum* has perplexed archaeologists just as the purpose of Hadrian's Wall has done.

Baradez himself believed the *fossatum* was part of a complex defensive system involving settlement of army veterans on frontier farms, where they combined manning an elaborate chain of forts and watch-towers and repelling invaders from the desert with being 'dry farmers', irrigating their plots in order to grow trees and some crops.

But as a military barrier against raiders from the desert, the *fossatum* does not make sense. It is not continuous; and its separate lengths are puzzling in location. It makes much more sense, however, as a *civilian* barrier, or rather filter, constructed to help the army control the movements of the pastoral tribes who pastured their flocks and herds inside the Roman provinces in the summer, but wintered in the desert south of the frontier. The aim was the same: to protect the crops of the settled regions further north.

In fact, it is most unlikely that there was any intention of preventing the pastoral tribes going north to their summer pastures; not least, because their animals were needed every year to fertilize the fields. But with the increasing cultivation of the most fertile areas it became more and more important to make sure that the tribes did not arrive from the south before their labour was needed for the harvest; and, once arrived, that their animals did not overrun the fields before the crops had been gathered. The policing of the frontier was practical, not hostile.

Most forts and towers – and indeed the settlements – have not been closely dated, although inscriptions indicate that they represent successive building programmes, and were the work of centuries rather than decades. Although the policing was done by the army, it would be left to auxiliaries; and it is very unlikely that many veterans settled there. A soldier would receive a substantial cash grant at the end of his years of service, enough to buy better land, or he would be granted land on the imperial estates in the much more fertile regions north of Lambaesis. The farming of the southern frontier was certainly a civilian achievement, though the nearby presence of the army – and the money wages soldiers had to spend – undoubtedly stimulated it.

Following this theory, the location of the different segments of *fossatum* makes sense. The desert is fringed with a line of salty *chotts* which fill up with rainwater in winter and spring; they afford excellent winter grasses. The sections of *fossatum* were intended to funnel the flocks and herds on their journey north from the *chotts*, towards certain 'control' points; there,

---

1 In any case the beginnings of irrigation systems probably pre-date the Roman occupation.

they would be halted, or waved on; not permitted up certain routes (for instance into the Aurès), or diverted to better ones – and taxed.

Among the most informative inscriptions found in Numidia are two early third-century customs tariffs, one found at Lambaesis, and one found at Zarai, some fifty miles to the north-west. It was long thought that these tariffs represented the regulation of trade between Roman Numidia and Roman Mauretania, since the frontier between the two provinces ran north-south nearby. But both places lie directly on the transhumance route between the Chott El Hodna, in the case of Zarai, and the Chott Melrhir, in the case of Lambaesis, with their excellent winter pastures, and the cereal-growing plains of the Sitifis and Cirta regions to the north.

Between them the two tariffs suggest the passage of exactly the goods one would expect for such a society: animals (horse, mule, donkey, cow and calf, sow, pig and piglet, sheep and lamb, goat and kid), woollen goods, leather, hides, glue, wine (three sorts), figs, nuts, dates (from the oases), resin and pitch (from the mountain forests); slaves; and, perhaps surprisingly, sponges, which probably came from the Gulf of Gabès.

In this context, it is particularly interesting to note that the Roman forts were built, approximately, along two east-west lines across north-west Africa. The outer *limes*, or frontier, followed the 100-millimetre rainfall line which divides the desert from the regions which can support a certain amount of dry farming, from Castellum Dimmidi (Messaad), which was to be founded by Septimius Severus at the end of the second century, through Hadrian's Gemellae and all the way to the Tripolitanian hinterland. The more northerly line of forts ran eastward from Pomaria in western Mauretania to Tébessa – following pretty exactly the 400-millimetre rainfall line, north of which cereals grow.

Was Rome's entire frontier policy in Africa based on the regulation of transhumance? C.R. Whittaker has called the vast area between the outer, southern *limes* and the inner, northern *limes* the Waiting Zone – where those pastoralists who wintered in the desert were let through, allowed to travel north, but then held until the corn was ripe.

6

GRANARY OF THE EMPIRE

The previous inhabitants of north-west Africa had already discovered that corn grew readily enough in the broad river valleys of Tunisia and on the Great Plains of northern Algeria and the far west, and both the Africans and the Phoenicians had learnt to improve on nature by crop rotation and irrigation where it was needed. Pliny the Elder reported that the country was so fertile that one grain would produce a stalk bearing a hundred and fifty new grains (and three times that figure had been known, it was claimed). As an average yield, this was clearly over-optimistic; all the same, African harvests were prodigious. By Caesar's day, Africa Nova alone produced nearly fifty thousand tons of grain every year. Now, with the extension of Roman rule, there was the prospect of far more: and a century after Caesar north-west Africa's cornlands provided two-thirds of the wheat the population of Rome required.

Imperial policy was dominated by the agricultural situation in Italy.

Team of oxen: detail of a second-century mosaic of rural life, now in the Bardo Museum

Italian agriculture had been devastated first by the Hannibalic War and then by the social wars of the last fifty years of the Republic, and the dispossessed peasantry had flocked to the overcrowded capital. The new urban population needed food, and Italy could no longer keep herself in corn. Corn had to be provided by the provinces, notably Egypt and Africa.

Remains of a quern for grinding flour at Timgad

All suitable land in north-west Africa was put under the plough. No doubt the mixed farming economy which the Carthaginians had built up on their estates had been literally trampled underfoot during the wars, and there was little question of actually uprooting healthy trees and plants. The historian Sallust, who went out to govern Africa Nova in 46 BC, had declared firmly that 'the soil produces good crops of grain and good pasture, but is unsuitable for the cultivation of trees,' which is not true, so it suggests that he saw few plantations or orchards. The only olive groves of real importance at that time were in Tripolitania. They were already important enough in Julius Caesar's day to furnish an annual tribute of a million litres of oil (penalty for fighting against Caesar at Thapsus) – and were left undisturbed because most of the land was too dry for wheat. The cattle and market gardens which the soldiers of Agathocles had admired in Cape Bon two hundred years before were, however, replaced by corn and barley: by the first century AD, when the Elder Pliny was writing his *Natural History*, the country was given over to the worship of the harvest goddess, and certainly many sanctuaries which survive from this period were dedicated to Ceres. A hundred years after Caesar's day, the province of Africa – which now included Tripolitania and Numidia – produced nearly half a million tons of grain annually, a tenfold increase.

Roman north-west Africa was fundamentally a farming economy. The Carthaginians had built their fortunes on a virtual monopoly of the maritime carrying trade; their farms, at least until the last few decades before the destruction of Carthage, had simply fed their own population. The tribes living further inland lived primarily off their livestock, which provided them with milk products and wool and leather for clothing, and went hunting for their meat;[1] they grew crops, but only enough for their own needs. The efforts of Masinissa's fellow-chieftains to settle their subjects on the land had not turned the Numidian and Moorish kingdoms into exporting nations – except for Masinissa himself, who exported considerable quantities of wheat and barley, even before he annexed Carthage's cornlands.

But under the Romans part of north-west Africa – roughly, the area of northern Tunisia – began to export foodstuffs on a vast scale; and she kept it up for centuries. It says a great deal for her agricultural wealth that even after the tax-gatherers had taken their tithe she still had a sizeable surplus to sell abroad.

LANDLORDS AND SERFS, TOWN AND COUNTRY

All land of conquered territories belonged to and remained the property of the *senatus populusque Romanus*. Naturally the senate and people of Rome could not exploit the land themselves, but immediately after the conquest individual senators were able from time to time to buy up confiscated estates not needed for town lands, which they then left in the hands of bailiffs. Later, under the Empire, confiscated land was automatically classed as imperial estates.

The pattern of land ownership was extremely complex. Many who had been 'fixed' on good agricultural land by the Carthaginians or the Numidian and Moorish kings were left in possession of their small properties. The old Phoenician cities and Numidian townships which had taken the side of the Romans in the wars were allowed to keep their city territories. In some townships, colonies of veterans or Italian immigrants were settled, so the city land had to be extended or redivided to give the newcomers a share. But most army veterans and other colonists from Italy were settled in townships on good land confiscated from Carthaginian and Numidian landowners, or expropriated from the tribes who were still grazing their flocks on the richer pastures within the province. These new

---

1 The tribes' livestock was their capital, too valuable to kill for food.

Third-century AD mosaic showing a peasant working near one of the
typical straw huts (*mapalia*). Now in the Bardo Museum

settlements, too, were endowed with a surrounding territory.

New towns and old alike, except for a handful on the coast which
had a cosmopolitan admixture of merchants and shippers and traders
of all kinds, were basically settlements of landowning or tenant farmers
with their families and servants. Although the accidents of inheritance
impoverished some – while it enriched others – by and large these
farmers, whether Roman colonists or previous inhabitants, employed
or sub-let to peasants or labourers who actually worked the land. Such
agricultural labourers sometimes lived in the towns, on the fringes or
in poor quarters; but most lived on the land, in the small hamlets of
mud-walled *gourbis* which can be seen throughout North Africa to this
day, or even in caves or straw huts (called *mapalia*) in desperate poverty,
wearing skins and supplementing their diet of barley and millet with
snails and crickets. They had no rights of citizenship in the cities to which
they were attached, and may have had virtually no ordinary legal rights
under Roman law.

Only one in six North Africans – perhaps as few as one in ten – lived in
the towns; directly or indirectly, and usually directly, the town-dwellers'
wealth was founded on the labour of the remaining population, the rural
poor. But the majority of the rural poor did not work on municipal territory.
For although the territories of the townships sometimes adjoined each
other, they were usually more like islands in a sea of the estates or *saltus*
(called *latifundia* if they were large enough), which belonged either to rich

citizens of Rome or, increasingly, to the Emperor himself.[1] Large areas, especially in Tunisia which was already well-cultivated and where much land had been confiscated from the conquered Carthaginians, had been bought up by speculating Roman noblemen. They had seen in Africa the prospect of easy money, since they could export their corn to Italy for good prices. These estates were an investment; the owners did not live on them, any more than the Emperor lived on the imperial domains.

Both kinds of estates were exploited under the supervision of an imperial agent or, in the case of rich Romans' land, a bailiff; or by companies of tax-farmers. But even though large numbers of the inhabitants had been enslaved after the fall of Carthage, the Romans had soon learnt to be wary of exploiting conquered territory by setting armies of slaves to till the soil until they dropped; the slave revolts which punctuated the last decades of the Republic originated in just such gangs of down-trodden men. One theory has it that the Emperor Nero, in the mid-first century, put to death six Roman senators who had acquired huge estates in Africa because they persisted in the habit of employing slave labour in gangs. It seems more likely, however, that he coveted the land itself, for taking it over would mean that he could extend the territory on which he could enforce the collection of rent.

By the first century AD the pattern of the Roman exploitation of north-west Africa had settled down. The large estates, both imperial and private, were, like the municipal lands, divided into individual holdings. The land was let either directly to the peasants who tilled it, or to *conductores* or tenants, who in turn sub-let it to peasants. In either case the peasants occupied the land in return for one third of their produce and a few days' work on the home farm.

Farming in the ancient world – as in many parts of the modern – required a vast labour force. It was as much as a man and his family could do to produce enough for themselves and, on top, half as much again for their masters. When the bad times came it was the peasants who were required to produce the extra taxes, or who suffered the consequences of any localized crop failure.

Fortunately, there was a vitally important side-effect of the judicial fiction that the provinces belonged to the Roman people and not to individual landowners; it meant that the law could regulate the relationship between landowner and tenant, which it could not do in Italy. An agrarian law of 111 BC had already given the provincials security of tenure in return for a part of their harvest; by the first century AD they could sell or leave the land they occupied as they wished, and with it their homes, on condition that the new tenant did not interrupt its cultivation, and its provision of tribute, for more than two years.

---

1 The Emperors confiscated the property of any Roman who died without an heir.

Detailed regulations governed the tax – or rent, in the case of imperial estates – they had to contribute. An inscription cut on an altar dedicated to Trajan in AD 116–17 on one of the imperial domains, at Henchir Mettich in northern Tunisia, lays down that the peasant shall 'give to the owners, lessors or stewards of this estate ... one third of the wheat from the threshing floor, one third of the barley from the threshing floor, one fourth of the beans from the threshing floor, one third of the wine from the vat, one third of the oil from the press, one sextarius of honey from each hive'. (They were allowed to have up to five beehives.) This estate was known, significantly, by the name of Mappalia Siga – perhaps because every harvest-time the *mapalia* of the tribes were to be seen in the fields, when they brought their flocks north in summer.

Another famous inscription from the site of the imperial Saltus Burunitanus (near Souk El Khemis) shows that the lessor, Allius Maximus, with the connivance of an imperial procurator above him in the administrative hierarchy, had attempted to demand more than the normal six days' work on the home farm from the peasants of the domain, and, when they had complained, had sent soldiers to seize and torture them '... and this forces us unhappy men to seek your divine aid. We ask, therefore, most sacred Imperator [Commodus], that you succour us; that in accordance with the clause of the *lex Hadriana* we owe not more than two days' work per year of ploughing, two of cultivating, two of harvesting ... So that through the kindliness of your majesty we, your rural workers, born and raised on your estates, may no longer be harassed by the lessors ...' The Emperor's instruction to the procurator is also recorded: 'In view of the law and of my decision, procurators shall not demand more than thrice two days' work lest any unjust exaction be made by you ...'

Such peasants had rights, at least some of them knew it, and the Emperor was prepared to listen to them. No doubt many were browbeaten by their superiors; no doubt justice was frequently not done to them, especially in the depths of the countryside, far from the towns and the opportunity to lay a complaint, and perhaps even the knowledge that it was possible; but they were *petits propriétaires*, with security of tenure, fixed taxes and a right of redress, even if not all were so fortunate as those who lived on the Saltus Burunitanus.

THE HARVESTER OF MACTAR

Some peasants had no fixed residence, and theirs was the hardest lot of all. They were obliged to hire themselves out by the day, how and when they could, living in straw huts in the fields, travelling the country in gangs, like nineteenth-century navvies, to help with the harvest on the large estates.

Yet the son of one such homeless peasant of the second century, in spite of his poor start in life, rose high in the Romano-African hierarchy, after years as a farm labourer. This man was a harvester of Mactar, who somehow acquired – he claims by his own labour and by his frugality – enough property to become a *censor*, someone of wealth and importance in his city. He left behind him when he died in the third century an inscription in verse on his tombstone (now in the Louvre) which records pride in his rise, if not to fame – his name is unknown – at least to fortune:

'I was born of poor parents; my father had neither an income nor his own house. From the day of my birth I always cultivated my field; neither my land nor I ever had any rest ... When the harvest-gangs arrived to hire themselves out in the countryside round Cirta, capital of Numidia, or in the plains of the mountain of Jupiter, I was the first to harvest my field. Then, leaving my neighbourhood, for twelve years I reaped the harvest of another man, under a fiery sun; for eleven years I was chief of a harvest gang and scythed the corn in the fields of Numidia. Thanks to my labours, and being content with very little, I finally became master of a house and a property: today I live at ease. I have even achieved honours: I was called on to sit in the senate of my city, and, though once a modest peasant, I became censor. I have watched my children and grandchildren grow up round me; my life has been occupied, peaceful and honoured by all.'

Was his 'field' sub-let to him, part of Mactar's town lands? It is of course possible that he inherited the lease – or perhaps even a freehold – from a relative other than his father. But that is not what the inscription suggests. On the contrary, it suggests that he saved out of his wages. Even more intriguing: were the 'harvest-gangs' tribesmen coming up from the south to their summer pastures, in time to sell their labour to help bring in the corn?

The harvester of Mactar, whatever the origins of his wealth, was not typical. Yet he was not the only African who told a similar story. For it was possible for a family's fortunes to change dramatically from one generation to another by accident as well as by effort. One Sicinius Aemilianus of Zarath in Tripolitania, who in later life achieved a minor immortality as one of those who accused the African writer Apuleius of black magic, had only one small field in his youth and was so poor he was obliged to cultivate it himself, although he belonged to a rich family. But the family was also large – and subdivision of the property between them all had reduced him to virtual penury. Then an epidemic carried off most of his relatives, and he found himself wealthy.

The market in land was free, and a generation or two of subdivision, or of buying up from neighbours who had to sell, meant a great variation in the size of properties, even on the imperial estates. Those who got into debt and failed to pay what they owed 'on the threshing floor' would have to give up their land, which could then be let to one of their fellow tenants, who thus increased the size of his holding, or perhaps to a landless peasant like the harvester of Mactar.

Peasant picking up a windfall: detail of a second-century Four Seasons mosaic from La Chebba, Tunisia, now in the Bardo Museum

A MIXED ECONOMY

It would be wrong to imagine that the corn-growing regions of north-west Africa bore any resemblance to the wheatfields of Nebraska, even in the first century AD when the main crop was wheat. The use of a simple wooden plough drawn by a donkey and an ox (or a woman, said Pliny) gave little scope for that kind of mass production. The rural population must always have grown other crops and raised domestic animals. There is little mention of them in the records; the extra produce would have amounted to no more than a diminutive vegetable patch, a fruit tree, probably poultry, a sheep or a goat; the better off may have had a donkey, perhaps an ox as well. The tenants with sub-tenants under them, and the farms of the imperial and private bailiffs must have had all these. With transport expensive and slow, in spite of the new Roman roads, townships and *saltus* alike had to produce everything they needed. Many grew barley, cheaper than wheat, for themselves; animal-owners grew it for their animals. And large numbers of beasts of burden would be needed for the transport of the vast quantities of grain to Carthage for enshipment to Ostia.

The moment there was enough security to grow plants like vines and olive trees, which needed years to come to maturity, any peasants with access to a few square yards of land to spare near their homes must have begun to cultivate them for themselves and their families. And it is unthinkable that the Roman administrators in the towns or on the estates would have been content with a diet of couscous and bread. By the beginning of the second century a mixed economy was commonplace: the imperial tenants of the Saltus Beguensis near Haïdra and the *saltus* at Henchir Mettich had bees, for instance, besides a variety of crops.

Naturally, even in the first century, the pattern of land exploitation was not the same all over north-west Africa. In Tripolitania, olives were always the main crop; the land was too dry for more than a modicum of hard-won wheat and barley. But recent British archaeological surveys (first by Richard Goodchild, David Oates and Olwen Brogan and then by Barri Jones and Graeme Barker) have shown that a good hundred miles inland a substantial region which is now uncultivated pre-desert became extremely prosperous during the Roman period, no doubt partly in response to demand from the cities of the coast, and supported a much larger population than either before or since. Scrupulous – and expert – water management of the heavy, intermittent rainfall which otherwise caused flash floods down the wadi-beds enabled sedentary farmers to grow barley, olives and perhaps vines, and to raise sheep and goats. It looks as if these intensive farms were worked by the local tribes (as in the Fezzan further south) and not by Roman or Italian colonists, as previously believed. There is evidence that the technology of water control in the wadis was in use long before the Roman period. And it is now known that the impressive ruins of immense fortified farm buildings, which for many years were thought to represent part of a defensive military system organized by the Emperor Septimius Severus, were originally built on local initiative – perhaps in self-defence against neighbours, because of population pressure on scarce resources of water.

Round Carthage itself, there was more horticulture than agriculture; the figs which reached Trimalchio's dinner table in the *Satyricon* of Petronius, which was written in the first century AD, came from her market gardens, like other exotic fruit and vegetables such as pomegranates and truffles, that appealed to the Roman taste; and artichokes were certainly grown in quantity for the citizens of Carthage. The forests, too, were not ignored. Those of Algeria and Morocco were hunted by the army for lion, leopard, panther and bear for the amphitheatres of Rome – and, once they were built, those of Africa. Elephant, too, until it became extinct in the first century AD, was hunted for its ivory. North Africa's rare woods were also much prized by Roman plutocrats: Cicero himself had paid the ancient equivalent of thousands of pounds for an African thuya-wood table-top, carved in one piece.

Meanwhile, all over Roman territory, there were still large areas of tribal occupation. Part of the former grazing grounds of the Musulamii between Madauros and Theveste (Tébessa) were taken over, after the crushing of the revolt of Tacfarinas, for a town territory, a *saltus* (the Saltus Beguensis), and a private estate; the Musulamii themselves were granted a 'reserve' nearby. The tribe of the Musunii Regiani were allowed to remain near Thelepte (Fériana), and land was set aside for the Nybgenii near the city territory of Tacapae (Gabès). There were many other tribal areas in the unsurveyed, unregistered hills and forests further west. The inhabitants continued to live mainly off their flocks, perhaps travelling great distances between their winter and summer pastures – and, in summer, prepared to hire out their labour to the farmers to earn money or grain to eke out their livelihood; setting up their famous straw huts, or *mapalia*, in the fields for a few weeks at harvest-time – a practice still followed by the modern transhumants whose portable straw shelters strongly resemble the *mapalia* which are frequently illustrated in Roman African mosaics.

The Romans, no horsemen themselves, recruited the famous Numidian cavalry auxiliaries among the inhabitants of the hills of the Maghreb, as the Carthaginians had recruited cavalry there before them, for service in other provinces of the Empire. By the second half of the first century, the Third Augustan Legion was raising local recruits for service in Africa too. There was little to fear, any longer, from the native Africans. Their pacification had long since begun, and many more were beginning to settle to a sedentary life in or around their own tribal townships.

Regular winter rains, mild springs without frost, long ripening summers unthreatened by sudden storms: Africa was blessed in its climate, and its harvests were reliable. If there were bad years, whether from drought or locusts, they left no record of widespread famine, and there was always wheat for Rome. After barely a century of direct Roman rule, the province had displaced Egypt as Rome's principal supplier of corn: two thirds to Egypt's one third. Not the least advantage from the Roman point of view was that the sea journey from Africa was so much shorter, and therefore both cheaper in transport costs and less liable to shipwreck. For more than three hundred years, Africa sent about half a million tons of corn to Rome every year.

In the nineteenth century, with the introduction of modern agricultural methods and the bringing into production of land which, since Roman times, had fallen into disuse, the population of French North Africa doubled in the hundred years after 1830; and although no Roman censuses for Africa survive it is very possible that the population of Roman north-west Africa also greatly increased between AD 50 and 150, and continued to rise. By the beginning of the third century it may have numbered between six and seven million and was possibly as much as eight million. It was only centuries later, when the security and settled conditions necessary for farming, particularly in the dry regions where the upkeep of dams and canals is essential to agriculture, finally vanished, that numbers declined to their pre-Roman level. By the mid-nineteenth century El Kef – the ancient Sicca Veneria – perched defensively on its bluff was the only sizeable community in the upper Bagradas valley, which had once supported dozens of thriving cities.

AGRICULTURE'S GOLDEN AGE

There was certainly a rapid growth in the size and numbers of the cities of Africa, and a dramatic extension and development of agriculture.

In the first century, according to Pliny, all the glory of the country was in its grain harvests. In the second century, pressure of numbers – combined, possibly, with the exhaustion of even that well-phosphated soil in certain over-cropped areas – dictated the spread of agriculture to less fertile land unsuitable for wheat: the hillsides and wooded heaths within the cornlands, and the dry regions to the south. Much of the glory was now to be shared by great groves of olive trees.

The new policy was actively encouraged by the Emperors. At the end of the first century the first of the provincial Emperors rose to the purple. This was Trajan, a Spaniard, a capable and far-sighted administrator. By this time, too, Italian agriculture had declined yet further; Italy was no longer producing enough olive oil and wine for her own needs, let alone those of the rest of the Empire. The peasants of north-west Africa were now officially encouraged to bring into cultivation uncultivated land on the fringes – land which could not be used for wheat.

The Henchir Mettich inscription previously quoted makes clear that, in return for the fixed shares to be given to the owners or lessors, 'permission is given to those who live on the estate of Villa Magna Variana, that is of Mappalia Siga, to bring under cultivation those fields which are unsurveyed on the terms of the *lex Manciana*, namely that he who brings the land under cultivation has provisional title'. Another inscription from Aïn El Djemala shows that peasants were allowed to plant vines and olive trees for themselves both outside and inside the domain. The peasants are appealing to the imperial administrators: 'We ask, procurators, that ... you grant us those fields which are swampy and wooded, that we may plant them with olive groves and vines in accordance with the *lex Manciana*, on the terms applying to the neighbouring Saltus Neronianus ...' Hadrian's procurators reply: 'Since our Caesar in the untiring zeal with which he constantly guards human needs has ordered all parts of land which are suitable for olives or vines, as well as for grain, to be cultivated, therefore by the grace of his foresight the right is given to all to enter upon even those parts of said land which are included in the surveyed units of the Saltus Blandianus and of Udensis [and others] ... and which are not exploited by the lessors.' New occupiers had the usual right to leave the new property to whom they wished, and must in return pay a rent of a third part of the produce. But anyone planting olive trees or grafting them on to wild olives need pay no part of the crop for ten years. An instruction to the imperial agent is added: 'If any fields lie fallow and are untilled, if any wooded plots or swamps [exist] in this district of *saltus*, [do not hinder from cultivating the same] those who desire [to do so] ...' There were certainly some aims shared by the Emperor and his rural subjects.

Forests were cut down, both to supply wood for fuel and timber and to make room for farming and stockbreeding.[1] Uncultivated hillsides and heaths were cleared, terraced and gradually planted with orchards, olive groves and vineyards, or stocked with cattle and horses, sheep and goats. There is no reason to suppose that matters were much different in the city territories, or on the private estates. A famous second-century mosaic, now in the Bardo Museum in Tunis, shows a typical private domain in the valley of the Miliana at Uthina (Oudna), just off the road between Tunis

Hunting wild boar. From the evidence of this mosaic from the House of the Laberii at Oudna, it was a 'mixed economy' estate. Now in the Bardo Museum

and Zaghouan. There are wheatfields, which were the source of its wealth still, but also olive trees and pastures for sheep and goats; there are cattle

---

1 It is ironic that the Roman occupation set in train the erosion which is now so conspicuous over large areas of the Maghreb, when at the time the inhabitants took such care with their barrages and dykes to prevent it. But once the waterworks were allowed to decay there were not enough tree roots to prevent the winter rains carrying away the topsoil for ever.

and horses, a donkey and, in the surrounding scrub, partridge, wild boar and even panther. There were probably no game reserves as there were in Italy, although it is possible that game birds were raised in the farmyard along with other domestic poultry. Hunting, particularly of gazelle and of hare, which is a favourite theme of African mosaics, was important for rich and poor alike: for the former for pleasure, for the latter for food, and for both to protect the crops from gazelle or wild boar. The mosaic was found in a town house; there is no villa on the domain, only farm buildings. Perhaps it was near enough to Uthina for the owner to dispense with a hunting lodge; his bailiff too probably lived in the city. What is really significant however is the presence of olive groves and meadows in the corn country. There was now enough labour, no doubt because population was increasing, to make use of hitherto unused land.

Mixed farming of this kind flourished, particularly in northern Tunisia, where the larger estates were to be found. The wetter plains south-east of Algiers and in the far west in Mauretania continued to concentrate on cereals, just as in Tripolitania olives were always the main produce.

But the land left uncultivated within the *saltus* and the city territories was not enough – either to satisfy the pressure of population, or to meet the demand for agricultural produce. There was a gradual expansion of agriculture west and south. The tribal reserves were hemmed in yet further, or pushed south, which caused constant clashes between transhumants and farmers, and occasional outbreaks of more serious fighting. Many of the transhumants, however, themselves took to the settled pasturage and farming which needed less elbow-room.

It was perhaps partly in response to this expansion that Trajan extended the old frontier which ran north of the Aurès to the south of that mountain range. The Romans wanted to encircle and control the mountain tribes of the Aurès, whose flocks and herds might endanger their crops and orchards; and indeed there was soon to be an imperial estate right in the heart of the Aurès. A military road was built from the oases of the Chott Djerid directly west through Ad Majores (Besseriani) and Vescera (Biskra). Trajan's successor Hadrian, who visited the army in Africa twice during a reign spent in constant travels round the Empire, founded several army outposts along Trajan's old frontier – in some sectors a kind of curtain wall of forts and running barriers – to keep an eye on the tribes of the desert; both these Emperors expanded the network of roads running west towards Mauretania Tingitana from Oppidum Novum (El Khadra, due south of Cherchel), a town founded by the Emperor Claudius in the first century and largely peopled by veterans. Either Trajan or Hadrian moved the Legion's headquarters to its final, westernmost home at Lambaesis. Within the new frontier it defended, more and more of the Maghreb was brought into cultivation until, by the end of the second century, the Christian apologist Tertullian was writing: 'Smiling estates have replaced the most famous deserts, cultivated fields have conquered the forest, flocks of sheep have put wild beasts to flight . . . certain proof of the increase of mankind!'

THE IMPORTANCE OF OLIVES

The main agent of this civilian colonization in the drier regions of the interior was the olive tree. It is impossible to exaggerate its importance to the prosperity of Roman North Africa for, if wheat enriched the conquerors, the oil was to enrich the native inhabitants also. It was one of the main commodities of commerce in classical times, for in the ancient world olive oil was as much used in cooking as it is round the Mediterranean today; there was, besides, no other soap, no other base to fix perfume, and it was virtually the only fuel for lighting. Most of the countries to the north of the Mediterranean were able to produce all the olive oil they needed, now that they had a taste for Roman comforts. But Italy did not fulfil her own needs, and the north-west African provinces were able to fill the gap, and in so doing profit themselves.

The olive tree's immense advantage to north-west Africa was that it does not require much water – less, in fact, than the palm tree. Of the total land area of north-west Africa north of the Sahara desert, about half has an annual rainfall of more than 400 millimetres, which is what corn needs, and the other half a rainfall between 100 millimetres – which is what the olive tree needs – and 400 millimetres. The olive tree's potential was enormous – provided the demand for oil was there, and it was.

Nor does the olive tree necessarily need fertile land – although it dislikes salt: it could not be grown in the *chotts*. In north-eastern Tunisia, it was planted not only on ground which had never been cultivated, but on land which had been under the plough since Carthaginian times, and had been exhausted by over-cropping. It is also remarkably hardy: in the hills of Numidia, it was planted well above the three thousand-foot contour (much higher than it is planted today), in spite of the danger from frost. It was even planted on land that was more suitable for wheat. Along the whole length of the east coast, it virtually ousted grain, and there is a famous mosaic pavement from Caesarea (Cherchel) in the comparatively wet, lush west which shows an early third-century estate dominated by olive trees and vines, with corn growing in their shade.

Another virtue of olive culture is that, although it is necessary to wait ten or more years for the tree to bear fruit, it requires little upkeep and little labour for a good return. Since oil was more profitable than corn, and less bulky, it was comparatively cheaper to pay for its transport. For the peasant, this meant that taking over virgin land on the borders of the domain where he worked his smallholding was not an impossible burden; and he could look forward to being able to sell his surplus oil in the local market when his trees at last began to bear fruit. The *pax Romana* and the

Famous mosaic of the early third century showing cereal-growing under olive trees, and viticulture. Note curious throwing action of the sower – still seen in Algeria. Cherchel Museum

agrarian laws enabled him to be confident that the trees would still be there, and still be his, that far ahead. The large landowners had enough capital behind them to buy large tracts of land for olive groves, and then wait years for their long-term returns. But for them, too, the saving in labour was an important consideration. If there was still slave labour in Africa, it was declining since most slaves were manumitted after a number of years' service, and one source of supply of new slaves, as part of the booty of war, was drying up. By the mid-second century the Empire had virtually given up foreign conquest, and even if slave-owners bred replacements there was less competition for free labour. The career of the harvester of Mactar suggests that hired hands could command a good wage, for to rise to the position of censor he must have amassed a large capital. Were his wages as a reaper 'for another man' and then as 'chief of a harvest gang' substantial – perhaps as much as those of a legionary (and it was certainly possible for soldiers to save considerable amounts)? Those who owned land in Africa could well have been glad to grow olives, which saved them so much of the cost of labour.

But the most important extension of olive culture was the establishment of vast groves all over the dry country of southern Tunisia and southern Numidia, to match the olive groves which already flourished in Tripolitania. The whole of the area round Thysdrus (El Djem) became a vast olive grove, with trees planted some twenty or thirty yards apart. Elsewhere, where rainfall was lower, the olive tree required more space for its roots to spread. It could support a large and thriving population, but not a concentrated one: a day's work covered a larger area than in the corn country. Thysdrus itself, in spite of the enormous amphitheatre which could have held thirty thousand spectators, had a population a fraction of that size: but it was at the centre of an area of prosperous peasant villages, whose inhabitants could come into the city for the spectacles or the chariot-races, or for market days to buy the other food they needed with the money they earned from the sale of their surplus oil, even if their place of work was too far for a daily journey. Further west, round Cillium (Kasserine) and Sufetula (Sbeïtla), the olive trees abounded; a recent survey round Kasserine found signs of an amazing number of olive presses. Again, the wealth of these cities' public buildings is out of all proportion to the number of people who actually lived there. Other crops were grown, of course, and livestock raised for local consumption, but in more modest quantities. The olive tree was king.

Still further west, olive trees were planted on the more fertile northern slopes of the Aurès mountains, where the Legion had built its base and its veterans' colonies; even more dramatic, they were also planted along the southern slopes overlooking Trajan's and Hadrian's frontier, and the desert beyond – slopes which are now quite barren.

Although there are signs that the Africans themselves had begun to irrigate certain of these regions before the Romans arrived, large-scale water management in the pre-desert zone could not be undertaken until the Romans had pacified the tribes along the southern frontier and established control over their seasonal migrations. This was the object of Hadrian's *fossatum* and the eventual development of the *limes*, or frontier-in-depth.

THE GREAT IRRIGATION SCHEMES

The southern frontier was not totally dry country. But even as far north as Lambaesis, normally well-watered, the rain could not be relied on. The author of the *Historia Augusta*, a collection of lives of the Emperors, says that Hadrian was particularly loved in Africa because when he arrived to visit his army in AD 128 rain fell for the first time in five years. Three centuries later, St Augustine was reminding his parishioners in Hippo Regius, on the north coast, how lucky they were compared to those who lived in the south: 'Here, God grants us rain every year ... there, He sends it rarely, if in great quantity.'

Rain fell, in fact, but intermittently – and violently. In Tripolitania, floods swept one concrete Roman barrage hundreds of yards downstream. In the Aurès mountains there was frequently snow on high ground. Although enough water sank to be trapped for wells it tended to run off over the dry ground and flow in floods down the beds of the few rivers towards the desert, where it was lost to evaporation. It was the same all over the desert fringe. The land was not infertile, or the tribes would not have wanted it for grazing. It merely remained to use every drop of what rain there was.

It was essential to prevent the water disappearing as fast as it came and to prevent any snow melting in a sudden flood. In parts, especially around Theveste, the tribes of Numidia had themselves already begun this task; but its vast extension belongs to the Roman period. Traces have been found of whole hillsides terraced not for cultivation but to hold rainfall or melting snow long enough for it to sink in gradually and fill the water-table for wells. Horizontal walls were built along the slopes, at intervals of thirty yards; similar ones can be seen today on hillsides throughout Tunisia. These walls have the secondary function of preventing erosion, for the washing away of soil can be an even more serious problem.

Sudden rushing of water down the oueds was prevented by damming them and constructing water channels to direct the water to crops and trees where it was needed. Enormous numbers of these barrages have been found in what is now semi-desert: there were at least sixty in the neighbourhood of one tiny settlement in Tripolitania. Elaborate regulations were worked out for the fair distribution of the water: similar regulations exist today in the palm groves of the oases. Wells were dug, and such was Roman technical skill that they could tap a natural water vein even in a predominantly mineral water area, or sink a well to a depth of fifty or sixty feet. Artificial basins were built to collect rainfall, and cisterns to hold it. The inhabitants of the pre-desert fringe practised in miniature, but with an even more compelling motive, what was practised in the more populous and more fertile regions with a higher rainfall.

It would be wrong to imagine a kind of green belt the whole length of the frontier; there were never enough people to develop it all, and there was not enough water, except in western Mauretania where in any case Roman penetration was not so thorough. The only farming was dry farming: widely-spaced olive trees and a few hard-won subsistence crops for people and animals. Yet the remains of dozens of small mills and olive presses and even the stumps of olive trees have been found in what is now barren land.

This was a countryside which was soon to become very prosperous. And the evidence of its prosperity was to be the number of substantial cities, and countless villages, which the olive groves, like the cornlands further north, were shortly able to support.

CRAFTS AND INDUSTRY

The wealth of Africa was in these primary agricultural products; there was almost no industry except on a small scale. The grain was threshed by the peasants themselves on the domain threshing-floors when they paid their tribute; perhaps there were municipal threshing floors also. In any case, the work was not specialized. But machinery, however simple, was necessary for the extraction of olive oil before it could be transported in amphorae to its destination. Wooden presses were common in well-wooded areas; only traces of their post-holes have been found, but no doubt they were similar to those still used in north-west Africa by the Berbers. What have survived are countless stone oil presses; not only single presses, but whole factories, some with as many as a score of ruined but recognizable presses. The surplus for sale was too great for the peasants to process themselves.

Huge quantities of pottery have also been found, especially on private domains in the olive country of Tunisia and Tripolitania, where amphorae to carry the oil had to be manufactured, and where the landlords may have found such manufacture a useful way of increasing the return on their investment in large tracts of land. Many North African amphorae have been found all over the western Mediterranean provinces: an oil amphora from Tubusuctu has been dug up in Rome. Lamps, of many different types, are another very common find in excavations. With oil plentiful and cheap, all but the poorest could afford to have artificial lights,[1] and there was a steady market for them. Lamps from Hadrumetum (Sousse), for instance, have been found in Sicily, Sardinia and Italy. Vessels with a fine red slip were also produced and exported widely, and in such quantities that Africa came to dominate the market. Votive statuettes were also manufactured, and some bricks also, although most bricks appear to have been imported from Italy. Pottery remains a thriving craft in north-west Africa to this day. Much of it must have been sold rather as it is today – from open markets or in special streets in the *souks* of the towns.

At Simmithu (Chemtou) – the only city of Roman north-west Africa which could remotely be called industrial – the yellow and dark rose marble so much prized by the Roman world was quarried. Africa was rich in quarries, which provided both stone[2] and marble, in the enormous colour-range of the *tesserae* used in the mosaics; but, like the mines, they all belonged to the Emperor and were largely worked by slaves. There was some mining also, for copper, lead and iron, but it remained a minor part of the economic life of the time.

---

1 St Augustine was astonished, when he lived in Italy, to find that artificial light – something he took for granted in Africa – was a luxury there.
2 The cliff quarry at El Haouaria, from which stone was cut for Carthage, is one of the most impressive sights in Tunisia.

Game of dice: pottery lamp from Tébessa

The importance of wood has to be assumed: though copses and wood-land on the domains were cleared by the peasants themselves, or by such slaves as there were, there may have been some kind of gang labour to cut and transport the enormous quantities of wood needed, in both Africa and Italy, to supply timber for the construction of buildings and for fuel for the public baths. Shipbuilding, too, must have been an important activity in the cities of the coast.

Leather and textiles also leave little evidence behind them. There was naturally spinning and weaving of wool from domestic animals for local use (see the Dominus Julius mosaic on page 166); but Africa had long been celebrated for its fine textiles, and continued to export them throughout the Roman period.

Without doubt the most important producers of wool and leather, as they are to this day, were the tribes; and – as they still do – they must themselves have made up much of their raw material into clothing and other finished goods. There is the evidence of the customs tariffs of Zarai and Lambaesis already mentioned; and the celebrated Price Edict of

Diocletian's day (late third century) itemizes Numidian hooded cloaks, buckled cloaks, shirts and carpets.

Some processes took place in the towns. Dyeing with the purple of the murex shell was a source of wealth for the inhabitants of Mogador in Morocco, Meninx on the island of Djerba and Chullu (Collo) on the north coast. Dyers, fullers and curriers, tanners and shoemakers have left evidence behind, and there must have been other ancillary trades. Most of this activity was in no sense industrialized; for the one large tannery found at Tipasa,[1] dozens of one-man artisan workshops have been identified by archaeologists. These textile crafts must have resembled the small-scale manufactures in the *souks* of modern Tunis, Fez and Marrakesh. One can well imagine such craftsmen sitting in their tiny shops in the side-streets of the cities, just as their modern descendants do. It is worth remembering, too, that both Timgad and Djemila, both army towns on important transhumance routes, had separate cloth markets.

The same is true of the modest manufacture of metals. Hardly a mention of them survives – a rare inscription here or there about a blacksmith, a goldsmith, a silversmith. Gold and silver working, however, were state-controlled industries, carried out under government licence.

The production of *garum*, a tunny-fish paste which was a popular delicacy in the Roman world, was also an 'industrial' process, and has been detected at several sites south of the straits of Gibraltar and along the Mediterranean coast as far as Tripoli.

The major industry of north-west Africa, the one which has left the clearest and most impressive evidence behind it, absorbed wealth rather than created it, except indirectly. The building and upkeep of five or six hundred stone cities, countless aqueducts and twelve thousand miles of roads must have called for substantial numbers of builders and masons. The Third Augustan Legion and its veterans built a handful of the cities and roads of the frontier provinces – it was a way of keeping soldiers occupied once the tribes were regulated and pacified, and they had too little policing work to keep them busy. Such building would cost the locals, or the Emperor, very little, since army labour was essentially free.

The rest were built by the natives. Virtually nothing is known of their organization. Perhaps they were masons who travelled the country in gangs like the harvesters; more likely they were recruited from the local inhabitants themselves, on a permanent or temporary basis. Certain skilled workers came from abroad – to work for Juba II or, much later, for the Emperor Septimius Severus at Leptis Magna, for example – but in general masons were not imported, for the old Punic unit of measurement, the cubit of twenty inches, rather than the Roman foot of twelve, was commonly used, and the walls of town houses – upright orthostat blocks every

---

1 Similar tanneries can still be seen at Fez and Marrakesh.

few yards filled in with small stones or bricks set in mortar – owe more to local antecedents than to standard Roman methods.

But if wealth was spent on building cities, and the waterworks and roads which supplied them, it was made there also; on the buying and selling, the processing and transporting of Africa's rural produce.

Ancient tannery still in use at Fez, Morocco

7

THE SIX HUNDRED CITIES

The harvester of Mactar grew up and spent his working life in the country-side; but as soon as he had enough money he went to live in the town. There was no question in the second century AD of him or any other rich African wanting to become a country gentleman, living in a mansion in the middle of his land. The very rich might have a suburban villa in order to escape the heat of the towns in the height of summer, or a hunting lodge in the hills; but even the proconsul's villa was in the suburbs of Carthage, hardly more than a mile or two from his palace in the city itself. The Carthaginians had made permanent homes of their country houses; but the Roman-African rich of the first three centuries were essentially city-dwellers. The great country villas which are so familiar from the mosaics of north-west Africa all belong to the late third and early fourth centuries AD, when life in the towns had become a great deal less agreeable.

In the golden age of the High Empire the Africans took to city life with enthusiasm. In the cities of the eastern Mediterranean, with their memories of a greater past and their resentment of an exploiting conqueror, Greeks, Jews and Asiatics bewailed the loss of their former independence. But, to the better-off African, Roman rule meant not subjection but opportunity – not merely to become a Roman citizen, but to help govern his city, to join the imperial bureaucracy, to be freed perhaps from the usual taxes and tribute and even, if he were rich enough, to become a senator in Rome itself.

There were several kinds of city in Roman North Africa: the old Phoenician towns, almost all on the coast, which had always had a sizeable immigrant population and were throughout the Roman period much the most cosmopolitan, among which Carthage was pre-eminent, with Leptis Magna not far behind; the old native settlements – especially the tribal capitals of Volubilis, Siga, Iol Caesarea, Cirta, Dougga and Zama; the purpose-built Roman veterans' colonies like Diana Veteranorum and Timgad, as well as other Roman towns that grew up around the forts and fortresses; and, by far the greatest number, the modest cities of the interior, which were essentially market towns which grew out of native villages

Two sides of the Roman genius: visible column and unseen sewer at
Sabratha, Libya

and hamlets. There was some overlapping, of course; Carthage was rebuilt
as a *colonia* by the Romans, and many veterans' colonies were settled in
former native or Phoenician towns, while market towns developed over
the course of time next to garrisons, or replaced them when the Legion
moved on – as happened at Haïdra and Tébessa.

By the third century, there were five or six hundred cities. Two hundred
of them were in the rich farmlands of northern Tunisia. In places they were
no more than six or eight miles apart, and in the valley of the River
Bagradas (Medjerda) there was almost a kind of ribbon development along
the main road from Carthage to Theveste (Tébessa). Few were cities as we
think of them today, for their population was too small, most probably
between five and ten or fifteen thousand; many had even fewer inhabitants.
Probably only Carthage ran to a six-figure population, and Leptis Magna
may have had perhaps eighty thousand. At Caesarea the main aqueduct
alone could supply water for a population of forty thousand. Another
dozen or so cities had between twenty and forty; most of them were major
ports like Sabratha in Tripolitania, Hadrumetum (Sousse) in eastern Africa
Proconsularis, or Utica, Hippo Regius and Hippo Diarrhytus on the north
coast. The only inland cities of comparable size were Juba's old capital in
the far west, Volubilis; Cirta, long the capital of the kings of Numidia and
for centuries past colonized by Italian immigrants, which was strategically

101

placed on a major crossroads; and Thysdrus (El Djem), in the heart of the olive groves of Tunisia. There was a scattering of cities with nearer twenty than ten thousand inhabitants; the rest were no bigger than large villages.

They were cities not by virtue of their size but by virtue of their function, and the privileges granted by Rome. Very few started as cities: there were only seven in the days of the Republic – Punic towns like Utica which had sided with the Romans, and new Roman colonies. The remainder achieved city status when they had grown large and prosperous enough to govern themselves, administer their own justice and collect their own taxes, for it suited the Emperors to delegate most of the burdens of rule to their subjects. There was a whole hierarchy, from the true city or *colonia*, whose inhabitants were full Roman citizens; through the *municipium*, whose government was also modelled on that of Rome, with a council similar to the senate and two *duumvirs* elected, like the consuls, for a year, but whose inhabitants had lesser rights and were not necessarily Roman citizens unless they or their forebears had been magistrates or had received citizenship as a favour from the Emperor for other services; right down to the native towns (*civitates*) and villages. These last, too, with increasing population and wealth, could aspire to higher status.

As the tribes found their grazing areas restricted, many of them took to more settled forms of stock-raising, and to farming, still under the leadership of their hereditary chiefs.[1] They, too, had built villages; numbers of cities originated in this way, and developed in time into Roman *civitates*. Others developed on the *saltus*: as land on the fringes was brought into cultivation, there was extra produce for sale or exchange, and the landowners, whether private or imperial agents, founded a weekly market. Groups of *saltus* arranged between them a cycle of market days, so that each held its market on a different day.[2]

Local trade combined with a rising population attracted traders and merchants. Gradually the market grew larger and richer, and acquired its own municipal territory from the domain: it made no difference to the Emperor, by now much the largest landowner in the province, whether taxes and *annona*, or corn tribute, were collected through imperial agents or through municipal authorities. If the township was on a main road, so much the better; here a *mansio* might be built by the army, at which the *annona* was collected and where the army and the imperial functionaries could collect their share before the remainder was despatched to the coast. This meant more trade, a larger entrepreneurial class, and artisans like potters and shoemakers to cater for the needs of people with money to

---

1 In Carthaginian times, the 'chiefs' of some native townships had adopted the title *sufes*, after the Punic chief magistrates – and Leptis Magna continued to have *sufetes* in Roman times.
2 A custom enshrined in the names of their present-day counterparts, for Souk El Arba means Wednesday market, and Souk El Khemis Thursday market.

spend. The army itself was enormously important in stimulating both agriculture and trade wherever it was stationed, simply because soldiers were paid in coin, and had to be provided with food and clothing. The Third Augustan Legion brought a money economy to southern Numidia, and its cities were prosperous and important.

Most of the villages which grew into cities were in the corn-growing plains of Tunisia and Algeria; in the far west of Morocco, where the tribes still had extensive grazing grounds, and in the dry south and in the Tripolitanian hinterland even villages were fewer. But remains of plenty of substantial towns have been discovered in the wild mountain country of central Algeria, where modern towns are few and far between, and villages an impoverished huddle of shacks.

BUILDING TO IMPRESS

The inhabitants of Roman north-west Africa eagerly followed their new masters' example: their towns were built of stone, and embellished with handsome and often grandiose temples, forums, market places and public baths. Though the Emperors sometimes allowed money for public buildings,[1] in hundreds of cities the money for building was provided by new-rich citizens.

In the ancient world there were few investment outlets for profits. Some rich men invested their money in shipping, which was extremely lucrative, and was the source of many African fortunes in the coastal cities; but the profits still had to be spent. There was little industry to invest in – money was not used to finance an industrial revolution which might, eventually, have raised the basic standard of living of the very poor. Instead, it was spent on conspicuous consumption and, like the Suffolk and West Country wool fortunes of the English Middle Ages, on buildings.

All the natural competitiveness of the rich second-century African, frustrated by the *pax Romana* from its traditional expression in war, was poured into the improvement of his native city, into a determination to rise in the local hierarchy to the highest magisterial posts, and into the pursuit of prestige in the eyes of his fellows.

The typical Romano-African town strayed a long way from the geometric ideal laid down at Timgad. A veterans' colony attached to an older town might follow the set square; but when the pre-Roman town was developed the former street plan usually remained. When a market town grew up beside a colony or a garrison, the new buildings were constructed without much semblance of order on the perimeter, doubtless on the sites of the earliest camp followers' shacks as and when they were pulled down

---

1 Some of the most spectacular remains at Leptis Magna, for instance, were built by its native son the Emperor Septimius Severus.

Auditorium and *frons scaenae* of the theatre at Djemila. The eroded hills
in the distance were once flourishing farmlands and orchards

to make way for improvements. Native villages were on the crests of hills;
when the slope was sharp, the main street was obliged to zig-zag from one
end of town to the other. It would have been impossible to impose much
order on the abrupt site of Thugga (Dougga), an old native settlement; and
even at Cuicul (Djemila), which was founded by veterans of the Third
Augustan Legion, although the main road runs straight along the narrow
spur on which the city was built, expansion meant that the later streets
extended the city further along the ridge. At Lambaesis, the fortress was
built with admirable regularity; but the town on the rising ground to the
south was not compressed into the same mould.

Nonetheless, the core of a Roman town had a pattern. The two principal
roads, the *decumanus maximus* and the *cardo maximus*, which were its arteries to the outside world, crossed at right-angles in the centre. All the other
streets of the city were, ideally, built parallel to one or other of these. Like
the agricultural land, cities followed the original survey system of the
province.[1]

---

1 The *cardo maximus* of Carthage, which ran south-west out of the city to become the main
road to Theveste, seems to have been for most of the province the base-line from which
were calculated the innumerable holdings of land in the survey.

Main street – the *decumanus* – of Tipasa. Tipasa is one of the most
picturesque Roman sites in north-west Africa

At the main crossroads was the forum – the heart of a city, the square
where public life was visibly lived. This, like the main streets, was always
paved (though wheeled traffic was forbidden), and frequently colonnaded
against the sun. It was the site of the *curia*, or city hall. As in Athens and
the city states of the Greek world, the comings and goings in this open
place in front of the seat of local government played a vital part in fostering
the sense of community, and collecting news and trade from the further
world. Sometimes, as a city expanded, a second forum was built, as at
Cuicul and Thubursicu Numidarum[1] (Khémissa) and Leptis Magna; but
the most important forum remained that which contained the *curia*. Often
an inscription records the name of the private citizen or Emperor who
donated the money for it or contributed towards rebuilding; the old forum
at Leptis Magna was repaired in AD 53 by Gaius, son of Hanno (whose
Punic descent is obvious from his father's name, and who had plainly not
suffered from the Roman conquest), while the new forum was donated a
hundred and fifty years later by the Emperor Septimius Severus.

The forum was also normally the site of the basilica, or court of justice;

1 The Numidae were a local tribe – and perhaps the origin of the word Numidia.

One of the two kiosks in the market place at Leptis Magna, with columns
of the original octagonal portico

usually there were shops and bars as well, and on market days it commonly
served as a market-place. Special market-places were, however, built
in the wealthiest cities. The market at Leptis was built by one Annobal
Rufus Tapapius, another benefactor of Punic origin, who generously gave
Leptis its theatre as well: both date from AD 1–2. The market had booths
along the sides and two kiosks[1] in the middle for the officials who settled
disputes or collected taxes and generally saw to good order. Timgad's
market was also donated by a private citizen called Sertius, who erected
statues of himself and his wife Valentina there, and both Timgad and
Cuicul boasted separate cloth markets, no doubt important outlets for
the woollen and leather goods of the tribes. The food market at Cuicul still
has a *ponderarium* of standard weights and a table with circular standard
measure cavities.

Temples were built to various gods and to Emperors – whose cult was
of great importance – and even to abstractions such as Concord, which
must have seemed invested with magical powers in that once war-torn
land. The richest cities built capitols – temples dedicated to the three

1 One kiosk, shown above, has been restored to its full height.

Tables with standard measure cavities in the market-place at Leptis
Magna

Temple of Juno Caelestis at Dougga, built between AD 222 and 235 just
before the inhabitants of this part of north-west Africa were converted
to Christianity

principal gods of the Roman pantheon, Juno, Jupiter and Minerva. Some
must have had libraries, although only one, at Timgad, has been identified.
Streets, forums and market-places were embellished with statues of

107

emperors, gods and leading citizens anxious to impress themselves on their neighbours: many were well over life-size.[1]

The semi-circular library at Timgad

Of all Rome's provinces, Africa is today the richest in examples of the triumphal arch. It was intended more as a kind of monumental street furniture than as part of the outer defences of a city, for which, with its open arches, it would have been useless. Surmounted by long-vanished bronze statues of gods or Emperors, frequently in chariots pulled by horses, they were permanent reminders to the inhabitants of the might of Rome. Often they were erected at the approaches to a city, some distance away; sometimes they formed a kind of roundabout at some public place. There is a fine triple arch at Timgad, other generously-columned arches at Cuicul; even a tiny hill-top city like Tiddis, near Constantine, has its own modest arch across the main street. But the finest is the magnificent four-way arch at Leptis Magna (recently restored), even though it has long since been denuded of its processional friezes, which are now in the Tripoli Museum and are among the greatest works of Roman sculpture in Africa.

At Ammaedara (Haïdra), at Mactar, at Cillium (Kasserine), on the edge of the desert, in the depths of the countryside, the traveller is constantly astonished at the sight of vast, pedimented, pilastered mausoleums inscribed with the career of a man or a family in whose memory they were

---

1 Those found at Bulla Regia make a visit to the gallery in the Bardo which now houses them a claustrophobic experience.

Arch of Caracalla at Djemila

erected. Rich Africans were not content with a dedication in a market-
place or a forum to remind posterity of their existence. They also built
these elaborate memorials, perhaps on land which belonged to them, for
themselves and their families. The earliest examples date from pre-Roman
times; the most celebrated, outside Dougga, dates probably from the
second century BC. It was erected, in the Roman style, in memory of a
prince of Numidia. Such tombs are found in many places from eastern
Algeria to Tripolitania, and continued to be built until the fourth century
AD. Some think it may have been a hangover into Roman times of the old
Libyan ancestor worship, and that surviving relatives may have made
expeditions on feast days or anniversaries to worship at the tomb of the
head of the family.

BUILDING FOR PLEASURE AND COMFORT

The Romans built for pleasure on as grand a scale as they did for piety or
government. Some two dozen theatres have been found in North Africa;
others no doubt have yet to be discovered; still more, of wood, must have
perished. No city of any size was without one. Usually they were cut into
a hillside; where no slope was available, the semi-circle of seats was built
up over huge curving galleries, as at Sabratha, where the late second-
century theatre has been restored by the Italians to something approaching
its original splendour. Here, between the imposing triple-storeyed *frons
scaenae*, its architectural style almost as much Renaissance as Roman, and
the exquisite bas-reliefs of the screen, modern revivals of classical tragedy

Arch of Trajan, Timgad: travellers from Lambaesis arrived by this road.
The grooves worn by wheeled traffic are clearly visible

The Emperor Septimius Severus and his sons Caracalla and Geta: part
of the frieze from the four-way arch at Leptis Magna. Now in the Tripoli
Museum

Fine mausoleum inscribed with a 110-line poem at Kasserine (ancient Cillium), Tunisia

have sometimes been staged. Roman African audiences, however, clamoured for entertainments like the pantomime which the African writer Apuleius describes in *The Golden Ass:* musical comedies with half-naked dancing girls, clowns and mimes. The theatres of the time were sometimes more palaces of varieties than temples of dramatic art – although many performances had an important religious role. They were as popular as the cinema in the first half of the twentieth century, and leading actors enjoyed the reputations of film stars – even though, as a profession, acting was looked down on, and actors could not hope, even had they wished, to become city dignitaries. To finance a free show was expected, however, from aspiring magistrates; the city of Cirta even had its own permanent acting company. It was a mark of imperial favour when the Emperor Caracalla lent his finest actor, Agrippa, to Leptis Magna.

The theatres were not the only places of public entertainment. The Legion brought with it a taste for gladiatorial combat, and for contests with wild beasts, and many towns had at least a modest amphitheatre too. The civilian population took to these cruel spectacles with avidity; they became the recognized method of putting to death prisoners, criminals and, in the third century, Christians. One of the finest North African mosaics (see page 155), from Zliten in Tripolitania, shows just such a scene

111

Roman theatre overlooking the Oued Derb at Kasserine near Sbeïtla,
Tunisia

of carnage: two naked prisoners strapped to little carts are being thrust
forward into the jaws of wild beasts. There is a small orchestra, no doubt
to drown the shrieks of the victims, which includes a woman player.

Many amphitheatres must have been of wood, but with increasing
prosperity were replaced by stone constructions. The most famous is the
great amphitheatre at Thysdrus (El Djem), which was as large as Carthage's
own; only Rome's Colosseum surpassed them in size. But by the third
century few of the more prosperous African cities were without an amphitheatre of their own. Nearly thirty are known.

Chariot racing was also followed with as much enthusiasm as motor
racing today. A leading charioteer was the Grand Prix winner of his day,
and won fame, fortune and considerable social status, however humble
his origins. The leading horses were immortalized in the mosaic floors of
their owners' homes. The elongated hippodromes where the races were
held have rarely survived, except as sites; only six have been discovered.
The fine one found at Leptis Magna was excavated, by a British team, in
the 1970s.

Naturally, the richest cities had the greatest number and variety of public
buildings, donated either by private citizens or by the Emperors and their
representatives.

The Romans also believed in making living conditions as comfortable

The amphitheatre at El Djem (ancient Thysdrus), central Tunisia. It is
nearly as big as Rome's Colosseum

as possible. There are at least two hundred and fifty days of sun every year
in North Africa; in summer the heat can be suffocating, so shade and water
are vitally important. Scarcely a city worth the name was without its own
public baths, and preferably several different establishments: Timgad had
thirteen. North-west Africa had more great baths than any comparable
part of the Empire. They were as important in the social life of a city as the
forum and the *curia*.

This was one Roman import which made more difference than any other
to the ordinary comfort of Africans of both sexes. They offered coolness
and cleanliness in that stifling climate, and also companionship: they were
like clubs, where people might agreeably spend the whole day and be sure

113

Fourth-century AD mosaic from Dougga (ancient Thugga) of Eros, a
charioteer, now in the Bardo Museum

Chariot-race: late second-century mosaic from Carthage, now in the
Bardo Museum

of meeting half their acquaintances. Women could use them on ladies'
days, or bathe in separate rooms. The poor too could bathe there – for the
rich donated money for their running costs and the baths were often free,
sometimes every day, sometimes on certain days of the week only.

Public baths were constructed in considerable style. Cleanliness rivalled
godliness, and indeed the remains at Leptis Magna and Carthage, in their
size and solidity, seem more like cathedrals than other secular buildings
of the time. This is partly because they had vast vaulted ceilings. The huge
barrel-vault had been made possible by the Roman discovery of a concrete

from which all air had been expelled (which was not improved upon until the advent of Portland cement in the nineteenth century), and the sophisticated skill with which they used it. Certainly the baths were utterly unlike the temples of the day, which were four-square and sturdy and had pediments and pitched roofs; for where temple architecture concentrated on an imposing outward appearance, with marble-columned porticoes and fine flights of steps, those who built the baths were primarily concerned with the interior: the exterior simply followed the internal spaces. From the outside, to judge from the Hunting Baths at Leptis Magna, which survive in a remarkable state of preservation – complete with frescoes and central heating ducts – they must have looked like giant versions of the modest barrel-vaulted houses to be seen all over North Africa today.

Inside, there were various baths – hot, cold, tepid; plunge baths and steam baths. Latrines were provided for both men and women, and there are still fine examples, whole rows of them, at Leptis, Djemila and Madauros, which once were continuously flushed by running water. There were exercise rooms where young men could wrestle; rest rooms; even small shops and bars. Naturally not all baths were so elaborate, and only the richest had columns of granite imported from Egypt or Corsican marble; but lavish mosaics and marble facings on floors, walls and ceilings were usual. Beneath the main rooms was all the apparatus of water supply and

Row of latrines at Djemila (ancient Cuicul), Algeria

water heating: furnaces, conduits, drains, hypocausts and fuel stores.

No inscriptions record the names of the architects of these monuments, for they were built to the greater glory of the gods or the Emperors, the donors or the cities. Architecture was a trade like any other, and without much prestige in the Roman world since it was left to underdogs like

Greeks and Orientals. Much of Leptis Magna, which bears striking similarities to the Roman cities of Syria, may have been designed by Syrian
architects – especially since the Emperor Septimius Severus, who donated
many of the buildings that survive, was married to a Syrian princess. The
magnificent decorations in the Great Basilica at Leptis were most probably
the work of skilled craftsmen from Asia Minor – perhaps from the island
of Proconnesus, in the sea of Marmara, from whose quarries the white
marble came. But there were certainly also skilled local architects and
craftsmen, and there are signs of an African 'school' by the second century.
Most of it was basically provincial jobbing architecture, but in a style far
superior to any the Carthaginians appear to have followed.

Streets and private houses were also well provided with water; there
were public fountains in forums and market-places (there is a fine example
at Djemila), and many cities had great *nymphaea*, or water basins, with
fountains and statues, often sheltered by a portico: the *nymphaeum* at Leptis
is one of the most remarkable among that wealth of splendid ruins.

This lavish use of water was made possible by the most scrupulous
water-collection. Every Roman house had its own cistern, in which rainfall
was collected: one constantly stumbles into their barrel-shaped remains,
used now as garden sheds or chicken huts, in the gardens of houses all
round Carthage. Wells were sunk, sources tapped, the local oued or wadi
dammed. Water was stored in underground reservoirs. Private enterprise,
however, was not enough; water management was a municipal responsibility. Public baths used vast quantities, and needed it at greater pressure
than could be provided by wells. As towns grew, local wells and carefully
hoarded winter streams were soon exhausted – or at least did not provide
enough for the public baths and fountains. Water had to be imported,
sometimes from great distances, by aqueduct. Because water was so
important, it was treated with some reverence: often splendid colonnaded
monuments surrounded the distant mountain source where it was tapped,
as at Zaghouan, which supplied Carthage, and the beautiful marble
'temple' outside Timgad; and fine 'water houses' were erected to store the
water in the cities. Dedications to Neptune, who was the god of fresh water
as well as the sea, abound. From the water houses an elaborate network
of canals led to every part of the city, sometimes overground, sometimes
under the streets. In one residential quarter of Volubilis the underground
conduits have been traced in great detail: each house was fed from the
municipal supply, and a similar network of drains carried away sewage.
Volubilis was, like Timgad, a planned city, but the visitor to almost any
excavated Roman city in North Africa will detect somewhere, from the
hollow ring of feet on the stone, the presence of a water channel beneath
the flagged street.

Certain cities had their *raison d'être* in water: Hammam Lif near Tunis,
for instance, was in Roman times a spa, as it is today. Apuleius went there

to take the waters. Carpi (Korbous) in the Cape Bon peninsula was known as the African Baiae.

There is no record of North African city-dwellers dying of thirst: the quantity of baths suggests that they had all they needed. But they had it because, either with the army's help or following the Roman example, they took the trouble to get it.

Shade was as important to health and well-being as water. Often there were public gardens, and cemeteries were always planted with trees. Trees were sometimes grown in the streets. The streets themselves were usually very narrow – often only one chariot-width, even the main streets of major towns (just as they are in modern Arab villages) – so that the buildings on one side shaded those on the other. The forums, and certain streets, were lined by arcades against the sun; most public buildings had generous open porches, and private houses were built facing inwards round an inner courtyard.

AT HOME IN A TOWN HOUSE

The North African house plan, which was originally Hellenistic, probably reached Carthage in Punic times; but it suited the climate so well that it survived the Arab invasions. The Arab *dar* is its direct descendant: virtually

Underground house at Bulla Regia, Tunisia

blank-walled against the glare of the outside world, or using the outside wall for tiny one-room shops as the Roman Africans did, the only light inside coming from the open courtyard in the middle.[1]

Occasionally an extreme solution was adopted. At Bulla Regia, houses of the second century had suites of rooms which were constructed underground. Even at this depth, there was a proper water system, mosaic floors and columned courtyard. Often, too, on sloping sites, houses were cut back into the hillside.

Running water was frequently laid on to private houses, and occasionally water was siphoned up to first-floor level. Not that water was actually laid on to the kitchen, where it would have saved the household staff the trouble of fetching and carrying it; there was no shortage of domestic servants, and that kind of labour-saving never occurred to the Romans. Water was primarily for the use and enjoyment of the master and mistress and their family – sometimes for private baths, above all for fountains in the inner courtyards.

Very few private town houses were large. The lives of most men, at least, were lived in public or out of doors – either on their land if it was near the city, or in the *curia* and the forum, or in the market-place. Leisure time, too, was spent in public places – the baths, the amphitheatre – so the Roman Africans spent their money there, and private houses were fairly simple.

Yet the site museums are full of mosaics taken not only from public buildings but also from private houses – which, when not paved with

The good life for a rich man in Roman North Africa: detail from a mosaic in the Bardo

1 The other notable survival is of course the Roman African bath-house, with its barrel vaulting, today seen in every *souk* and casbah, and not only for the *hammam*.

marble, were often decorated with mosaics of mythological scenes, portraits of the mythological characters known as the Four Seasons and scenes from daily life: banquets, spectacles, hunting, fishing and the agricultural round of the countryside. This passion for interior décor is a major source of our knowledge of the daily life of the time. It also inspired one of the principal art forms of Roman Africa. Many mosaics, especially of mythological scenes, were local copies of well-known eastern models; others were designed and made up in squares abroad, and then imported to be laid by local workmen. But some North African mosaics have no affinity with other Roman mosaics. No doubt many a new-rich landowner or merchant commissioned mosaics in the international style; but it was African patrons who first commissioned hunting and circus scenes to commemorate their giving of games in the amphitheatre, and here and there, at Acholla for instance, a local craftsman developed a style of his own; while at Djemila, where the museum boasts some of the most original examples, a minor provincial school seems to have developed. Timgad specialized in a wonderfully ornate 'floral carpet' style.

The best work is distinguished by a lively naturalism, where the artist has used his eyes as well as his sense of fitness to depict what he saw and knew for himself: a chariot race, oxen ploughing, the trapping of wild beasts. At least forty of the famous mosaics at Piazza Armerina in Sicily were either made in a Carthage atelier, or executed by African craftsmen specially imported to do the work.

Agriculture, not unexpectedly, was a favourite theme; but so, too, was the sea, and heads of Neptune and marine scenes are found inland as well as on the coast. The celebrated mosaic now in the Bardo which shows twenty-three different types of ocean-going vessel was found at Medeïna (Althiburos), nearly a hundred miles from the sea. Most marine mosaics, however, followed conventional models of the day; but their popularity suggests that many a rich citizen of the interior owed at least a part of his prosperity to investment in shipping.

If town life was sweet for the rich, it was also more agreeable for the poor, whether they lived in their masters' households, or in their little one-room workshops, or in tenements in a poor quarter (as at Carthage), or in hamlets and villages near the cities. They, too, could visit the baths, see life and exchange views in the market-place and forum, flock to the theatre or the games or the chariot racing. They may have had little money to spend, but much was available to them free. They could share a few, at least, of the pleasures of Roman life.

Some of the increased prosperity came their way even more directly. Many rich people kept open house, and it was often possible for the poor to pick up a free meal, perhaps when someone anxious for election to public office gave a banquet.

Meanwhile, the rich, who were so ostentatiously devoting themselves

This elaborate decorative style was a Timgad speciality

Forum of Septimius Severus, Leptis Magna

to the good of their cities, were hoping to be rewarded not only by the gratitude of their fellow citizens, but by that of the Emperor. They began to seek, and to find, a wider fame.

8

CAREERS OPEN TO TALENT

In the nineties of the first century AD, a literary jury at Rome reached a unanimous verdict: the prize for poetry should be awarded for the first time to an African, P. Annius Florus. But the young man never received it. At the last moment, the Emperor Domitian, who had instituted the prize, refused to ratify the jury's decision. It was unheard of – unthinkable – that a provincial should carry off his prize from under the noses of Italian competitors.

The Emperor's veto caused a sensation in Roman literary circles; Florus himself said later that his rage had nearly driven him into insanity. It was also absurd: it was flouting the temper of the times. For Italy's economic decline was matched by political and cultural decline. The old colonial Empire, with Italy at its head, was changing into an Empire in which the separate provinces had more and more influence. Provincials were even about to ascend to the throne of the Caesars, and not two years after Domitian's death in AD 96 a Spaniard, Trajan, succeeded to the purple. The pre-eminence of Italy was over. For those with eyes to see, it had long been obvious; Spanish influence in Rome had been strong for some time.

Then came the turn of the Africans. For most of the second century they were to dominate the intellectual life of the Empire, and by the 180s nearly a third of the Roman senate was of African origin.

There had already been harbingers: the playwright Terence, who reached Rome as the slave of a senator in the second century BC, was a Berber. His owner, won over by his beauty and charm, freed him and gave him an education; and he left his African origins so far behind that he became a friend of the Scipio who destroyed Carthage. (To Terence we owe those most familiar Latin tags 'homo sum; humani nil a me alienum puto', 'hinc illae lacrimae' and 'quot homines tot sententiae'.[1]) Manilius, too, a poet of the early first century AD, was probably African. More significant for the future, though, was the career in the middle of the century of Cornutus, a teacher

---

1 'I am a man, and reckon nothing human alien to me.' 'Hence these tears.' 'As many opinions as there are men.'

of rhetoric and philosophy at Rome; for it was as leading orators and philosophers, and above all as jurists, that the Africans of the Antonine Age were to play a leading part in the intellectual life of the Empire. Even Apuleius, the greatest of them, was – among a variety of other things – an orator and advocate, who prided himself more on being a *philosophus Platonicus* than on being the author of *The Golden Ass*.

Quite modest cities provided a decent education for the sons of the rich and those sons of the poor whose gifts attracted the patronage of munificent citizens. Apuleius himself went to school in the small town in Numidia where he was born; two hundred years later, St Augustine also spent part of his schooldays at Madauros, and was helped to further education by a rich friend of his father's. Girls, too, could sometimes hope for an education: in the 170s a rich citizen of Sicca Veneria (El Kef) left money for the education of 200 girls as well as 300 boys, and Christian women like St Monica, St Perpetua, Melania and Lucilla could all read. Local schoolmasters were respected citizens, comparatively well paid out of municipal funds; if cities vied with each other in the splendour of their public monuments, they also took pride in the renown of their local grammarian.

Surprisingly for so practical a people, Roman education was devoted almost entirely to the written, and above all the spoken, word. Arithmetic was taught, as well as reading and writing, in the elementary schools, but thereafter the aim of schooling was to turn an educated man into an orator. Rhetoric and grammar were the main subjects; the teaching of other subjects was left to the rhetoricians, for there was little specialization. Indeed, the local schoolmaster might also be the local doctor.

In these circumstances, there could be little serious study of, for instance, science. Such science as there was was lifted wholesale from books; original research was virtually unknown. Apuleius, with his exceptional curiosity, dissected fish and made optical experiments with mirrors; but to his compatriots such activities smacked of black magic. The great Roman historians of the Republic and the Augustan age were read, or dismissed, for their prose style. When it was not simply a pastime, literature was studied for its moral examples.

Still, it was better than nothing. It was certainly better than what had gone before. The Latin language is a marvellous instrument for the expression of both thought and feeling; and the freedom and liveliness with which Africans like Apuleius learnt to use it suggest that their ancestors had little literature because their languages, Punic and Libyan, lacked flexibility and vocabulary. Latin gave Africans a tongue. At a time when Latin was declining in Rome in favour of Greek,[1] and the nobility spoke the language of their erstwhile enemies, rather as Tsarist aristocrats spoke French at home, African scholars and lawyers and writers gave it a new

---

1 The Romans were the first people to teach a foreign language as part of the regular syllabus.

lease of life. The great Christian apologists of Africa, Tertullian, St Cyprian and St Augustine, played an important part in ensuring that the language of the Catholic liturgy bequeathed to the Middle Ages was Latin and not Greek, its original language.

After school, clever boys went to Carthage for further study. 'What better or more certain title for praise,' Apuleius wrote years later of his *alma mater*, 'than the celebration of Carthage, where every citizen is a cultivated person and where all devote themselves to all fields of knowledge, children by learning them, young men by showing them off, and old men by teaching them? Carthage, venerable mistress of our province, Carthage, divine muse of Africa, Carthage, prophetess of the nation which wears the toga?' By this time the population of Carthage probably numbered a third of a million; it was as large as Alexandria, Antioch and Seleucis; only Rome was larger. It was not, in any technical sense, the capital of north-west Africa, since the Mauretanias and Numidia had their own capitals which were the seats of independent Roman governors; but only Africa Proconsularis had a proconsul as its governor, and his seat, Carthage, was also the most important port for trade. It was no minor provincial town; it was, and remained for centuries, a major intellectual city in the Roman world.

Even so, the rich young men of North Africa went abroad to complete their education. The universities of Athens and Rome were full of them. The Roman Empire was international, and in nothing more than this. Its schools taught Latin and frequently Greek, and people could make themselves understood in one or other language from one end of the Empire to the other. For the educated classes there was no language barrier, and for no one a national barrier.

Indeed, Africans were achieving positions of considerable eminence in Rome early in the second century AD. Florus himself, whose career as a poet had begun so stormily under Domitian, became a famous Roman rhetorician. Old slights forgotten, he devoted himself to extolling the glories of the capital. The poet Juvenal, who died during Apuleius's youth, described Africa as the 'foster mother of advocates'; and if he meant merely that all Africans were naturally litigious, there were plenty of professionals among the barrack-room lawyers to add force to his dictum.

By the middle of the second century, two of the most renowned lawyers in Rome were African-born. Marcus Cornelius Fronto was born at Cirta (Constantine) at the beginning of the century; and although he was probably descended from the Italian immigrants who had always formed a large minority of the population of the old Numidian capital, he proudly claimed descent from Libyan nomads. He had been east to complete his education, and by his early twenties had established himself in Rome. There he rapidly became more Roman than the Romans themselves. His devotion to Latin took the form of a scrupulous pursuit of the *mot juste*, a pursuit which too often led him into artificiality and archaism. But his

Arch of Marcus Aurelius in Tripoli, Libya

enthusiasm for perfection made him much in demand as a teacher, and he had considerable success at the bar. Hadrian, who shared some of his literary tastes, appointed him tutor to the adopted sons of his designated heir, Antoninus, one of whom was the future Emperor Marcus Aurelius. Imperial patronage no doubt helped Fronto to become the centre of that intellectual circle which Aulus Gellius (also perhaps African-born) describes in his *Attic Nights*. It also helped him to wealth and status; he became a consul in AD 143, and had the refusal of the proconsulship of Asia. He married a close friend of Marcus Aurelius's mother, and was able to buy the gardens of the legendary Maecenas in Rome. His friendship with Marcus Aurelius was lifelong, although the future Emperor disappointed his tutor by turning to the Stoic philosophy, with which Fronto had little patience. Marcus Aurelius speaks of Fronto's integrity, and their correspondence, copies of which came to light early last century, is full of mutual affection. The over-conscientious pedagogue[1] was clearly redeemed by courage and sweetness of character.

---

1 Aulus Gellius describes Fronto breaking off a conversation with the architect who was building him some baths, in order to discuss at length – in spite of being tormented by gout – the correct usage of *praeter propter*.

The other great African lawyer of second-century Rome was Salvius Julianus, born at the turn of the century into a knightly family from Hadrumetum (Sousse). While still very young he became head of one of the schools of law at Rome, and made himself very useful to Hadrian. He became a senator, and was commissioned by the Emperor to disentangle the legal position between the inhabitants of Rome and visiting strangers in civil actions. He also became a governor – of Germany and of Spain – and proconsul of his native Africa in AD 168.

Young Roman boys were also flocking for their secondary education to the classes of Sulpicius Apollinaris, a Carthaginian, who was the leading grammarian of the capital. The future Emperor Pertinax was one of his pupils.

If education was one way to a distinguished career, wealth was another. Many Africans were now rich enough to be admitted to the Roman knights class; there were perhaps three or four equestrian families in the average-sized African city, and members of these families could make careers for themselves in the imperial administration or as officers in the army. There was no racism in the Roman Empire; these new rich, after a generation or two, certainly felt themselves the equals of Roman bureaucrats in the proconsul's suite at Carthage or in the administration of the imperial domains. Other, richer Africans, like provincials from elsewhere, were being admitted to the senatorial order (much depleted by the executions and confiscations of Nero and the Year of the Four Emperors in the sixties of the previous century). These local plutocrats were of modest fortune compared to the millionaires of Rome itself; but there were huge profits to be made in shipping, which the Romans (only exceptionally a seafaring people) left in African hands, and the *navicularii* of the ports were great magnates. Their work was so important in the eyes of the Emperors that they were frequently excused the expenses of civic duties, and enjoyed a privileged position at Ostia, the port at the mouth of the Tiber which Hadrian enlarged to handle the corn shipments for Rome.

The first African to become a senator had been a citizen of Cirta, who was ennobled by Vespasian in the seventies of the first century AD. A hundred years later, there were a hundred African senators. Many of them emigrated to Rome, there to pursue conventional Roman political careers, and an African lobby seems to have developed. Their influence at court became stronger than that of any other province. They remained loyal to their native cities; individual senators frequently became the patrons of their birthplaces, interceding with the Emperors to raise them from *municipium* to *colonia*, or pleading for favours for compatriots newly arrived in Rome. A young African coming to trade or study there would find himself among willing friends and allies.

Sixth-century Byzantine fortress at Madauros, Algeria – birthplace of
Apuleius

APULEIUS OF MADAUROS

Meanwhile Africa itself, feeling its own strength, was no longer a culturally
unregarded province. It had its own rich men, its own hierarchy, its own
romanized civilization. Students were beginning to come to Carthage not
only from all over Africa, but from other parts of the Empire, to learn from
the teachers of the university.

The best-documented career – and in certain ways a typical one – in this
new-rich, newly confident society is that of the greatest of second-century
Africans, the mercurial, many-talented Apuleius. Born in Madauros
around AD 120, he was the son of a municipal *duumvir*. Like M. Cornelius
Fronto he boasted of his part-Numidian descent. After schooling in Madauros and Carthage, having been left a substantial legacy by his father, he
went to Athens to learn Greek. He also studied Platonic philosophy and
was indoctrinated into the mysteries of the goddess Isis, which play such
a significant part in his writings. Then he went to Rome where, as he says
himself, he set himself to study Latin – a language he certainly already
spoke, but not like a native Italian.

It was the time when Fronto and Salvius Julianus were in the ascendant,
and an African link was extremely useful. But men such as these, lawyers
and career politicians, were not the sort to hold Apuleius. In any case, he
had run through his share of the family money during his years abroad –
he was now over thirty – and Rome was no place for the indigent. He was
down to his last three slaves: only just enough to keep his head in the air.
So it was in Africa that Apuleius chose to make his career; significantly he

was content to do so, even when a turn in his fortunes would have enabled him to return to Rome.

He went home by way of Oea (Tripoli), where by a happy chance he was introduced by a former fellow-student to the latter's widowed mother, whom he shortly married. Aemilia Pudentilla was comparatively rich (she owned some four hundred slaves). She was also about ten years older than Apuleius, and had hitherto resisted remarrying; her suspicious relatives accused him of obtaining her consent by magic. Brought before the pro-consul at Sabratha, probably in AD 158, on one of the Roman magistrate's visits to the city to administer justice, Apuleius conducted his own defence with wit and skill. The *Apologia* he delivered is one of the works that have survived; it reveals, besides many details of his personal history, how well he had 'set himself to study Latin', his considerable knowledge of both Greek and Latin authors, and how much, both as orator and advocate, he had learnt from the study of Cicero. He was acquitted; and – presumably with his bride – he spent the rest of his life either at Madauros or at Carthage, as a teacher and public orator, devoting himself principally to the interpretation of Plato.

The Golden Ass, or *Metamorphoses*, was his masterpiece. It recounts the picaresque adventures of a young man who is turned by magic into an ass, and eventually returns to human form through the intervention of the goddess Isis. The hero's conversion to the worship of Isis is a wonderful account of a religious revelation, such as Apuleius himself must have experienced. The exquisite version of the story of Cupid and Psyche, which the hero is told on his journey, is immeasurably superior to its known predecessors; and the whole work is the finest surviving romance of the ancient world. It owes much to Apuleius's years in the eastern Mediterranean, but the racy style, the uninhibited enjoyment of low life and high life alike, the passion for both the pleasures of this world and the mysteries of the other, are Apuleius's own. Just as mediaeval alchemy owes something to Apuleius's scientific curiosity and taste for magic, so mediaeval romance owes something to this pagan tale; and nearly two thousand years later it is still read with pleasure.

SOLDIERS FROM AFRICA

Literature, law and politics were not the only careers open to talented Africans. More astonishing and much more spectacular was the military career of the Moor, Lusius Quietus, who was certainly of purely African origin – 'from the unknown desert', said one ancient authority. He was the chieftain of a Moorish tribe, still nomadic, on the fringes of Mauretania; his father had already fought for the Romans during the Moorish uprising led by Aedemon after the murder of King Juba's son Ptolemy by the Emperor Caligula, and had been rewarded with a Roman name and Roman citizenship. Lusius Quietus was promoted to equestrian rank by Domitian for military achievement at the head of his Moorish cavalry, but was soon cashiered for insubordination. His gifts as an officer, with the formidable *goums* under his command, were, however, too striking to ignore; and Trajan reinstated him to fight on the Danube against the mounted warriors of the Dacians. The Emperors, in their wars against the northern barbarians, whose horses made them too nimble for the normal tactics of the Roman legions, were forced to rely more and more on other barbarian horsemen to repel them. Lusius's bare-headed cavalry are immortalized on Trajan's Column in Rome, and Lusius was awarded the *dona militaria* and the governorship of Mauretania. Then he was given the command of regular Roman troops in Trajan's Asiatic war, for which he was promoted, though rather irregularly, to the senate. This move incensed his new colleagues: it was early days for a barbarian to appear in the highest councils of the Empire. Lusius went from strength to strength. A ruthless rearguard campaign against the Parthians even brought him a triumph and the governorship of Palestine, a much more important province than Mauretania; and finally the consulship. It looked for a moment as if nothing could stop Lusius succeeding Trajan as Emperor.

But Trajan's circle was too strong for him. When Trajan died, his widow hurriedly announced that just before his death he had adopted his old favourite Hadrian, another Spaniard, as his heir. Hadrian had Lusius's infantry disarmed and, when Lusius's cavalry rebelled against the Romans, had Lusius himself put to death.

Lusius was not the only African to whom the Emperors entrusted high military rank. Trajan gave command of the First Alpine Cohort to a soldier born at Thuburbo Maius, later entrusted him with the supervision of the unloading of the *annona* at Ostia and its transfer to Rome – and finally made him, too, governor of Mauretania. One of Marcus Aurelius's best generals was a citizen of Thibilis (Announa), to whose son the Emperor gave his own daughter in marriage. The man who subdued most of Scotland for the Romans and built the Antonine Wall, Lollius Urbicus, was a citizen of Tiddis, a small township in the mountains just north of Cirta (modern Constantine). One family of a city near Thugga (Dougga) produced two prefects of the Praetorian Guard – which by that time meant not merely the command of the troops at Rome itself but virtually the premiership of the Empire.

Then, in the late second century, Aemilius Laetus of Thina (near Sfax), who rose to the prefecture during the disastrous reign of Marcus Aurelius's son Commodus, actually turned king-maker.

Since the assassination of Domitian in AD 96, the Emperors had at least not died by the swords of their subjects. By chance, Marcus Aurelius, who died in 180, was the first of the second-century Emperors to have a son. His predecessors had chosen as their heirs the most promising member of

Private house at Thuburbo Maius, Tunisia

Remains of Christian chapel at Tiddis, a hill-top city near Constantine
and birthplace of Lollius Urbicus, who was to build the Antonine Wall
in Scotland

the Roman senate, a practice which, while it might seem more open to
argument as a method of succession than primogeniture, had distinct
meritocratic virtues. Marcus Aurelius, however, chose his son Commodus,
who was totally unlike his philosopher father in everything that mattered.
Marcus Aurelius hated war, but dutifully spent his last years with his army
on the northern frontier. Commodus hated war too, but his duty was his

last consideration; he paid no attention to the Empire and its problems. The imperial bureaucracy, by now an efficient international civil service, was left to administer, and the army was left to fight, while Commodus indulged in excesses that recalled those of Caligula and Nero. He corrupted the discipline of the Praetorian Guard; he squandered the imperial finances on vulgar extravagances; he put to death senators who complained that he had made peace with the Germans; and he spent most of his time in the amphitheatre, where his cruel tastes – which included taking part himself in the arena – sickened even the hardened inhabitants of Rome.[1]

He met his deserts in AD 192. He and Aemilius Laetus, by now prefect of the Praetorian Guard, shared a mistress, Marcia, who, discovering that Commodus intended to have Aemilius Laetus put to death, poisoned him. The African then became effectively master of Rome. He and the Praetorian Guard, with the senate's agreement, chose a career soldier to be Emperor. This was Pertinax (the former pupil of Sulpicius Apollonaris), who had been governor of Britain, and was at that time proconsul of Africa. Pertinax showed every sign of becoming a strong and efficient ruler in the old Antonine tradition. But eighty-seven days after the proclamation of Pertinax as Emperor, the Praetorian Guard murdered him (for reasons which remain obscure: the role of Aemilius Laetus himself is not known), and put the Empire up for auction to whichever senator would pay them the highest bribe. The 'winner', Didius Julianus,[2] though he reigned for an even shorter time, took the occasion to have Aemilius Laetus and his mistress put to death.

But the African connection was about to become stronger than ever. For the legions in the provinces, enraged at the presumption of the Praetorian Guard, had proclaimed their own Emperors, and two of the three new candidates were African.

---

1 'Little chick', his tutor Fronto used to refer to Commodus in letters to Marcus Aurelius. Grown up, the little chick referred to himself as 'Amazonius' or 'Exsuperatorius'.
2 Didius Julianus was a distant relative of the African Salvius Julianus who had been a leading lawyer a generation earlier.

9

THE FIRST AFRICAN EMPEROR

Septimius Severus, Julia Domna and their sons Caracalla (right) and
Geta – whose head was erased after his murder on Caracalla's orders.
Painted wood panel in the Staatliche Museum, Berlin

In the first century AD a citizen of Leptis Magna, the son of a Punic father
who had been granted Roman citizenship, bought himself a property in
Italy, near the old Etruscan city of Veii. His son, one Septimius Severus,
became a well-known rhetorician and a friend of the poet Martial, who
congratulated him that nothing in his looks or his speech betrayed his
Punic origin. He was wholly italianized.

Back home in Leptis Magna a kinsman, also Septimius Severus, became
the leading citizen of his native city when Trajan granted it the status of
colonia in AD 110, and his family were raised to the equestrian order. Two

of his sons followed their relative to Italy, where they entered the senate and became consuls, no doubt with help from their influential connections. The third, who took little part in public life, remained in Tripolitania. It was a son of this provincial branch, another Septimius Severus, who became the ruler of the Roman world. Unlike his namesake of Veii, however, he never lost his African accent, and his Punic-speaking sister, on a visit, is said to have shamed him with her broken Latin.

THE SLOW RISE TO POWER

Septimius Severus was born at Leptis Magna in 145. Since Leptis Magna had been raised to the status of *colonia* its freeborn citizens were automatically citizens of Rome – and those who were rich enough were eligible to join the senatorial order. Septimius's elder brother Geta had already embarked on a senator's career in Rome, and it was to Rome that Septimius, not yet twenty years old, also went to enter public life. There, in 162, the Emperor Marcus Aurelius awarded him the broad stripe of the senatorial order.

The details of Septimius's early career are not clear – except that, unusually, he did not become a military tribune, normally an essential stage in the *cursus honorum*. He may have studied law – for between 167 and 169, when he appears to have been back in Africa, he was prosecuted for adultery and conducted, successfully, his own defence. All his life he took a particular interest in legal affairs.

Back in Rome in 169 he would have entered the senate automatically once he was in his twenty-fifth year, and become a *quaestor*. He served as *quaestor* first in Rome and subsequently in Sardinia. Then between 173 and 174 he was one of the three legates of the then proconsul in Africa – who was another distant cousin and namesake, one C. Septimius Severus. Young Septimius's sphere of responsibility was most probably the easternmost part of the province based on Hadrumetum and Leptis Magna. The story was told of him that, when an old acquaintance insisted on embracing him during an official visit to Leptis Magna, he had the man flogged for such over-familiarity towards a representative of the Emperor. Certainly his name appears on a monumental arch put up at that time on the outskirts of the city.

After his year in Africa he returned to Rome, and served a year as tribune of the people – he had the honour of being one of the Emperor's own candidates – with, it was said, 'great rigour and energy'. The post involved watching over the work of the magistrates and protecting the rights of private citizens. It was probably at this time that he married. His wife, Paccia Marciana, was also from Leptis and, to judge from her name, descended from Punic stock. Virtually nothing is known of her, except that she died some ten years after the marriage, and seems to have had no children. Years later, when he was Emperor, Septimius had statues erected to her memory.

In 177 he became one of the eighteen praetors. This could well have meant his taking on further legal responsibilities, presiding over the permanent courts and the judges. But the eye of the Emperor was still on him, for he was soon appointed deputy head of the civilian administration of Hispania Tarraconensis (northern Spain, based on Tarragona).

In 180, the year the Emperor Marcus Aurelius died and was succeeded by his son, Commodus, Septimius Severus received his first military posting: commander of the Legion IV Scythica in Syria – where the gifted ex-schoolmaster turned soldier, Helvius Pertinax, was already governor. This was an important appointment and gave Septimius his first experience of the life of the Roman frontiers – and his first taste of the Orient. For Syria was the homeland of the woman who was to become an immense influence on him, his second wife Julia Domna. Julia Domna was a member of the priestly family which controlled the famous Temple of Emesa, where an enormous conical black stone representing the Sun God was an object of profound veneration. It is possible that Septimius met her at this time – and more than probable that he learned then that her horoscope had foretold that she would marry a king. All his life Septimius Severus was immensely conscious of omens and dreams: they seem to have been a constant theme of the autobiography[1] which he wrote late in life, and which was drawn on by his biographers. The historian Cassius Dio says that he consulted a local oracle of Baal (Syria was, after all, the original homeland of the Phoenicians who had a thousand years earlier colonized Carthage and Leptis Magna), who quoted Homer's description of Agamemnon to him:

> *Eyes and head like Zeus who delights in the thunder,*
> *Like Ares his waist, his chest like Poseidon.*

Was he, too, to be a king?

But by 182 there was a setback. In response to political intrigues in Rome, both Pertinax and Septimius Severus were dismissed from their Syrian commands. Septimius prudently withdrew from public life, and went to Athens 'to study, and for religious purposes, and to see the monuments and antiquities' – rather like his fellow-African, Apuleius, half a century earlier. It was better to be out of the way of the dangerous whims of Commodus and his favourites.

However, the fall and death of the Emperor's principal favourite led to the reinstatement both of Pertinax – first as governor of Britain, then as proconsul of Africa – and of Septimius, who also became, for the first time,

---

1 The autobiography itself has not survived.

a governor. He was appointed legate of Gallia Lugdunensis – roughly, the northern half of France, with its capital at Lyons. It was while he was at Lyons that his wife Paccia Marciana died, and – after making enquiries about the horoscopes of potential brides and having several dreams which fortified him in his belief that he was destined for far greater things – he made Julia Domna his second wife. She bore their first son, Bassianus (later known as Caracalla), in April 188. A second son, Geta, was born in 189.

That summer Septimius moved from Gaul to do a year's tour of duty as proconsul of Sicily. The following year he achieved the consulship back in Rome; but since it was a year when there were twenty-four consuls, and in any case the real power was now in the hands of the prefects of the Praetorian Guard, it was not a striking promotion. He was forty-five; he had had an honourable but not particularly impressive career – nothing like as impressive as that of Pertinax, whose father had been a slave, and who had just been appointed to the other key post of prefect of the city of Rome when his year as proconsul of Africa was over.

That very year, however, an economic crisis and shortage of food precipitated a revolt of the Roman mob who, recognizing the realities of power, demanded the head of the then Praetorian prefect, a Syrian. The Syrian was succeeded by the African Aemilius Laetus, who was anxious, in order to secure his own position, to fill important military posts with fellow Africans. There were three principal governorships of frontier provinces available at that time, all of them with command of two or more legions: Britain, Upper Pannonia (on the Danube) and Syria. Distant Syria Aemilius Laetus left to a nonentity, an Italian called Pescennius Niger; Britain he secured for Clodius Albinus, who came from Hadrumetum; and Septimius Severus he made governor of Upper Pannonia. It was an unexpected appointment, for Septimius had had little experience of army command – and none of warfare – yet now found himself with three legions at his disposal.

Commodus hardly cared what was happening. What had been implicit for some time was soon to become clear: the army was the real master of the Empire – or those legions which were able to impose their will. It was Africans who made this situation clear, and an African who was to profit from it.

When Pertinax, so briefly Emperor after Commodus's murder, was himself murdered in AD 193, both Pescennius Niger in Syria and Septimius Severus on the Danube were proclaimed Emperor by their armies as soon as the news reached them, and it was rumoured in Rome that Clodius Albinus in Britain entertained similar ambitions. Septimius Severus was nearest to the capital and seized his chance. He made a forced march to Rome, where Didius Julianus (to whom the Praetorian Guard had 'sold' the throne after they had killed Pertinax) had been hurriedly murdered when news of Septimius's arrival in Italy reached the city. *Force majeure*

Marble bust of the Emperor Septimius Severus in the museum at Djemila

obliged the senate and the Praetorian Guard to recognize Septimius as Emperor. He at once disbanded the Praetorian Guard, and reconstituted it, mostly with his own provincial troops, to safeguard his rear while he dealt with his rivals. Keeping Clodius Albinus quiet with false promises of the succession, he turned east. He eventually defeated Pescennius Niger in AD 194, and went on to campaign successfully against Niger's allies in Mesopotamia, beyond the Euphrates. Meanwhile the senate, who disliked Septimius as an upstart and a threat to their order, began to intrigue with Clodius Albinus, who was from a senatorial family. The latter rapidly realized that Septimius Severus's ambitious wife Julia Domna would never allow him to succeed in place of her two sons, even though they were still very young; especially since Septimius declared himself to be the son of Marcus Aurelius, and his elder son was renamed Marcus Aurelius Antoninus, thus making his own dynastic ambitions startlingly clear. In 196 Clodius Albinus set off to Rome with his legions, but when Septimius Severus defeated him near Lyons early in AD 197, he committed suicide.

Back in Rome, Septimius put to death twenty-nine members of the senate who had supported Clodius Albinus. More than a third of them had family or landowning interests in Africa Proconsularis, and the executions broke the back of the African lobby. Ironically, it was never again to have such influence as it had done under the Spanish Emperors and during the reign of Marcus Aurelius. Though the new Emperor later introduced other Africans into the senate, senatorial power had so declined in the face of his military dictatorship that it made little difference. The senate was at a discount, because Septimius Severus favoured the less powerful, less wealthy equestrian order. Army officers increasingly took over major civil governorships from the senatorial order, and the higher ranks of the army were staffed with *equites* from Africa and the east. He opened the Praetorian Guard to soldiers from all over the Empire. He depended on the loyalty of the army to himself personally, and greatly increased their pay. He permitted soldiers to marry – hitherto, they were only able to marry on retirement – and added to the number of legions. Even his civil administration was more like a general staff than a bureaucracy.

THE SEAT OF POWER

Septimius's travels were far from over. Like his admired predecessor Marcus Aurelius, he ruled the Empire from its frontier provinces. Once securely on the throne – and by now his elder son had been made Emperor-designate – and with his own men in key appointments, he left Rome with Julia and their sons for the east, to ensure the security of his newly-created province of Mesopotamia. He conquered the Parthian capital, Ctesiphon, but failed twice to take the desert city of Hatra – where Trajan, too, had failed a hundred years earlier. It was during this tour, so Cassius Dio reports, that he once more consulted the oracle of Baal at Apamea. This time, the oracle quoted Euripides: 'Your house will utterly perish in blood.'

Early in 199 Septimius moved on to Egypt, which no Emperor had visited for more than sixty years. Long ago in Athens, he had been a tourist and even a pilgrim: now he could be both again. 'Subsequently,' says the Augustan History's *Life of Severus*, 'he always indicated that he had enjoyed this tour, because he had taken part in the worship of the god Serapis, had learned something of antiquity and had seen unfamiliar animals and places.' He almost certainly went up the Nile as far as Aswan: he saw the pyramids, the Sphinx and the 'singing statue' of Memnon.[1] He sacrificed at the tomb of Pompey at Pelusium, and visited the tomb of Alexander the Great at Alexandria, which he ordered to be sealed so that he should be the last person to look on the great Macedonian's embalmed remains.[2]

More important, Septimius reorganized the structure of Egypt's government. Its principal cities were granted their own councils, and its citizens

---

1 It never again gave off its peculiar sunrise song (caused by temperature change), for it was 'repaired', no doubt on the Emperor's orders.
2 The site of the tomb has long been lost.

given the right to enter the Roman senatorial order if they were qualified. He ordered the construction of public baths, a gymnasium and a temple of Cybele at Alexandria. He attempted to improve the lot of the peasantry. He administered and improved the law: one papyrus listing a number of his legal decisions has survived.

At long last, after another visit to Syria and tour of inspection of the Danube army, he and his retinue returned to Rome early in 202. He celebrated by holding public games and distributing ten gold coins each to the soldiers of the Praetorian Guard and the urban *plebs* – 200 million sesterces worth, the largest amount ever distributed. But he did not stay long. In 202–3 he and his family were in Africa. He did not forget his origins. Leptis Magna, where they probably spent the winter, owes him a host of monuments. He was by now exceedingly rich, largely from the quantity of property confiscated from his rivals, and from those who had supported them in various parts of the Empire.[1] He imported the very best architects and sculptors to begin work on a new forum and basilica, and an immense temple perhaps dedicated to his – and Leptis's – tutelary gods, Bacchus and Hercules. The harbour was rebuilt, the circus enlarged and restored, the water supply improved, an arcaded main street planned – and the whole embellished with dozens of statues, mostly of the Emperor and his relatives, including the great four-way arch decorated with reliefs of the imperial family and imperial victories, which are among the glories of Roman art. Leptis, Carthage and Utica were granted immunity from provincial taxation. Many other cities in North Africa received gifts from him.

His reign also saw the reorganization of the defences of the north-west African provinces. Anicius Faustus, who had been governor of Numidia from 197 to 202 and was himself African (from Uzappa, near Mactar), had on Septimius's orders extended the frontier well beyond Hadrian's old southern limit, down to Castellum Dimmidi (Messaad) in south-west Numidia – founded in 198 – and to Ghadames and Bu Ngem in modern Libya, well to the south of the Tripolitanian coast. Numidia became a separate province.

Now the Emperor himself went on campaign against the tribes of the desert. The fourth-century African writer, Aurelius Victor, says he 'freed Tripolitania from fear of attack by crushing most warlike tribes'. He was accompanied by his sons – both, by this time, recognized as co-Emperors – and no doubt detachments from the Third Augustan Legion under Anicius Faustus. To these years, too, belong military activities of some sort in the Mauretanias, although Septimius is unlikely to have travelled much further west than the Legion's headquarters at Lambaesis.

---

1 In Tripolitania Septimius's estates were perhaps extensive enough for him to grant free olive oil in perpetuity to the Roman people. Some of it even reached Britain.

Temple of Septimius Severus, Djemila

In the summer of 203 the Emperor returned to Rome. His stay this time was to be the longest he spent there. Another great arch in his honour was built in the Forum, the Forum of Peace was restored, the imperial palace was improved, other public buildings were constructed; the Pantheon had already been restored. Great games normally held only every 110 years were held in 204 – for the seventh time in Rome's history – with all the traditional religious ceremonies which mattered so much to Septimius. Meanwhile the great jurist Papinian was given preferment, and together with Ulpian and Julius Paulus provided the fundamentals of Roman law which were eventually codified by the Emperor Justinian in the sixth century, and formed the basis of much of mediaeval Europe's legal system. The reign was a golden age of jurisprudence.

All the same, it was not free of the judicial terror and uncertainty which had disfigured the reigns of so many of Septimius's predecessors. He was guilty – though his elder son wielded the weapon – of the murder of his oldest and closest associate, and a relative through his mother, the Praetorian prefect Plautianus; and there were other victims, too, during these years.

Cassius Dio is the only contemporary whose eye-witness accounts have come down to us. He describes Septimius thus:

'He was a small man, but physically strong (although he did become very weak from the gout). His mind was extremely keen and vigorous. He did not get as much of an education as he wanted, and because of

139

this he was a man of few words, although he had plenty of ideas. He did not forget his friends. His enemies he treated with a very heavy hand. He took a great deal of thought over all his plans; but he never gave a thought to what was said about him. For this reason he raised money from every source – except that he never killed anyone to get their money – and he met all necessary expenditures unstintingly.'

Septimius believed himself to be thoroughly Roman. He struck the Romans, however, as wholly alien, cruel and superstitious in spite of his concern for the improvement of the law: 'the Punic Sulla', some of them called him. Through his strong-minded and clever wife, who during these years in Rome seems to have sought out the company of writers and philosophers, Rome had its first taste of an older east than Greece.

Septimius may not have been displeased to get his quarrelling young sons away from the intrigues of Rome when, in 207, he was called away to Britain. This northernmost province was endlessly troublesome: its wars with Rome were famous from the works of the great historian Tacitus, and Septimius's own brother Geta had served there. The governor was yet another African, L. Alfenus Senecio, from Cuicul (Djemila).

Septimius appears to have had the ambition to conquer the whole of Britain. To the last, he was an 'expansionist' Emperor. But in Britain, where he spent the last years of his life, increasingly crippled with gout, he was only partly, and only temporarily, successful.

Septimius died in AD 211, after three years in Britain fighting the incursions of the Highlanders. Strange to think of this native African, who until he grew up had probably never seen snow, lying on his deathbed in York, where the icy winds of February blow straight from the Urals. Stranger still to think of his exotic family transplanted to the life of the camps, in that damp, thickly-forested land where, in Strabo's words, 'the mist holds on for long, so that in the course of a whole day the sun will only be visible for a few noontide hours'. The Emperor's last words to his sons were: 'Do not disagree between yourselves, give money to the soldiers, and despise everyone else.'

THE LEGACY OF SEPTIMIUS SEVERUS

The sons Septimius Severus left behind him, however, were no more successful than Marcus Aurelius's. The elder, who became famous under his nickname, Caracalla, soon murdered his brother (and thousands of Geta's supporters, including the jurist Papinian), and was eventually murdered in his turn, like Commodus, by the prefect of the Praetorian Guard. The prefect was yet another African, Macrinus, who, for want of a better candidate, was acclaimed Emperor in succession to Caracalla.

But Macrinus was not Emperor for long. When Julia Domna, who had been virtually regent during her son's six-year reign, killed herself in disappointment, her sister Julia Maesa soon seized an opportunity to push the dubious claims of two of her own Syrian grandsons, by pretending that the elder was a bastard son of Caracalla. Her plot succeeded; Macrinus was deposed, and for four years Rome was treated to the spectacle of Elagabalus, a teenage Emperor from Syria with sexual tastes depraved even by the standards of Rome, acting as hereditary priest to his Semitic Baal and marrying a Vestal Virgin. Affront could go no further; but when Elagabalus was assassinated the surviving women of the family quickly substituted his more moderate cousin Alexander. Alexander reigned for thirteen years – until the army murdered him, together with his mother (Julia Maesa's daughter), in AD 235. So ended the African dynasty, in oriental mysteries and petticoat government.

During the next half-century there were twenty-six Emperors, only one of whom died a natural death, before, in AD 284, Diocletian at last stopped the rot. The third century was a time of anarchy for the Roman Empire. Some of the causes of its long drawn-out disintegration were already apparent in the reign of Marcus Aurelius. It had virtually stopped expanding in Trajan's day. The Republic had grown rich on the spoils of the cities of the east; Augustus had financed the reorganization of the army and the bureaucracy from the loot of Egypt; his successors had profited from the increase and exploitation of the natural wealth, primarily agricultural, of the provinces he had bequeathed to them. The limits had largely been reached. Growing pressure from the barbarians in the north in the second century AD meant higher costs in soldiers and money, and there were to be no new resources to meet them. It meant higher taxes and desperate expedients like the debasement of the coinage. The extravagances of Commodus aggravated the crisis, and the civil wars in the north and east which followed his murder put a heavy strain on a tottering structure. Septimius Severus's strong arm policy and the stability which, somehow, the Syrian princesses maintained during the reigns of his successors only postponed more serious decline.

The north-west African provinces, meanwhile, free of major wars, were still quietly bringing under cultivation huge tracts of virgin land. Higher taxes were largely absorbed by a greater population and increasing agricultural production. There, from the second century to the fourth, the Africans enjoyed the high peak of their prosperity under the Romans.

THE GORDIAN REBELLION

However, the effects of the crisis of the Roman world brought a setback to one of Africa's provinces in the middle of the third century, when Africa Proconsularis became the cockpit of an imperial contest. An expatriate African (Laetus) had already played king-maker, an expatriate African

(Septimius) had won the crown; now Africa herself played the king-maker. The results were disastrous.

On the death of Severus Alexander in 235, the Thracian giant Maximinus had been acclaimed Emperor by the Rhine army which he commanded. He was the first professional soldier to become Emperor, and he recognized as clearly as Septimius Severus had done where his support lay. He doubled his soldiers' pay. More money had to be raised somehow, and taxes were increased; his critics complained at the time that he even confiscated the cities' public funds and temple offerings.

In Africa the imperial procurator set about the new tax-gathering with zeal, particularly in the whole area round Thysdrus, where the inhabitants had just demonstrated their prosperity – from the export of oil from their olive groves – by building the enormous amphitheatre which is still the major landmark of El Djem. 'Among other violent exactions,' reported the historian Herodian, a contemporary, 'the procurator in question had condemned certain wealthy young men of good family and attempted to confiscate all their ancestral fortunes at once.' Enlisting their peasants, the young men murdered the procurator and routed his soldiers. 'The deed done, the desperate young men realized that their only salvation was to venture even greater daring, to make the proconsul of the province share their enterprise and raise general rebellion.'

The proconsul was Gordian, a rich, elderly landed proprietor claiming descent from the Gracchi on his father's side and Trajan on his mother's. The young Africans rightly thought that 'he would welcome the imperial office as a culmination of his career, and the senate and Roman people ... would welcome a man of noble birth who had ascended to Emperorship by appropriate degrees' – a jibe at the hated Maximinus. After some hesitation, Gordian, associating his son Gordian II with himself, accepted the supreme honour, and the senate and the European provinces acknowledged his claim.

Unfortunately they reckoned without Capellianus, governor of Numidia and legate of the Third Augustan Legion, who remained faithful to Maximinus. He killed Gordian II in battle, whereupon Gordian I committed suicide. They had reigned for scarcely two months.

The future of the *imperium* was now out of African hands, but Capellianus took revenge. He executed half the aristocracy of Carthage, killed prominent supporters of the Gordians throughout the province and allowed the Legion to pillage the unprotected countryside as they wished. There was perhaps in this an element of the hatred of the soldiery (drawn from the poorer classes of society) for the rich olive-growers; but all suffered. Parts of the country never fully recovered, their prosperity so damaged that the new tax burdens – which were to grow heavier – were impossible to meet.

The loss of confidence is strikingly reflected in the archaeological evidence. The quantity of buildings erected by private donors had risen dramatically during the second century, and had continued steadily, on a lesser scale, throughout the Severan period. After the death of Severus Alexander, however, all such building virtually stopped for half a century. The only monuments put up were gifts either from the Emperors or from imperial governors. It is even possible that the El Djem amphitheatre was never used by the inhabitants of the Thysdrus region.

There was another consequence of the Gordian *débâcle*. A change of fortune brought Gordian I's young grandson, nephew of Gordian II, to the purple in July AD 238. One of the first actions of his principate was the disbanding of the Third Augustan Legion – perhaps for its part in the overthrow of his elder relatives. That same year, the garrison established in the desert by Septimius Severus forty years before, at Castellum Dimmidi well to the south of the old Numidian frontier, was withdrawn. The military left behind them, to be covered by the encroaching sand, a quantity of fine objects now in a museum in Algiers, for, like other regiments in important outposts of other empires, they had done themselves proud; but it was a sign of future times.

Magnificently carved pillars in the apse of the Severan basilica at Leptis
Magna. Early third century

143

10

THE NEW RELIGION

Meanwhile the cares of the world were beginning, for many Africans, to take second place to the things of the spirit. On July 17, AD 180, thirteen years before Septimius Severus became Emperor, seven men and five women from Scilli had been brought before the proconsul Saturninus in Carthage for refusing 'to swear by the genius of the Emperor'. The proconsul begged them to 'have no part in this madness'. But they persisted in their refusal and, when Saturninus offered them time to reconsider, one of them replied: 'When the right is so clear, there is nothing to consider.' Their refusal cost them their lives. When sentence of death was pronounced, 'they all said "Thanks be to God"'. They were the first recorded Christian martyrs of north-west Africa. It was the dawn of a new age.

Hitherto, the official Graeco-Roman pantheon of gods, with Jupiter at their head, had been accepted readily enough by romanized Africans alongside their old gods. Every sizeable city had a capitol for the worship of Jupiter, Juno and Minerva; Ceres and Neptune, Mars and Liber Pater (Dionysius), Venus and Mercury, Apollo and Aesculapius – all had their devotees. So had Oriental deities like Isis and Mithras, whose cults were spread throughout the Empire by merchants and soldiers and bureaucrats, and which the Romans had themselves adopted from their former enemies in Egypt and Persia – just as, in Hannibal's day, the worship of the gods of the Carthaginians had been introduced to Rome. If the grandest of old Roman families continued to look upon the eastern mystery religions with disapproval, most ordinary Romans regarded all gods, in the philosophical spirit of the time, as manifestations of the same divine principle, and therefore to be tolerated and, frequently, worshipped. When in Rome, do as the Romans do; with admirable broadmindedness the Romans suffered this principle to work both ways. And among the poor and uneducated, superstition prompted what philosophy taught the upper classes: a ready acceptance of new gods, new invisible powers to be propitiated.

So-called Temple of Minerva at Tébessa – once probably a Christian
church, then a tenement, a barracks, a prison and now a museum. It is
one of Africa's best preserved Roman buildings

SURVIVALS FROM THE PAST

The old local gods had not disappeared with the arrival of the Graeco-
Roman gods. In the African countryside the peasants continued to
worship the local *genii* of woods and sources, caves and mountains; and
sometimes even educated city-dwellers both worshipped in the new
Roman temples and followed the native cults of their forebears without
any sense of incongruity. If the gods were jealous, it was not of each
other. They were more like patron saints, or the *marabous* of the modern
Maghreb. The *dii Mauri* – Moorish deities – seem to have had a
considerable following in both the army and the civilian administration,
and not only in 'Moorish' areas.

The Punic religion, too, survived, although in part at least it underwent
a significant transformation. The city-dwelling Africans were adopting
Roman-style names and learning Latin (without which any career outside
a small town was increasingly impossible); and just as they themselves
were being romanized, their gods were romanized also. Tanit became
identified with Juno-Caelestis, Baal with Saturn, Shadrapa with Bacchus
and Melkart with Hercules. They were virtually indistinguishable. It was

145

Bacchus and Hercules, the romanized versions of Shadrapa and Melkart, whom Septimius Severus in deference to his origins adopted as his presiding deities. The enormous quantity of ex-votos dedicated to Saturn by the poor, and the disappearance of the Punic script by the end of the second century, suggests how far, at least in the neighbourhood of the cities of Africa, this romanization extended.

Yet the very popularity of Saturn (whose name only thinly disguised his original identity as Baal), in preference to Jupiter or Minerva, for example, also reveals the strength of old loyalties. For romanization, whether religious or cultural, was far from complete. It scarcely touched the old nomad hinterland. Many of the rural poor continued to bury their dead curled up and painted red, and went on speaking Libyan or a bastardized Punic long after the latter had ceased to be a written language. As late as the fifth century, St Augustine was urging his fellow-clergy to learn the local 'Punic' – the language the Carthaginians had brought with them from their Near East homeland more than a thousand years before – in order to make themselves understood by their parishioners.[1]

Linked with the worship of Baal was the Punic practice of naming children after the god: Given by Baal or Iatanbaal, Honoured by Baal or Hannibal. Hamilcar was similarly derived from Melkart. With romanization, the Africans took Roman names – but they were names formed on the old pattern and closely connected with worship, whether of Saturn-Baal or, later, the Christian God. Saturninus and Saturus recur constantly; so do Honoratus (Honoured by God), Donatus and Adeodatus (Given by God): the latter was the name St Augustine gave his own son. Rogatus, Fortunatus, Concessus – no one would take such names for Italian Latin. They have vanished utterly from modern North Africa; but in their place, the Arabs – also a Semitic people like the Phoenicians – name their children Abdullah ('Slave of Allah') or Muhammad ('His Prophet') ...

In the most romanized parts of the province, the well-off adopted Roman-style open-air cemeteries, where the vaults were furnished a good deal less sumptuously than had been to the Carthaginian taste; and after a thousand years in which their national costume had been virtually unchanged, they took to the toga. Their womenfolk followed the hairstyles of the women of the imperial family – publicized by the official statues of succeeding reigns – and wore, even to sleep in, the Roman *mamillare* or *strophium* (breast cloth or band). But for Africans outside the upper classes the toga never became more than a kind of court dress, worn for ceremonial occasions and tombstone portraits only. They remained attached to their

---

1 Not that this is unusual: more than six hundred years after Wales fell to the English monarchy, and nearly a hundred after the coming of the railways, some of its inhabitants still spoke only Welsh.

long sleeves and lively colours, their bangles and baubles. To this day the rural population of the Maghreb remains faithful to this style of dress – or to an even more ancient garment, the hooded Berber *burnous* of the North African shepherd which first appears in pre-Roman rock engravings. The toga – even the simple tunic – might never have been.

Arch of Caracalla at Tébessa, an early third-century four-way arch, set in ramparts built by the Byzantines

Even in the greater cities, where romanization was naturally more successful, it took a long time. Two hundred years after the death of Julius Caesar, the future Emperor Septimius Severus was speaking Punic in his Leptis Magna nursery; and at the turn of the second century, when he was in a position to do so, he made Punic one of his native city's official languages. Old habits died hard, in religious matters as in language. In the temples at Thuburbo Maius dedicated to the new worship of Aesculapius, with whom was now associated the Punic god Eshmoun, the injunction to abstain from pork and beans and from the pleasures of bath and bed for three days before admission to the sacred precinct was merely a temporary version of the permanent vows of the old Punic priesthood. But, both in the cities and the countryside, the unreformed Punic religion survived alongside the new. For not all its adherents welcomed its Roman garb. The *kohanim*, its priests, watched with dismay as the Roman language was introduced into its rites and their knowledge of Punic was no longer

147

indispensable, and as new temples to the romanized gods were built on the sites of the prophets of old. They retreated to neighbouring heaths and forests, from where they stirred up the faithful against these hateful innovations with the desperate fervour of supporters of a losing cause. Some, it was said, still practised the infant sacrifice which the Romans had been at such pains to stamp out; one second-century proconsul crucified some *kohanim* who were alleged to have sacrificed children in a sacred wood near Carthage. They fomented unrest: when the future Emperor Pertinax was proconsul he had to put down what appears to have been a religious rising in Carthage itself.

There were political and social undertones to this discontent, no doubt, a hard core of resentment against the new order, which may have had something to do with the continuing devotion to the old religion. But discontent was soon inflamed by a new and passionate enthusiasm. For in the third century, Africans of the lower classes, who were the first to suffer from rising taxes and rising prices, turned to the one religion which the Romans could not tolerate, and which therefore offered, as well as hope of better things in the next world, a way of demonstrating against the masters of this.

THE CULT OF LOYALTY

In this motley host of cults, there had been little difficulty about the introduction of Emperor-worship in the first century AD. What was one religion more among so many? For most of the Empire it did not go against the grain to worship the mortal representatives of a nation which, for all its faults, was god-like in its beneficence and power. The Jews, it is true, refused to do so; from long custom, and because they made no attempt to make converts, the Romans excused them from participating in the ritual worship of the Emperors.

But, for all other subjects, the Romans insisted on the veneration of the Emperors. This was the one cult which the Romans took seriously. More than the worship of their national gods, worship of the genius of the Emperors was the symbolic bond that united the diverse peoples under their rule. They also organized it seriously. All public office, whether imperial or municipal and however modest, required an oath of loyalty and the sacrifice of a pinch of incense. Not to sacrifice meant not being able to take any part in public life; not to do that signified to the Romans *odium humani generis*, the equivalent of an anti-social attitude.

There were special provincial assemblies, composed of deputies from among the leading citizens of the cities, which met in the various capitals to celebrate with appropriate ceremony the rites of the Emperors. These assemblies had other functions: they were a useful method of sounding provincial public opinion, and they were able, at the end of a proconsul's term of office, either to make him an address of thanks, if merited, or complain of his behaviour. Protests could, indeed, be made from lower down the hierarchy: the Younger Pliny records his own and Tacitus's part in the trial of one discreditable proconsul of Africa who had during his year of office condemned seven innocent men to death for money, and against whom complaints had been laid at Rome by the municipal *curia*. Nor was the equivalent of tomato-throwing unknown: Vespasian when proconsul in AD 51 – his reward for conquering the Isle of Wight and much of Wessex – was pelted with turnips at Hadrumetum, where the inhabitants were exasperated by his meanness. But it was the provincial assemblies which mattered; it was a great honour to belong to them, and it gave the deputies a happy sense of self-importance to journey to the chief city of the province and feel they were involved in deliberations of state. The threat of their publicly-expressed disapproval was also, usually, a useful check on at least the worst excesses of proconsular behaviour, and reinforced the supervisory activities of the imperial procurator who was the Emperor's personal representative in the province.

Nevertheless, there is no doubt that their real importance in imperial eyes was as cheer-leaders in the worship of the Emperor. Their chief officer was nominally a priest, the *sacerdos provinciae*, whose principal function was to lead the province in the correct observance of these religious duties. Not that the tone of the ceremonies was reverent, once the official rites of sacrifice to the Emperor had been celebrated: Apuleius, who regarded the honour of being *sacerdos* as the summit of his professional career, organized magnificent games at Carthage. There were processions and feasts, and for the populace such occasions were mostly excuses for behaviour of a kind familiar still in Europe during Fasching or Mardi Gras. Long after Apuleius's day, Tertullian was inveighing against Carthage being turned into a tavern, wine flowing in the mud, and the people 'giving themselves over to outrage, indecency and the pleasures of the libertine'. The Emperor's birthday, in fact, was a good excuse for a party. But the excuse was also the *raison d'être*, a matter of policy; the occasion for the expression, through its representatives, of the provinces' devotion and loyalty.

So long as allegiance was sworn and formal sacrifice made to the Emperor, his subjects could worship whatever gods they wished. International religions like Mithraism and the worship of Isis (Apuleius was a follower of Isis) were accepted because their adherents were prepared to sacrifice to the Emperor. Local cults were tolerated for the same reason, or because their devotees were so poor that their absence from public life was to be expected.

The Jews were tolerated because their religion was also, in a sense, a local cult. But religious toleration broke down in the face of Christianity.

THE EMERGENCE OF CHRISTIANITY

At first those renegade Jews, the early Christians, were believed by the authorities to be merely a sub-cult of Judaism. For several decades they were protected by this confusion; like all Jews, they were allowed to be conscientious objectors.

But the Christians were a light unto the Gentiles, and the Romans soon noticed that this Jewish sect was not confined to Jews, and that its beliefs were spreading all over the east and even in Rome itself. Like Judaism, it forbade Emperor-worship, but unlike Judaism it was a missionary religion. It was both international and disloyal – dangerously disloyal, simply because it was international. It was an explosive combination, which the Romans could not ignore. Christianity called in question the kingdoms of this world; and by obliging its numerous converts to become conscientious objectors to the worship of the soul or genius of the Emperor it represented a potentially serious loss to public service and public finance.

Nero had already discovered that this new mystery religion was a useful scapegoat – although few, even at the time, believed that the Christians were actually responsible for the burning of Rome. Equally, no one any longer believed the conventional charge that the Christians ate children or indulged in nameless orgies at their secret 'love-feasts'. But by the second century AD the Emperors were forced to take seriously this canker which was eating the heart out of the public life of almost every province.

The general policy of suppression was formulated by Trajan in his famous correspondence with the Younger Pliny, then governor of Bithynia, when Christianity – 'this wretched cult' – had numerous followers in Asia Minor. 'These people must not be hunted out,' Trajan wrote. 'If they are brought before you and the charge against them is proved, they must be punished, but in the case of anyone who denies that he is a Christian, and makes it clear that he is not by offering prayers to our gods, he is to be pardoned ... Pamphlets circulated anonymously must play no part in any accusations. They create the worst sort of precedent and are quite out of keeping with the spirit of our age.' The punishment was death, but there was to be no witch-hunting, no listening to tale-bearers. The Emperor did not want martyrs, but recantations.

In practice, persecution was erratic. It depended on the whim or temperament of the Emperor, or the arrival of some natural disaster like plague or earthquake, when the pagan crowd would clamour for someone's blood, and the local governor yielded to their demands. The noble army of martyrs during the two and a half centuries which separated the first persecution from the last numbered fewer than the victims of the Catholic Inquisition in the sixteenth century – to name only one of the Church's own heresy hunts.

Not the least of the Christian Churches' strengths has been their devotion to the written word, to keeping records, publishing sermons, translating the Bible (the Scilli martyrs had 'the Book and the letters of a just man, one Paul'), writing letters, keeping each other and the world informed. Martyrdom, and with it martyrology, was a vitally important element in the history of the early Church. Nowhere was this more true than in Africa.

However, nothing is known of when or how Christianity reached Africa. Its first converts were probably the Jews in the seaports. It may well have been introduced by sailors and merchants, perhaps from the east, perhaps from Rome itself: from the beginning it seems to have been a Christianity more Latin than Greek. The first African bishop of Rome, Victor I (189–?199 – a contemporary of Septimius Severus), was also the first bishop of Rome to write in Latin. From the synagogues it spread rapidly, above all among the poor; by the third century AD the north-west African provinces were the most Christianized in the west.

The followers of the new religion were in a minority, but a substantial one. Only seventeen years after the execution of the Scilli martyrs, Tertullian (another contemporary of Septimius) was claiming in his *Apologia*, published in AD 197: 'We are of yesterday, yet we have filled all that is yours, cities, islands, villages, free towns, market towns, the camp itself, tribes, town councils, the palace, the senate, the forum; we have left you your temples alone ... If we abandoned you for some far country you would shudder at your solitude, at the silence, the stupor of a dead world.' Even if he exaggerated, Tertullian wrote in the expectation of being believed.

It was impossible to root out the new sect. The Romans soon discovered that persecution rebounded on their own heads; making an example of individual Christians or groups of Christians did not work. An example was set, certainly, but from the official point of view it was the wrong one. Martyrs did not make recusants of their fellow-believers; they made converts of pagan onlookers.

Many Roman magistrates who had to carry out the persecutions felt great distaste for the task. The proconsul Saturninus, for example, gave the Scilli martyrs as much leeway as he could, urging them to recant, offering them thirty days to consider (which they refused). And it was not long before the imperial officials – and the pagans in general – realized that what the Scillitans said of themselves was true of other Christians also: that they paid their taxes, and held the Emperor in honour even if they refused to sacrifice to him. They were good neighbours and peaceable citizens. So at many times and in many places, the obligation to sacrifice was quietly relaxed.

During some reigns, for decades at a time, there appear to have been no persecutions at all. Even under Septimius Severus, who decreed that Christians, especially the newly converted and those who had converted them, should be actively sought out for prosecution by the State, a public figure like Tertullian was able to broadcast his faith and opinions to the world without, so far as is known, being so much as admonished, let alone threatened.

Detailed knowledge of the persecution of Christians we owe primarily to the shorthand writers in the law courts. The Christian *acta*, among which those of the Scilli martyrs are the earliest surviving for north-west Africa, are transcripts of the trials; copies of them were later sold on the side to the faithful, and jealously preserved and recopied as a permanent reminder of the glorious dead.[1]

The *acta* sometimes have an additional connecting narrative or explanation – although unfortunately this rarely includes any indication of how the defendants were brought to trial, or why they, rather than their fellow Christians, should have been arrested. But for the most part they consist of simple question and answer exchanges. The strong emotions, whether the faith of the accused or the reluctance of the prosecuting magistrates, shine through the direct speech.

There were also unofficial records, no more affecting but often fuller and more dramatic. These *passiones* were usually eye-witness accounts by other Christians, such as the celebrated Letter of the Churches of Vienne and Lyons to their co-religionists in Asia and Phrygia describing the fearful martyrdom of the heroic slavewoman St Blandina and her companions in AD 177. The most famous of African *passiones*, however, was largely written by the victims themselves, on the eve of their martyrdom. This was the Passion of St Perpetua and her companions, written, according to the third-century editor who prepared it for publication, by St Perpetua and St Saturus 'with their own hands'. It is one of the most moving documents in the history of African Christianity.

THE MARTYRDOM OF ST PERPETUA

In her single-minded courage, Perpetua is of the company of Dido and Sophonisba and the wife of the defending commander of beleaguered Carthage. She and Saturus, with Saturninus, Secundulus and the slaves Revocatus and Felicity, were arrested and tried at Carthage in AD 203, during the reign of Septimius Severus.[2]

There is nothing to show why Perpetua rather than her brother – known to be a Christian also – should have been arrested, but from the editor of the Passion, who provided an introduction and an account of the final horrors in the amphitheatre at Carthage, we learn that she was twenty-two, well-born, well-educated (and Saturus reveals that she spoke Greek

---

1 During the course of centuries the *acta* were, not unnaturally, frequently supplemented by later interpolations and forgeries – usually recognizable by the sensationally miraculous content.
2 Septimius Severus was in Africa at the time, but is not known to have had anything to do with the episode – and may have been ignorant of it.

'Here are the martyrs Saturus, Saturninus, Revocatus, Secundulus,
Felicitas, Perpetua, who suffered on the Nones (7th) of March':
inscription found on a tomb in the Basilica Maiorum, Carthage

as well as Latin), well-married and the mother of an infant son. For the
rest, he lets Perpetua and Saturus speak for themselves.

Perpetua's father was a pagan, and her story is full of his baffled fury at
her profession of Christianity, and her own grief 'for the sorrow that had
come on his old age'. But she did not falter.

She describes how they were questioned in the market place: 'There was
my father with my child ... beseeching me: "Have pity on your baby."
And the procurator Hilarion ... said to me: "Spare your father's white
hairs; spare the tender years of your child. Offer a sacrifice for the safety
of the Emperors." And I answered: "No." "Are you a Christian?" said
Hilarion. And I answered: "I am." And when my father persisted in trying
to overthrow my resolution, he was ordered by Hilarion to be thrown
down, and the judge struck him with his rod. And I was grieved for my
father's plight, as if I had been struck myself.'

Her steadfastness did not mean that she had no motherly concern for
her son. But she took it as a sign of God's blessing that when her father
refused, after the trial, to return the baby to her in prison to be fed, 'neither
had he any further wish for my breasts, nor did they become inflamed'.

Martyrs were constantly on the look-out for signs of divine favour. The
principal aim of Perpetua and Saturus was to describe the visions they
were granted. Perpetua dreamed twice of a dead brother who, at the age
of seven, 'had died miserably of a gangrene of the face', and whom her
visions showed her first in purgatory, unable to drink from a font placed
too high, and then, after she had prayed for him, drinking at a font low
enough for him to reach; and the wound in his face had become a healthy

153

scar. 'Then I knew that he had been released from punishment.' Her third vision, on the day before the games, was of the heavenly martyrdom to come. Saturus's vision was of himself and Perpetua in paradise, with angels and other African martyrs, in the presence of the Lord: 'We were all fed on a fragrance beyond telling.'

The slavewoman Felicity, who was eight months pregnant, was also granted a sign. The editor describes her distress that she would be unable, since it was illegal in her condition, to meet death with the others, and her fear that she would be executed with ordinary criminals after the birth. Her fellow martyrs therefore 'in one flood of common lamentation poured forth a prayer to the Lord two days before the games. Immediately after the prayer her pains came upon her,' and the baby was born.

Both the women were as spirited in word as in deed. When a prison warder jeered at Felicity that the sufferings of childbirth were as nothing to those she would endure in the arena, which she should have thought of before, she replied: 'Now I suffer what I suffer: but then Another will be in me who will suffer for me.' Perpetua chided the prison governor for ill-treating them: 'Why do you not at least allow us to refresh ourselves, the most noble among the condemned, belonging as we do to Caesar and chosen to fight on his birthday?[1] Or is it not to your credit that we should appear thereon in better trim?' The gaiety of men and women martyrs alike at the public feast on the eve of the games astonished the crowd: many, claimed the editor, were converted, among them the prison governor.

Some authorities have seen in the cruelty of the amphitheatre, in which criminals as well as Christians were torn to death by wild animals, not only a pandering to the bloodthirsty tastes of the onlookers and the reassurance (however illusory) of seeing justice publicly meted out in an ill-policed age, but a revival of the long tradition of human sacrifice. Wild beasts were sacred to the gods, and wore religious ornaments in the arena; their victims were sent to meet them either naked or in the costume of priests, so that their ordinary clothes should not profane the gods. A more ancient superstition hovered in the background: the games took place at set times of the year, ostensibly to celebrate the Emperor's anniversary or victories, but perhaps also to renew the fertility of the earth, and to placate the unknown forces of nature.

The Christian martyrs were, in a sense, the accomplices of their persecutors. Just as the Punic religion had taught that sacrificial victims became divine, so for them death in the arena was a certain passport to paradise. Martyrdom was already, and was to remain, an important part of African Christianity.

Perpetua and her companions went to the amphitheatre 'as if they were on their way to heaven, with gay and gracious looks; trembling, if at all,

---

1 Geta, younger son of Septimius Severus, was fourteen that day.

The horrors of the amphitheatre: detail of mosaic from Zliten, Libya, showing prisoners strapped to little chariots being attacked by leopards. Now in the Tripoli Museum

not with fear but with joy'. The editor recounts the end: how Saturninus was mauled first by a leopard, and then by a bear; how Saturus had to face a boar and the bear before the leopard got him in the throat; how the two women, one with milk dripping from her breasts (which scandalized the crowd), were enclosed in nets and tossed by a maddened heifer. He describes how Perpetua's immediate, instinctive action after being tossed was to tidy herself, to cover her legs with her tunic and fasten up her hair – for dishevelled hair, the sign of mourning, was inappropriate to the hour of her glory. Then she pulled the bruised Felicity to her feet, and together they left the arena, their 'turn' over. 'When are we to be thrown to the heifer?' were her first words: she had been in an ecstatic trance throughout the ordeal. She and the other survivors returned to the arena to be executed. Perpetua guided the sword of the gladiator to her throat.

THE FATHER OF LATIN CHRISTIANITY

There are good, if not conclusive, reasons for believing that the anonymous editor who witnessed the death of Perpetua and her fellow martyrs was the great Christian apologist Tertullian. He, like Perpetua, belonged to a rich pagan family of Africa. He was born into literary circles in Carthage, probably around AD 170. He wrote Greek and Latin fluently, and could well have trained in the school of rhetoric where Apuleius had been a pupil a generation before. His wife was a Christian, and he himself was a convert; he seems to have remained a layman. Little is known of his

155

life, except through his writings, which were composed between about 196 and 212. Although St Jerome, in his brief life written two centuries later, reports that Tertullian 'is said to have lived to an advanced age,' his date of death is not known, and he may not long have survived his last works.

A good deal more is known of his personality. An ardent, uncompromising man, who grew more uncompromising with age, he crusaded unceasingly against the evils of this world, whether the sins of the pagan community or the weakness of his fellow Christians. A Roman logic was married in him, sometimes uneasily, to all the wild undisciplined fervour of the African. A steady sequence of pamphlets poured from his pen, to confound faithless and faithful alike. He attacked Jews and heretics; he denounced military service and attendance at the games. Like other rigorists, his view of the deportment proper to women was harsh. Not only were they to dress with a decent modesty, but they were not to take second husbands. Fornicators and adulterers, he believed, should not be re-admitted to the Church. He himself ostentatiously abandoned the wearing of the toga as too much of a compromise with paganism. To follow all Tertullian's prescripts and to live in the world at the same time would have taxed a saint.

He was also something of a trial to the leaders of the African Church. He had little patience with the spiritual pretensions of the bishops, who were just beginning to set themselves up above their flocks and preparing, in their corporate capacity, to build the remarkable organization which was to survive the barbarian invasions and hand on to distant generations the remnants of the classical world into which the Church was born. It did not suit bishops to be told that wherever two or three lay Christians were gathered together in the unity of the Spirit, there the Church was. By the end of Tertullian's life there were some seventy bishops in Africa (the number is believed to have been based on that of the Jewish sanhedrin), and Tertullian's view had become revolutionary doctrine. He also extolled the virtues of seeking martyrdom with too much enthusiasm for comfort: bishops did not care for the idea of losing all the souls in their care, and they themselves had work to do in the Church Militant before joining the Church Triumphant. Tertullian vigorously denounced the understandable practice of fleeing from persecution – and his views were to lend a glamorous authority to the Donatist schism which was to plague the Church in Africa after the Great Persecutions.

Yet none of this prevented St Jerome from including Tertullian in his list of Eminent Men of the Church. Jerome was careful to omit any mention of what Tertullian's beliefs actually were, but the African was forgiven everything for his passionate defence of the Faith, for the wit and conviction with which he expressed the basic tenets of Christian belief, and the splendid vigour of a Latin style at once demotic, literate and rhetorical, to which the liturgy of the Church owed, and still owes, an enormous debt. A generation after his death St Cyprian, a greater and a wiser churchman, made a habit of reading Tertullian every day, saying to his servant: 'Hand me the Master.'

Gravestones from the Chapel of the Martyrs, Timgad

ST CYPRIAN, BISHOP AND MARTYR

St Cyprian himself was the greatest of the bishops of Carthage, the first African martyr-bishop and the man who, more than anyone, organized the African Church. His reputation in the west was such that the Churches of Gaul and Spain appealed to him as an arbiter. His importance in the development of Church discipline was considerable: like Tertullian, he believed that baptisms were invalid when performed by heretics or schismatics; unlike Tertullian, he believed that contrite sinners, even gross sinners such as apostates who denied the Faith, should be re-admitted to the Church after suitable penance. For in his view the Church, like the field in the parable, properly comprised both wheat and tares.

Cyprian was born into a prosperous pagan family around AD 200, shortly before the Severan persecution in which St Perpetua died. He held a chair in rhetoric at Carthage, and was converted only in middle life; indeed, Cyprian had been openly anti-Christian, like most of his class, which

157

had much to lose by turning Christian.[1] After his conversion, which was prompted in part by reading the works of Tertullian, Cyprian distributed most of his fortune to the poor. His natural authority was such that he was soon attending the episcopal councils which were becoming a regular feature of the life of the Church. He was already well known as an orator and pleader, and only three years after becoming a Christian he was elected bishop of Carthage. Such rapid promotion is familiar in the early stages of any new organization; and no doubt in a movement which found its chief support among the poor Cyprian's social and educational superiority marked him out for leadership.

His great intellectual gifts emerge clearly in the surviving dozen or so treatises on various aspects of the Faith. The tempestuousness of his master Tertullian is in Cyprian replaced by a calm, reasonable persuasiveness. He owes something, perhaps, to another contemporary of Tertullian, the Roman lawyer Minucius Felix – possibly also African by birth – whose *Octavius*, a subtle defence of Christianity in dialogue form, is a model of sophisticated debate. Cyprian is more straightforward than rhetorical, more concerned with substance than style. His letters, of which some sixty have survived, show the most devoted concern for the welfare of his flock as individual souls as well as for the maintenance of a disciplined, unified Church.

The unity of the Church was the major problem of St Cyprian's episcopacy. He maintained that unity in his own day, but did not lay it on secure foundations: half a century later, both the orthodox Catholics and the schismatics were claiming that his words or deeds were the justification for their own position.

The trouble arose principally from the perennial tendency of the Christian Church to split into two: the rigorist, evangelical wing (exemplified by Tertullian) and the more moderate believers who were prepared, indeed willing, to make some concessions to the temporal world. The earliest converts, not unnaturally, had been enthusiasts for the Faith, prepared to die for it or at least to renounce the world; but, with the spread of Christianity, weaker or richer converts were drawn in, who were less willing to give up all they possessed. The increasing number of converts had another consequence: a more formal organization was necessary, to handle donations and legacies (which were soon considerable), to administer charitable funds, to settle doctrinal disputes and personal rivalries; the clergy also received a stipend. By the time St Cyprian became bishop of Carthage, the Church was beginning to be rich and to acquire property; and the Church itself, as distinct from individual members,

---

1 Paganism remained common in the romanized upper classes, even after Constantine had adopted Christianity as the official religion of the Empire in AD 313. In the late fourth century, the family of St Augustine's mother had been Christian for several generations, but his father was still a pagan.

was finding a motive for some compromise with the Roman authorities.

For forty years after the persecutions during the reign of Septimius Severus there was peace for the Church: the faith of new converts was not tested. But in AD 250, when St Cyprian had been a bishop for two years, the first of the Great Persecutions was inaugurated by the Emperor Decius. All Christians were commanded to sacrifice to the genius of the Emperor, for which they would receive a certificate – on pain of torture and imprisonment or exile and confiscation of property if they refused.

It was soon clear that the quantity of Christians in Africa was now more impressive than their quality. 'Some did not wait to be arrested to go to the capitol [to sacrifice],' wrote Cyprian, 'did not wait to be questioned before denying their Faith. Many were defeated before the hour of battle ... did not even have the merit of appearing to submit by force ... many were in such a hurry that the magistrates were obliged to postpone their cases until the morrow.'

The bishop himself had gone into hiding, a prudent step which earned the scorn of Gibbon and would have shocked Tertullian. Cyprian did not believe in apostasy, but he believed discretion to be the better part of valour; and he counselled other Christians to flee. The Romans could have sought him out had they wished, for he continued to direct the affairs of the Church from his retirement, and messengers could certainly have been followed; but the authorities contented themselves with confiscating his property.

There were many, however, who thought, like Tertullian, that flight was itself apostasy: calling themselves martyrs, they preferred openly to refuse to sacrifice and to suffer for their Faith in prison. In their eyes, Bishop Cyprian no longer had any spiritual authority.

Meanwhile, the apostates, the *lapsi*, having by one sacrifice to the Emperor earned the necessary certificates, or *libelli*, were seeking re-admission to the Church. St Cyprian, still in hiding but closely in touch, decided that there were so many of them that it would seriously weaken the Christian community to excommunicate them all; and that after a suitable period the question of their re-admission should be considered.

He was forestalled. The martyrs in prison had already begun issuing pardons to the *lapsi*, particularly to friends and relations; soon pardons were being distributed wholesale, in an ecstasy of saintly forgiveness. As martyrs, they were, they believed, their bishop's spiritual superiors, and they were not the only ones to believe that: many of St Cyprian's own clergy were recognizing the validity of these *libelli pacis*, and re-admitting the apostates to communion. Church discipline had broken down in the face of this unlikely alliance between 'martyrs', the most zealous, and *lapsi*, the least.

Suddenly Decius died; the persecution was over. Cyprian, his authority badly shaken, came out of hiding and tried to repair the damage. The question of the *lapsi* was to be settled at a council (which eventually agreed that they should be re-admitted, at least on their death-beds after a suitable show of repentance); priests, too, should be forgiven, but not restored to office; meanwhile, all should be given pastoral care.

The unnatural alliance was soon broken; for although a number of purists, led by a priest who had been Cyprian's rival for the see of Carthage, formed a short-lived schismatic sect, the *lapsi* and many of the martyrs who had confessed them gradually returned to Cyprian's fold.

It was mainly a victory for diplomacy, but there was another reason for the bishop's success: Cyprian had a vocation for good works. During the severe plague which tormented Africa in AD 252, he and his priests and helpers succoured Christian and schismatic, heretic and pagan alike. Human charity added its persuasiveness to hope and faith.

Unfortunately, Cyprian's very success in luring back the followers and converts of the schismatics created another doctrinal problem. Some of them had been baptized while in opposition: should their baptism be recognized? Cyprian, whose views on the solidarity of the Church were well known, was adamant: they must be re-baptized, because baptism by heretics or schismatics was a ceremony outside the Church and therefore invalid. To his surprise, however, the bishop of Rome, where persecution had caused a similar problem of discipline, thought otherwise. For him baptism by the schismatics was valid, since the schismatics had left the Church on a point of order rather than of doctrine. Cyprian put the matter to a council of eighty-seven African bishops from all over north-west Africa in AD 256. Their support for him was unanimous; it looked as if a serious split might develop between Rome and Carthage.

This was averted by the renewal of persecution under the Emperor Valerian, and the martyrdom of both bishops. In AD 256 Valerian decreed that all bishops and priests who refused to sacrifice should be punished by exile. In Numidia, nine bishops were sentenced to the mines near Cirta; others were banished. In Carthage, the proconsul sent for Cyprian, and, after the routine question-and-answer exchanges in which the bishop testified to his faith, banished him to Curubis (Korba) on the bay of Hammamet. There he remained for a year, until the next year's proconsul summoned him back to Carthage to face death: Valerian had decided that Christians were to lose their rank and property, Christian women should be banished and all clergy should be executed at once.

On 14 September, AD 258, 'the day singled out of all days, the day of promise, the day of God', wrote St Cyprian's biographer, the deacon Pontius, Cyprian was taken to open ground surrounded by woods, escorted by an immense crowd of Christians, and there beheaded, having charged his friends to see that the executioner was given twenty-five gold pieces. The bishop's martyrdom united moderates and rigorists in his praise; each party claimed him for their own, and the breach between them did not reopen for nearly fifty years.

Six months later two Numidian bishops were put to death and, within the week, two deacons, Saints James and Marian, at Cirta, where the number of the faithful to be dispatched was so numerous that 'inventive cruelty arranged rows or lines drawn up in order, that the blade of the impious murderer might take the beheading of the faithful in a rush of fury'. Their *passio* was cherished by the persecuted Church alongside the *acta* of St Cyprian.

The persecutions stopped, almost as suddenly as they had begun, and for the moment Church and State lived in an uneasy truce. But within the Church dissension simmered, awaiting only its occasion.

The blood of the martyrs was the seed of the Church, as Tertullian had thundered warningly against the Roman authorities; the Christian tree grew straight and strong because it was pruned of its heresies. At least part of the strength of Christianity was its doctrinal intransigence. The Faith was not to be watered down by pagan tolerance; heresy was countered by intellectual argument – and argument was all too soon to be backed by force. Africa was spared the early struggles of the Arian controversy, and although Montanism – a sect embraced by Tertullian and Perpetua and her fellow martyrs – gained adherents it had little influence there; but the unsolved problem of the *lapsi* and re-baptism was dormant, not dead. From it was to sprout not merely a minor offshoot but a new branch of the Christian Church, which was finally destroyed only when the whole community of Christians in North Africa was overwhelmed by the Arabs.

THE REFORMS OF DIOCLETIAN

Meanwhile, there were other anxieties. The withdrawal of the Legion in 238 by Gordian III seems not to have led to immediate trouble; other troops were deployed along the frontier. In the far west, the Romans appear to have concluded a series of peace treaties with the Baquates tribe of Mauretania Tingitana, whose capital was at Volubilis. But by 253 it had become necessary to reconstitute the Third Augustan Legion in its old territory.

In that year a number of Christians had been kidnapped by 'barbarians' – St Cyprian's word – and the bishop had had to raise 100,000 sesterces, an enormous sum, for their ransom. The Church was indeed growing rich. The kidnapping was probably the work of opportunist brigands, since St Cyprian's letter does not mention any tribe by name, but no doubt they were taking advantage of a weakness in the forces of law and order; for very soon afterwards the tribes of the mountains of Mauretania Sitifensis and Numidia were, together and separately,

pillaging fields and settlements. The Bavares near Sitifis, the Quinquegentiani of the Grande Kabylie mountains and the Fraxinenses
(whose region of origin is uncertain) were allied in a confederation and
openly on the offensive. Order seems to have been restored by 262; but
it had taken nearly a decade.

Fifteen years on, the chieftain of the Baquates, one Iulius Matif, is for
the first time given the title *rex* in an inscription of 277 found at Volubilis.
His people are called *gens foederata*; and on his death his son Nuffusi is
also referred to as *rex*. They are allies, not subjects of Rome – such
words, however friendly, suggest that they were effectively independent.
It was the prelude to Rome's withdrawal from the west.

Between the late 280s and the late 290s warfare broke out again in
Mauretania, about which, once more, there are few details; but the co-
Emperor Maximian came in person to repress it. No Emperor could
afford to let the regular corn supply for Rome be threatened by insurrection. However, at the end of the third century the Romans withdrew
from the far west, leaving Mauretania Tingitana to be governed by its
semi-romanized chieftains; the surviving Roman province, a small area
round Tingis (Tangier), was made part of the province of southern Spain –
a belated recognition of the fact that North African communications were
easier by sea than by land. Maximian toured North Africa from the
Atlantic to the Bay of Tunis, and ordered a general repair of all military
roads and of the frontier defences which had fallen into neglect since
the days of the Severan dynasty. But, like a snail, Roman North Africa
was shrinking into its shell; and the shell was cracked.

By then, the Emperor Diocletian had come to the throne, and the
African provinces were suffering almost more from Diocletian's firm
government than from the previous anarchy.[1] Now, for a crucial twenty
years – Diocletian's reign lasted from AD 284 until his voluntary retirement in AD 305 – the Empire had strong, centralized government. It
worked – at a price. Diocletian's response to the problems of barbarian
pressure from outside and over-independent provincial initiative inside
was vigorous. He increased the size of the frontier army (possibly
doubling it) and divided the provinces into smaller and more tractable
units. Africa was divided into eight – Mauretania Tingitana (much
reduced in size), Caesariensis and Sitifensis; Numidia Cirtensis (northern)
and Militiana (southern); Zeugitana (northern Africa Proconsularis) and
Byzacena (central); and Tripolitania – instead of the original four. Except
for Mauretania Tingitana (which was linked with Spain), these provinces
were grouped together into the *diocesis* of Africa, under a *vicarius* (who
was to prove less powerful in practice, however, than the individual
governors). The frontier armies were put under the command of *comites*,

---

1 There had been more than twenty Emperors in fewer than fifty years.

or counts, and the troops of the peaceful interior provinces under that of *duces*, or dukes. Occasionally, dukes doubled up as provincial governors, though it was the usual policy to separate civilian and military roles. Diocletian also introduced cavalry into the Roman army proper, where earlier Emperors had left this important arm to barbarian auxiliaries. North-west Africa received nineteen squadrons – more than any other province.

He also divided the responsibility of ruling the Empire, by associating Maximian with himself as junior Augustus, and appointing two Caesars to assist them. There was an unhappy six-year dispute after Diocletian's retirement in 305, during which the army in Africa sided with the loser. The winner revenged himself by laying fertile farmlands waste, and by pillaging Carthage and Cirta. Only seventy years earlier another fertile part of the province had suffered in just the same way when the young men of Byzacena had nominated Gordian I as Emperor. Carthage itself suffered for a second time.

Another part of Diocletian's policy had been the conversion of the *imperium* into a form of monarchy, with all the ostentatious trappings of a court – the vast, secretive household, the atmosphere of mysterious royalty – and he had made his capital at Nicomedia, in the richer east, leaving Rome and the west to Maximian. His eventual successor, Constantine the Great, who reigned for a quarter of a century, followed his example – and transplanted his court yet again, from Nicomedia to a splendid new city on the Bosphorus, Constantinople. There the new regime, more durable even than that of Augustus, was to survive for a thousand years as Byzantium.

But it was all very expensive. A larger army, a greater number of provincial staffs, not merely one set of courtiers and bureaucrats but two: the Emperors required new supplies of money and men. The history of the later Roman Empire is a melancholy tale of their efforts to raise such supplies, efforts which were crushing when they succeeded and desperate when they failed.

As usual, taxes, in the absence of war booty and industrial or agricultural advance, were the chosen means of raising money. The senatorial class had always been excused taxes; so the burden fell most heavily on the poor who actually worked the land and on the middle classes of the cities who were responsible for tax-collection. It had once been an honour to become a magistrate of one's city, to join the class of *curiales*, an honour for which citizens were glad to pay entrance fees and annual dues; now it was a burden, and obligatory. Even in the second century AD, Trajan had had to appoint procurators in the cities to supervise the collection of taxes; in the third, magistrates were personally responsible not only for their own dues and taxes, but for any that they failed to collect. The *curiales* struggled to buy or bribe

163

their way into the senatorial class; otherwise they fled to the countryside or another city to escape municipal burdens, or vanished into the army, or the priesthood, or into a lower class.

Peasants also fled, when bad harvests or ill-fortune piled up debts they could never hope to pay off. Tiny freeholdings did survive until the end of Roman times, but many were swallowed up by richer neighbours when their owners were forced to sell. Often freeholders became tenants, and tenants, obliged to pay their debts by selling their rights in their land, became serfs; but the flight from the land, combined with the flight from the cities, was sufficiently serious for the Emperors to try to arrest it by decrees. For farming was still the necessary occupation: Rome still had to be fed by Africa's surplus, and municipal taxes had to be paid by someone. Diocletian and Constantine therefore decreed that men should be 'tied' to the occupations of their fathers, whether they were peasant-farmers, artisans or *curiales*. Such an arrangement also meant that the Emperors could demand from each city, each piece of land, a statutory number of recruits for the army, and a statutory amount of taxation, for which the *curiales* were responsible. Gradually they turned the citizens of the Empire into subjects, and classes into castes.

The poor grew poorer; but the rich grew richer. Not only were they spared taxes or were able to bribe their way out of them, but they could profit from the misfortunes of the poor. Every freeholder who sold out to them, every city-dweller who put himself under their protection, added to their wealth in realty or manpower. And the laws which tied peasants to the land were laws the rich welcomed. The population of the Empire appears to have been declining at this period, and landowners were as anxious as the Emperors that the people who tilled their estates should continue to do so. Though the Emperors took advantage of a tied population to demand soldiers from cities and landowners, the richest could resist or buy their way out of even this obligation.

A TASTE OF *LA DOLCE VITA*

The very pattern of upper-class life was changing. The archaeological evidence makes plain that many of the great landowners were at long last living on their estates. Life in the unhappy, hard-pressed cities was no longer the easy, civilized pleasure it had been a hundred years earlier. All those Roman Africans who could afford to do so, and whom office did not keep in the towns, retired out of harm's way to their country estates, where they built themselves houses and created independent little empires of their own. The rich turned into country gentry, and – although large tracts of Africa were still owned by absentee landlords such as the Emperor, the Church, Roman senators or those rich who had many estates – the feudal manor began to supplant the city as the basic unit of the provinces' economy.

Typical North African villa of the fourth and fifth centuries AD, with colonnaded living quarters on the first floor. Detail of mosaic from Tabarka, now in the Bardo Museum

It is to the late third century and the fourth that the great mosaics of African villa life belong. For the first time in representations of the life of the countryside, aristocratic dwellings appear alongside the stables and barns. They are real country mansions, often semi-fortified, and quite unlike the town houses of the second century. They are only exceptionally built round a courtyard; instead, coolness and shade are provided by the long Mediterranean verandah built the full length of the outside of the house. Sometimes, there are adjoining private baths, similar to the Moorish *hammam*. A famous mosaic found at Carthage and now in the Bardo, the mosaic of Dominus Julius, shows just such a house, with dome-roofed baths half hidden behind it. The house is turreted at the corners, with its living quarters on the first floor to afford some protection in case of attack in the troubled times of the fourth century; but as a portrait of rural life the mosaic is redolent of the *douceur de vivre* that was still possible for the rich. The house is surrounded by a pleasure garden; there are cereal crops and olive trees, domestic animals and poultry, huntsmen, servants and farm labourers. The master, in the time he cares to spare from the pursuit of game, watches over his domain; his wife, fashionably dressed in spite of exile from Carthage, gazes at herself in a mirror.

Estates like this one were beginning to develop into self-contained communities, sometimes with their own churches. The flight from the cities brought artisans and craftsmen out to the country, to seek the protection and patronage of the only people strong enough to protect them from tax-gatherers and bureaucrats. Africa was on the brink of the Middle Ages.

The Dominus Julius mosaic found at Carthage, showing the house and domain of a country gentleman. Note first-floor living quarters and domed bath-house. Bardo Museum

11

A CHURCH DIVIDED

The crowd which had watched St Perpetua and her companions die in the amphitheatre at Carthage had been hostile to them. Half a century later, the crowd which escorted St Cyprian to the scene of his martyrdom outside the capital had almost rioted in support of their bishop. For by the middle of the third century Christianity had become the dominant religion of the urban poor. During the half-century after the persecution in which Cyprian died, it became the religion of the poor in the depths of the countryside also. It spread from the romanized cities of the wheatlands to the olive country of the plains of Numidia and the semi-desert of the south, and to the tribal interior of the Mauretanias. Very little is known of this change, except that it was paralleled in other provinces in the Eastern Roman Empire, where, as in north-west Africa, it coincided with the survival of a native language; but, to judge from inscriptions, it occurred with startling suddenness. Within a generation, much of the African peasantry was converted from Saturn to Christ. The last securely dated dedication to Saturn in Numidia and the Mauretanias is for AD 272, less than a century after the deaths of the martyrs of Scilli.

There were also sensational conversions in the professional classes. Arnobius, for instance, a teacher of rhetoric at Sicca Veneria (El Kef), had been such an ardent pagan that he had difficulty in persuading his bishop that he wished to become a Christian. He was obliged to write *Adversus Nationes* to convince him.¹ Another convert was his pupil Lactantius, to whom Diocletian had given a professorship in Nicomedia; he became the author of *Divine Institutions*, and in AD 313 Constantine, the first Christian Emperor, appointed him tutor to his son Crispus.

Eighty-seven bishops had attended Cyprian's council at Carthage in AD 256. Fifty years later, there were probably three times that number. Admittedly, the vast majority of African bishops were more like parish priests than heads of dioceses – one reason why Cyprian, with the score or

---

1 This was at the end of the third century. Arnobius inveighed so strongly against paganism that it seems likely it was still widespread.

so of Carthage's parishes under his wing, could make himself undisputed primate of the province – and the authority of many, if not most, extended no further than one small town or a few villages, or one imperial or senatorial domain. However, every bishop represented at least one Christian community of sufficient size to have its own organization of priests and deacons, and probably its own holy books and sacred vessels.

But the Christianity of the African poor – and even of intellectuals like Tertullian – had much in common with the religion it displaced. The new Semitic God was, for the superstitious Africans, the old Semitic Saturn-Baal writ large: a God of Vengeance to be feared and propitiated, rather than a loving Father. It was 'a transformed popular religion, rather than ... conversion to a new religion'. Indeed, one of St Augustine's tracts suggests that many fifth-century Christians believed that God was Saturn re-christened; and the old god's nickname, *senex*, the Old Man, may have been applied by extension to Christian bishops, even though the name of Saturn seems to have vanished more than a century earlier. The correct and fanatical observance of ritual, rigorous acts of penance, devotion to martyrs and the pursuit of martyrdom were of fundamental importance, as ritual and blood-sacrifice had been in the old religion. Human suffering still bought the favours of the divine power, and persecution was still the passport to paradise.

THE CONVERSION OF NUMIDIA

The mass conversion was rapid and easy because it was less of a change than it looked. That does not explain it; but there was a significant social difference between Saturn-worship and Christianity in the third century which suggests a reason. Saturn, though based on a more ancient African god, had become romanized, respectable and official, with public temples and a recognized place in the accepted pantheon; the God of the Christians had not. His name, now, could be a rallying cry for dissent. And in the late third century, by the time Diocletian had become Emperor, there was strong reason for dissent.

In the olive country of Numidia and the south, the late third century onwards was an age of settlement and prosperity. Sites of well over a thousand villages have been listed in southern Numidia alone, a region which is mostly uncultivated steppe today, but which was becoming, then, as important a source of olive-oil as the groves of Africa Proconsularis and Tripolitania. Its increasing agricultural wealth attracted the attentions of the tax-gatherers, and an unfair share of Diocletian's new demands.

A rising standard of living is a common prelude to revolt; the thwarting of new aspirations is the spark that lights the fuse. The hopes and pleasures

---

1 W.H.C. Frend in *The Donatist Church.*

of city life, which had so much to offer men like the harvester of Mactar in the previous century, no longer functioned as a safety valve in the third. The rural peasantry turned to Christianity.

Looking down the nave to the apse of the late fourth-century Christian basilica at Tébessa (ancient Theveste). It is one of the largest Roman buildings in North Africa

Hardly had they done so than Christianity itself became respectable. The Edict of Milan, promulgated by the Emperors Constantine and Licinius in AD 313, ushered in not only toleration but the long alliance between Church and State. Almost simultaneously, the Church in Africa split in two, with perhaps at one time as many as half the Christians supporting the schism known as Donatism, so-called after Donatus, its most important figure. It was from the olive country of Numidia that the Donatist schismatics, hating the secular authorities and the *status quo* as much as they hated their religious rivals, and hating each the more for their alliance, were to draw most of their support. The instinct for dissent found its outlet after all, and for the remaining century and a quarter of north-west Africa's subjection to Rome its history is that of a people divided against itself, a history written not only in words, of which there were to be many, but in blood. Discontent simmered beneath, and sometimes on, the surface, until it was finally subsumed in the death throes of the Empire itself.

It would be wrong to see in Donatism merely a form of social protest, and certainly not a nascent African nationalism. It was always, as Peter Brown has pointed out, a schism solidly devoted to the Latin scriptures,

169

and led by romanized bishops who were based in important, prosperous Roman cities like Cirta, Carthage, Timgad and Calama (Guelma). Its famous battle cry – *Deo laudes* – was Latin, not St Augustine's *lingua punica*. Further, in the far west, where tribal chieftains always exercised considerable authority and Roman influence was much weaker, the population was converted to Catholic Christianity and not to Donatism.

But economic distress and the corruption and oppressive policy of the administrative machine certainly exacerbated religious tension in the potentially more prosperous parts of the province, and confirmed the Donatists in their refusal to yield when the rightness of their cause, both legal and moral, had long been disproved.

The Donatists were not heretics; they believed what the Catholics believed, and their forms of worship and organization were the same. The schism sprang from a difference of emphasis which had already been obvious in St Cyprian's day. Both sides had condemned the handing over of sacred books on demand to the Roman magistrates during the persecutions of the Christians in the 250s; both sides believed that such apostasy was a grave matter. But was a priest who handed over heretical or medical documents, pretending that they were scripture and thus avoiding blame, also a *traditor*? Was such a *traditor* priest thereby incapable of administering the sacrament of baptism? Did the parable of the field of wheat and tares refer to the Church or to the world – did the True Church admit only the virtuous, and exclude sinners? Was it wrong to have any dealings with secular authority?

To all these questions, to which the Catholic answer – developed over decades of argument – was now in the negative, the Donatists would have answered yes. They laid up difficulties for themselves. They fought test cases on shaky evidence. Some of their leaders turned out to be as guilty of apostasy as any on the other side. They, too, appealed to the Emperors for support. They were as vulnerable as any other group which claims moral superiority to the frailties of both flesh and spirit. Had their views on the necessary purity of the priesthood prevailed, whole communities would have been deprived of the Christian communion. For it is only God, as St Augustine was later to argue, who can divide the wheat from the tares.

Yet it is impossible to withhold sympathy from the Donatists. The Christians with their vast increase in numbers were no longer a band of dedicated souls; corruption and malpractices were as rife, even in the priesthood, as in the pagan community. And like other evangelicals, the schismatics appealed to something very deep in human nature, which was not merely a question of the poor against the rich. Thousands did die, willingly, for Donatist beliefs; their leaders were, in the fourth century, more distinguished both as Christians and as intellectuals than those of the Catholics; and neither the might of the State nor the genius of St

170

Augustine ever broke their hold on the hearts of half North Africa.

HOW THE SCHISM BEGAN

The schism began in tragedy: the Great Persecution of Diocletian of AD 303–5. There had already been during his reign a number of isolated executions in Africa of men who refused to serve in the army on the grounds that they were Christians. The son of a veteran was beheaded at Theveste in AD 295; a veteran at Tigava (El Kherba) met the same fate for refusing to re-enlist after being converted. In AD 298 the centurion Marcellus threw down his arms before the standards of the Legion stationed at Tingis (Tangiers), in the presence of his fellow-soldiers. He, too, was tried and executed, and the shorthand-writer at the trial, one Cassian, who had flung away his notebook and pen with an oath at the injustice of the sentence, of which he complained to the judge, was also beheaded. There were many Christians in the army, and although such crises of conscience were rare, at a time when every soldier was needed – it was the year the co-Emperor Maximian was in the province to suppress tribal revolts – the dangerous doctrine of 'I am a soldier of God, not of the Emperor,' could not be countenanced.

But in AD 303 Diocletian turned against civilian Christians too. Possibly at the prompting of the oracles of Apollo, by no means yet silenced (even if Saturn had lost his following), Christian meetings were suddenly forbidden, their places of worship were ordered to be pulled down and their scriptures burned. They were to be deprived of their rank and not allowed to bring court actions. When two fires mysteriously broke out in his palace, Diocletian further ordered the arrest of all bishops and priests.

In Africa this was taken to mean death for all who refused to recant or deliver up the scriptures. Most of the higher clergy persuaded themselves that compromise was to be preferred to martyrdom. Many bishops gave up the scriptures to the magistrates; Mensurius, bishop of Carthage, handed over heretical works which he pretended were sacred books. At Cirta (Constantine) Bishop Paulus, aided and abetted by his deacons, sub-deacons and priests, gave up various ecclesiastical objects, and after some prevarication disclosed the whereabouts of the scriptures; and the sub-deacon Silvanus officiously brought out of hiding from behind a barrel in the library a silver box and a silver lamp. It was all set down in official records. Years later, Silvanus had cause to regret his role in this scene.

But not all their congregations followed such episcopal examples. Many of the laity enthusiastically courted imprisonment, some even declaring they had scriptures hidden which they did not in fact possess. There were genuine martyrdoms: the most moving *acta* of the Diocletian persecution records the trial of the priest Saturninus of Abitina (where the bishop had turned *traditor*) and his flock of nearly fifty men, women and children,

171

including his own four sons. To almost every question put to them by the proconsul at Carthage, the simple answer came: 'I am a Christian.' Their fate is not known – it is possible that some or all of them died in prison; but their stoical courage under threat of torture was an inspiration to many. In Timgad the governor of southern Numidia, a convinced pagan, appears to have been given the opportunity to put many to death; those who gave him that opportunity were not forgotten, and their tombs became places of enthusiastic pilgrimage.

Meanwhile the Christians who were in prison began to pardon *lapsi* as they had done in St Cyprian's day. But this time they also unequivocally condemned their own clergy. In Carthage, they were soon openly accusing Bishop Mensurius's deacon, Caecilian, of starving the martyrs of Abitina to death by preventing food reaching them in prison. Whether that was true or not, Caecilian was known to be opposed not only to unnecessary martyrdoms, as St Cyprian had been, but hostile to martyrs. He was tactless enough to make this clear – something St Cyprian would never have done – and was soon the most hated man in Carthage.

TRAGEDY TURNS TO FARCE

The persecution lasted scarcely more than a year, but it left behind it an unbridgeable gulf between the *traditores* – those who handed over – and the anti-compromise party. The latter, which found its earliest supporters among the urban mob at Carthage and in the Numidian countryside, now began to force its own candidates into the episcopacy. The origins of the schism are remarkably well documented; each side kept detailed records, the better to confound its opponents. Both had plenty of ammunition – and the story turns from tragedy to farce.

At Cirta, for instance, when the *traditor* Bishop Paulus died, the leading citizens wished to elect a less compromised Christian as bishop. Unfortunately they allowed themselves to be overawed by the excited mob, who had set their hearts on a man of the people who had proved his worth by spending the previous few months looting pagan temples. Blinded by enthusiasm, they overlooked the fact that their man was that same Silvanus who had been a *traditor* alongside Bishop Paulus not two years before. Nor did they hold it against him when, on becoming a bishop, Silvanus promptly appointed a certain Victor as a priest in exchange for a bribe.

Silvanus then had to be consecrated, according to custom, by twelve bishops who – on St Cyprian's authority – were 'in a state of grace', which, as they interpreted it, meant bishops who were not themselves *traditores*. However, of the twelve who gathered for this purpose at Cirta soon after under Secundus of Thigisis, primate of Numidia,¹ Secundus himself was

---

1 The Church in Numidia was now strong enough to have its own primate.

suspected of being a *traditor*; four other bishops present, according to the minutes of the meeting, actually admitted to it; and the notorious brigand Bishop Purpurius of Limata, when taxed with murdering two nephews, replied: 'Yes, I did kill and I will kill anyone who acts against me.' Weakly Secundus decided that the sins of bishops could only be left to the judgement of God. The *traditor* bishop of a fanatically anti-*traditor* see was duly confirmed in his holy office by other *traditores* and a self-confessed murderer. It was tricky ground on which to fight for a Church from which the tares must be weeded out.

None of this prevented the bishops of Numidia, some time later, from virtuously protesting when the anti-martyr archdeacon Caecilian was elected bishop of Carthage on the death of Mensurius in AD 312, and consecrated by three bishops, one of whom, Felix of Apthungi, they claimed – wrongly – had been a *traditor*. It was true that the election and consecration had been rather hurried; true, too, that the number of consecrating bishops had been fewer than was usual; but the most serious objection was a point of pride. Since St Cyprian's day, the consecration of the primate of Africa had devolved on the primate of Numidia. His claims, which were not welcomed by the Carthaginian clergy, had on this occasion been ignored. Secundus set off at once for Carthage accompanied by a veritable army of seventy bishops.

An extraordinary intrigue followed. There were rumours of attempted embezzlement of Church treasures in the Carthaginian camp; an interventor appointed by Secundus was murdered in church; Purpurius of Limata threatened to break Caecilian's head during the service if any reconsecration took place; a wealthy dowager of Spanish birth called Lucilla, who had never forgiven Caecilian for reproving her for kissing a martyr's bone at communion, allegedly bribed Secundus's party to elect Majorinus, one of her servants, in Caecilian's place.

However it came about, there were two bishops in Carthage when Secundus finally left to return to Numidia a few months after he arrived. The schism was now in being, the sides about evenly matched, each convinced that it alone was the true Church. Its history might have been different had Caecilian enjoyed as much popularity as St Cyprian had in similar circumstances – or had shown such quality as a bishop; and had not the anti-bishop Majorinus been succeeded the following year, the year of the Edict of Milan, by a personality as remarkable as all but one in the history of African Christianity.

---

1 This date has been disputed. Mensurius may have died in 305.

DONATUS, ANTI-BISHOP OF CARTHAGE

Donatus led the anti-Catholic Christians – maintaining always that they were the true Church – for forty years. To him the schismatics owed what dignity and strength the movement was able to wrest from its unsavoury beginnings. Not that the scandals were over, or that mistakes were not made, or that the Donatist Church did not acquire its share of worldly goods and worldly ambitions; the schismatics soon acquired a lunatic fringe, were plagued by sub-schismatics of their own (such is the logic of purity) and, like the Catholics, found great difficulty in recruiting for the priesthood. Many of their priests were illiterate rabble-rousers. But Donatism attracted a number of the best intellects of the day, and throughout the fourth century men like Parmenian, Tyconius, Primian and Petilian took the initiative in an energetic war of propaganda. The Catholics were forced into a defensive role, and the mere titles of their tracts suggest men hurriedly plugging holes in the dam of orthodoxy, whenever and wherever it sprang a leak; Bishop Optatus of Milevis' *De Schismate Donatistorum*, or the whole string of works written by St Augustine in the twenty years after his conversion – *Contra Cresconium, Contra Epistolam Parmeniani, Contra Litteras Petiliani, De Baptismos Contra Donatistas, Psalmus Contra Partem Donati*. The following of Donatus had to be taken seriously, for their leaders, taking as their text Tertullian's alluring pronouncement, 'Nothing could be more foreign to the Christian than the State', could proclaim themselves the champions of the poor and oppressed.

Very little is known about Donatus himself: none of his works survive, there are no eye-witness accounts. He remains throughout his life a shadowy presence in the wings of the African scene. But the magnetism of his personality can be deduced from its effect on those whom posterity can still see in the centre of the stage. Not for nothing was the schism named after him: his followers – according to St Augustine – resented insults offered to him more than they resented blasphemy, and even his enemies saluted his integrity. He was plainly a born leader and orator, with the power to draw the crowds, and turn those crowds into impassioned disciples: many believed that he performed miracles. His reputation and his sayings survived long after his death, and some have seen in him a forerunner of the holy prophets of Islam who were to inherit, three centuries later, the fanatical devotion which could be awoken in the African heart.

He seems to have come, appropriately enough, from Casae Nigrae, far to the south of Tébessa, on the fringe of the great *chotts* of the northern Sahara, a harsh and unyielding land which suffered much during Diocletian's persecution. It is not known when or why he arrived in Carthage, but he was active on behalf of the Numidian bishops led by Secundus of Thigisis during their attempts to get rid of Bishop Caecilian. He may have been instrumental in rousing the Carthaginian crowd against Caecilian, and a useful ally for the rich Lucilla in her efforts on behalf of Majorinus. At all events, when Majorinus died Donatus was well enough placed to be chosen anti-bishop in his place. Almost at once, the bishop of Rome, Pope Miltiades – himself an African and suspected of being a *traditor* – found him guilty of re-baptizing lapsed clergy and forming a schism.

Stables of the hostelry for pilgrims attached to the Tébessa basilica – which was almost certainly a Donatist foundation

THE INVOLVEMENT OF THE EMPEROR

So far, the activities of the party of Donatus were simply a matter of internal Church discipline. They did not remain so. For they provided Constantine, the first Christian Emperor, with the chance to forge the first link in the long alliance between the State and the Church. Once Constantine had become a convert that alliance was perhaps inevitable; but it was the Church in Africa which played into his hands.

Constantine had already decided to take a part in the dispute. No Emperor could afford to have the major supplier of corn and oil for Rome racked by dissension, whether political or religious. Without enquiring into the matter very closely, he gave his support to Caecilian; property confiscated during the persecution was to be returned to the Church, Caecilian was to be provided with money, his clergy were to be immune from curial responsibilities – and his opponents brought before the magistrates. 'The Devil rewarded the lapsed clergy not only with the restoration of ecclesiastical honours, but also with royal friendship and earthly riches,' the Donatists pointed out sharply, but even they did not realize the momentous significance of Constantine's interference. Indeed, within a few days of the announcement they themselves forged a second link in the chain that was to bind the secular and the religious authorities together, by appealing to the Emperor to hear their side of the story and be their judge. They did not spurn imperial friendship until it was at length clear that they would not get it. Meanwhile, the damage was done.

Constantine was taken aback by this communication from Caecilian's opponents, which included detailed charges against the bishop he had chosen to support; he wondered if he had made a mistake. But he found it quite natural to be appealed to; he felt himself directly responsible to his new-found God for the peace and unity of His Church. As he wrote to Pope Miltiades, 'It seems to me very serious that in those provinces which the Divine Providence has spontaneously entrusted to my devotion ... the population should be found in a state of discord.' He asked Miltiades, with other bishops, to adjudicate; Donatus and Caecilian were summoned to Rome.

In October 313 the bishops found in favour of Caecilian; but the Donatists refused to accept the verdict, complaining that 'the bishops had shut themselves up somewhere and passed judgement as convenient for themselves'. They claimed that evidence against Felix of Apthungi, one of the three bishops who had consecrated Caecilian eleven years before, had not been taken into account. Constantine at once overrode the bishops' verdict: there must be a further council at Arles the following year, and the case of Felix should be re-investigated at Carthage. The Christians were no longer masters of their own Church. When the council at Arles confirmed the previous verdict, Constantine again hesitated to dispossess the Donatists: 'I consider it absolutely contrary to the divine law that we should overlook such quarrels and contentions, whereby the Highest Divinity may perhaps be moved to wrath, not only against the human race, but against myself.' Even when his own proconsul at Carthage found Felix innocent of the charge of *traditor* – after a trial which turned on the exposure of a forger – he continued to listen to Donatist appeals. It gave the Donatists a precious opportunity to establish themselves in the eyes of the world. 'What frenzied audacity!' Constantine complained, threatening to come to Africa himself. Instead, however, he suddenly sent for the forger and challenged Donatus and his party that if they could still prove anything at all against Caecilian he 'would regard this as if every accusation which you bring against him has been proved. May Almighty God grant peace everlasting,' he added optimistically.

THE FIRST APPEAL TO FORCE

It took Constantine three years – partly because of other problems – to make up his mind finally that Caecilian was the right man to back, and to decree that Donatist churches were to be confiscated and their leaders exiled. But those three years had given the Donatists a taste of recognition and, it should be remembered, of something more worldly: for the Church was extremely rich – both sides already had many churches, both sides disposed of valuable plate.

By this time the Donatists also had – not surprisingly – serious hopes that Constantine would change his mind yet again. The new decrees had still to be put into effect, and they had no intention of yielding while there was still any doubt. They announced that they would never communicate with Constantine's 'scoundrelly bishop'.

In this *impasse*, Christians for the first time appealed to the use of force against other Christians. The Church had called in the Emperor, and made a mockery of religious authority; Constantine had made a mockery of the law; and neither religious nor legal sanctions were now enough. The stage was set for the persecution of Christians by Christians.

Caecilian appealed to the army. Fatally, once force was decided on, the operation was conducted half-heartedly. Most Donatist bishops actually remained in possession of their sees; and the deaths that occurred, which included a 'massacre' outside Carthage, predictably served to divide the schismatics irrevocably from the Catholics. They also provided Donatus with his most persuasive slogan: the true Church is persecuted, not persecuting.

Nothing, now, could shake the following of Donatus, not even the belated revelation in AD 320 that the Donatist bishop of Cirta, the former sub-deacon Silvanus, had been a *traditor* fifteen years earlier. Silvanus, who had not mended his ways, had imprudently quarrelled with one of his deacons, had him stoned and excommunicated him. This man, who knew Silvanus's history, appealed to the civil authorities. At the trial, everything came out; the yielding up of the silver box and lamp, the taking of bribes, the embezzlement of money intended for the poor when Silvanus had accompanied Secundus of Thigisis to Carthage during the campaign against Caecilian in AD 312. Many of his fellow bishops were implicated with Silvanus; they were sentenced to exile by the governor. Yet the aftermath of the trial reveals Donatus's strength. Although Silvanus went into exile, Purpurius of Limata, who had also been exiled – and had raged at Silvanus when he first quarrelled with his deacon, 'You will kill us all' – remained impenitently in office.

The Catholic leaders, struggling to maintain the fiction of unity, had certainly been distressed by the violence involved in their attempts to implement Constantine's decision. So was Constantine, who, if he could not have peace and unity, of the two preferred peace. The following year, though he continued to support Caecilian, he extended toleration to the Donatists, and left the matter to the judgement of God. But he had put the Church at a considerable diplomatic and psychological disadvantage. With their connivance, he had judged ecclesiastical disputes, whether directly or through episcopal councils summoned on his authority; he had exiled bishops, seized Church property and forbidden religious meetings. If the Church had acquired a protector, that protector was also its master.

Much of the history of the remainder of the fourth century in northwest Africa is obscure; but Donatism went from strength to strength. The Donatists proselytized abroad, formed alliances with the eastern bishops against St Athanasius of Egypt, who was backed by Rome, and even recruited in Rome, where they supported a schismatic Donatist bishopric for a hundred years. They could thus claim with some justification that they too were 'Catholic', in the sense of universal, not merely provincial. They attracted many of the educated; they acquired wealth; and they built enormous churches – the most celebrated of which is the great Donatist foundation at Tébessa.

Remains of Christian basilica at Henchir El Kousset, near Kasserine, Tunisia

Just as, in the golden age of the second century, rival municipalities had vied with each other to create finer cities, so in the fourth the rival Churches struggled to outdo their opponents in the size and splendour of their

---

1 Constantine was now in a position to play a leading role in the Arian controversy which was threatening to disrupt the east. In the event, he took the chair at the Council of Nicaea in 325, and is credited with making a significant amendment to the Nicene creed. He was a convert of barely thirteen years' standing, with no theological training; he had not even been baptized. It was a notable triumph for a layman.

178

monuments. There was a difference: the cities had for the most part been built by rich private donors while the Churches must have been largely financed out of the pockets of the comparatively poor, for, until the end of Roman times and in spite of the patronage of the Emperors, most rich families remained pagan. And some of the finest basilicas in North Africa were built by the Donatists in Numidia – at Tébessa, for instance, where the ruins of the church are as impressive as anything else in the city, and at Timgad, where a total of seventeen churches have been discovered – more than the number of public baths. Even small places often had two or more, though it is not usually possible to tell which denomination erected them; all villages so far excavated in southern Numidia prove to have had at least one. Many Christian mosaics have been uncovered: mosaics cruder in workmanship than those of the classical period, and far removed in spirit – the figures front-facing, hieratic, symbolic rather than naturalistic – awakening echoes of the non-Roman workmanship of the votive tablets once dedicated to Saturn.

THE RISE OF TERRORISM

By AD 330 the Donatists could muster two hundred and seventy bishops. Their strength was such that, in that year, they seized the basilica which the Emperor had built for the Catholics at Cirta (now renamed Constantine in his honour) – and kept it, in spite of Catholic protests. Constantine merely gave the Catholics money to build themselves a new one. However, Donatus did not have everything his own way. When, some ten years after Constantine's death in AD 337, he appealed to his son, the Emperor Constans, for full recognition of the rightness of his cause, the two notaries sent to re-investigate the matter, Paul and Macarius, sided firmly with the Catholics. The Donatists rose in revolt, and found themselves being persecuted more harshly than they had been thirty years before. One Numidian bishop who had raised a private army among the Donatist peasantry was besieged and massacred with his followers in his own basilica; another bishop, who became one of the great martyrs of the Donatist Church, was humiliated and executed, and his followers were flogged; riots at Carthage were suppressed by Roman troops; Donatus himself was exiled. Although this persecution did not last long it inflamed enmity. For decades afterwards, Donatist apologists stirred up the faithful with reminders of the *tempora Macariana*.

Donatus continued to lead the schism from exile until his death in AD 355 and within a few years the Donatists were as strong as before. They continued to bear witness not so much against the State (they did not hesitate to appeal to the pagan Emperor Julian) as against the world, in the persons of the imperial administrators – almost wholly recruited from and identical with the great landowning class.

The Catholics, too, offered them plenty of ammunition; the Church hierarchy appears to have been as corrupt as the secular administration, devoting more time to money-lending and intrigue than to their calling. The Donatists' hopes were revived when Julian the Apostate succeeded the sons of Constantine as Emperor in AD 361. Almost his first action was to restore exiled Christian leaders of every sect all over the Empire, and if his aim was to create discord among them he succeeded. The surviving Donatist ring-leaders exiled with Donatus appealed to him and were granted back all the property which had been confiscated from them in AD 347. It proved the signal for an outbreak of religious warfare – fuelled, no doubt, by the value of what was at stake. The Donatists, half drunk with triumph, set upon their Catholic adversaries in a frenzy of revenge – killing, humiliating, pillaging, looting. Two Donatist bishops led an armed gang in an assault on a Catholic church in Numidia and slaughtered two deacons. In Mauretania, gangs led by Donatist bishops virtually sacked the city of Tipasa. Many Catholics, terrified, turned Donatist themselves. The extremists were in control.

The religious hatreds of the 340s, feeding upon social inequality and rural poverty, had led to the rise of a new phenomenon: footloose bands of itinerant peasants, both men and women, who were fanatically devoted to the Donatist cause – and, it seemed, to freeing slaves and reversing the established order. They soon acquired the name of *circumcelliones* – whether because they congregated round the martyrs' shrines, or *cellae rusticanae*, attached to so many of the Donatist churches in Numidia, or because they were landless labourers temporarily attached every harvest-time to the barns – *cellae* – is still disputed. Were they similar in origin to the harvest teams of which the celebrated citizen of Mactar had been a hard-working member, their numbers swelled by grossly oppressed labourers and tenants of the *latifundia* of Numidia and Mauretania? Or were they primarily wandering ascetics, a genuine religious movement? Even St Augustine, although he deplored their activities, was to compare them to monks, and allow their womenfolk the term *sanctimoniales*. Either way, to such men and women Donatism, with its detestation of the established order, and its invitation to martyrdom, made a strong appeal. It would have suited the Donatist leaders, when their rivals could call on the army, to put such forces into the field against them. Neither the Donatists, however, nor the secular authorities were able to keep these bands under control and it is likely that at least some of their outbreaks were provoked by official attempts to settle them on the land.

They had their own rude disciplines and communal organization, their own rituals (including drunken orgies), their own battle-cries – of which *Deo laudes* was the most characteristic – and even their own style of dress, a rough habit. They appear to have made regular pilgrimages to martyrs' shrines, and recent archaeology has turned up what appear to be dwellings and storage places for grain and olives associated with such shrines. Perhaps that was where the local villages gave them food and shelter on their journeys. 'They lived as robbers,' as St Augustine – a partial witness – later put it, 'died as *circumcelliones* and were honoured as martyrs.'

They actively courted martyrdom; if a religious skirmish was not available, they would challenge passing travellers to stand and kill them, or be killed; occasionally whole groups would throw themselves over a cliff into salt lakes, or burn themselves alive in an ecstatic fervour. They exerted a terrorist pressure on the hated landlords and usurers; they laid waste villas and churches, sometimes independently, sometimes led by the wilder Donatist clergy; they prevented the collection of debts and had been known to force rich men out of their carriages in favour of their own slaves, and make them run behind. They could be compared to the outlaws of Sherwood Forest, operating their own kind of rough, Robin Hood justice against the sheriff's men and the feudal barons.

The pagan Julian's reign was brief. With the advent of a new Emperor, State and Catholic Church were once more united in persecuting the Donatists and trying, in vain, to stamp out the *circumcelliones*. Even the Donatists were alarmed at their excesses; one Donatist bishop disowned them, and went into schism with several colleagues. And the great Parmenian, who was Donatist bishop of Carthage from AD 363 to AD 391, never countenanced violence. But they were not so easily got rid of; half a century later, St Augustine's letters are full of them. And to make matters worse, the unhappy province was now consigned to the care of a *comes* who, for corruption and greed, rivalled the most iniquitous governors of the Roman Republic against whom Cicero had once inveighed.

THE REBELLION OF FIRMUS

The story of Count Romanus, which has come down to us in the pages of Ammianus Marcellinus, eloquently exemplifies the horrors which had overtaken the imperial administration. His arrival unfortunately coincided with the devastation, after centuries of peace and prosperity, of the city lands of Leptis Magna by the tribe of the Austuriani. It was the first time any tribes had struck in such strength from this part of the desert.

Romanus's first duty was to protect the provinces under his command; yet when the citizens of Leptis appealed to him he held them up to ransom, demanding payment in advance of full provisions and four thousand camels. Having had their lands laid waste, the citizens were unable to meet these demands, and Romanus simply took the army away and left them to their fate. The Austuriani raided Tripolitania twice more, emboldened by the lack of opposition; olive trees and vines were cut down. The

---

1 Or possibly 400: some authorities believe 4,000 to be an impossibly large number.

three cities (Sabratha, Oea, Leptis Magna) never recovered, and Leptis itself seems to have been more or less deserted within half a century.

But this neglect of duty, shameful though it was, was not what prompted Ammianus Marcellinus to record that 'even Justice herself has wept'. After Romanus's first desertion – he may indeed have depended on supplies which failed to arrive, or genuinely lacked money to pay his soldiers – the people of Tripolitania sent envoys to the Emperor to complain. The Emperor sent a commissioner to enquire into the matter, and money to pay Romanus's army. Romanus, however, used the money to bribe the commissioner to give a false report to the Emperor. This done, the original envoys and other leading citizens of Leptis were sentenced to death for having made unjustified complaints against Romanus. When the truth emerged ten years later (a compromising letter was discovered in Romanus's papers), although the guilty commissioner committed suicide, Romanus himself escaped punishment.

Romanus's fiscal administration, based on Carthage, was all of a piece with his notions of justice, and led to the most serious uprising which the Romans had had to face since the revolt of Tacfarinas early in the first century. In AD 372 his inordinate tax demands and the way in which his troops lived off the land – Ammianus Marcellinus maintained that his devastations were worse than those of the barbarians – provoked into rebellion a romanized native chieftain in the Kabylie mountains south-east of Algiers. This was Firmus, who belonged to the powerful Jubaleni tribe,[1] who had become romanized landowners, and responsible for providing a good deal of corn for Rome – but who also retained some of the prestige which had belonged to the old princes of Numidia. Firmus quickly found allies among the Donatist peasantry of the highlands, and his revolt spread rapidly as far as Calama (Guelma) in the east, and west to the plain of the River Chélif beyond Caesarea (Cherchel). The insurgents proclaimed Firmus king.

The revolt failed. Although one of Firmus's brothers captured Caesarea and held out there for three years, the rebellion was finally overcome by one of the great soldiers of the later Roman Empire, the *comes* Theodosius. Firmus himself was halted at the walls of the Catholic city of Tipasa, whose citizens celebrated their victory by adroitly attributing it to the miraculous intervention of a thirteen-year-old Catholic martyr.[2]

The Donatists could now be represented not merely as erring schismatics, but as traitors. Yet the persecution which followed was brief, for the new *vicarius Africae*, although an imperial official, was himself a

---

1 The Jubaleni tribe were perhaps descended from King Juba – or both had adopted the name of an African god.
2 St Salsa's ruined basilica can still be seen on Tipasa's rosy cliffs. The supposed corpse of the saint has, however, turned out to be that of a woman in her sixties.

Basilica of St Salsa, built in the fourth or fifth century AD, at Tipasa,
Algeria

convinced Donatist and the Catholics were naturally unable to enforce the
regulations. Both sides were led by moderate men; the passions aroused
over the election of Caecilian had long since faded, and a generation had
passed since the *tempora Macariana*. Both sides seem to have settled down
to live in peace if not harmony. The Catholics, though they had the law on
their side, were still at a moral disadvantage. The most distinguished
Christian in the diocese of Africa was the Donatist theologian Tyconius;
when his thinking took him beyond the accepted Donatist position towards
the Catholic belief that the Church must be a mixture of wheat and tares,
to be separated only by God on the Day of Judgement, and Parmenian felt
obliged to excommunicate him, it never occurred to Tyconius that he
should join the Catholics.

THE REBELLION OF GILDO

While religious controversy preoccupied the provinces of Africa, the
Empire itself had other, more serious problems to face. During the fourth
century it had become impossible any longer to keep the barbarian tribes
of northern Europe outside the Empire, even by withdrawing from the
frontier lands. In the middle years of the century, when Constantine's sons
were on the throne, Gaul was ravaged by the Franks and the Alamans.

183

During the reign of Valens, in the late 370s, the Visigoths had to be permitted to settle peacefully within the Danube frontier. Even Theodosius the Great (AD 379–95), the last really effective Roman Emperor with a tough military and social policy, was obliged to allot yet more territory to tribal settlements; and his death ushered in the permanent division of the Empire, and the long minorities of his two young sons, Honorius in the western Empire and Arcadius in the east.

It was Honorius's guardian, the brilliant Vandal Stilicho, who had to deal with Gildo's rebellion barely twenty years after that of Firmus. Once more, it was the Jubaleni tribe which set in train the events which brought down on the Donatists the vengeance of the State; but this time, the Catholics were able to inflict a moral defeat on them as well.

The Jubaleni, in the shape of Firmus's brother Gildo, had been restored to imperial favour. Gildo, who had fought for the Romans against his brother, was appointed *comes Africae,* and one of his daughters was married into the imperial family. But after a decade of loyalty to Rome, ambition reasserted itself. In AD 397 Gildo held up the corn supplies for Rome. This could not be ignored by Rome, for Africa was Italy's only large supplier, since the founding of Constantinople as capital of the eastern Empire and the diversion there of Egypt's annual corn harvest. With most of the western provinces in the hands of the Germanic invaders, who were poised, in the person of Alaric, king of the Goths, to invade Italy itself, the western imperial court, now at Ravenna in northen Italy, was more than ever dependent on its African granaries for food.

Gildo was declared an enemy of the State, and this time the Donatists were made to seem deeply implicated. The most intransigent and fanatical of their bishops, Optatus of Thamugadi (Timgad), had acquired Gildo's support in a private quarrel with an offshoot of Donatism, had summoned into being his own army of *circumcelliones* – now equipped with swords as well as their traditional staves – and was already (according to St Augustine) 'scorching all Africa with tongues of flame'. His new cathedral was the most magnificent in Africa, he himself had an almost royal power, and he was threatening to convert the province by force to Donatism. But his reliance on Gildo meant that, if Gildo failed, Optatus would fail with him.

Gildo proved his own worst enemy. In a family feud he murdered two nephews, and his brother fled to Italy where he was given troops to take to Africa to avenge his sons. Gildo's army was utterly defeated near Theveste, and Gildo himself died a fugitive – leaving behind him estates so enormous that their confiscation by the State required the appointment of a special governor, *comes patrimonii Gildoniaci.* Bishop Optatus was executed, and although the Donatists awarded him the martyr's crown, at last, after nearly a century, their grip on North Africa was about to slacken.

By their association with Gildo, the Donatists had condemned themselves in imperial eyes as the party of disunity and rebellion. From now on, the Catholics could count on the political as well as the religious support of the government. They could also count on the support of new allies – the many Roman aristocrats who were at this time fleeing from the perils in Italy to seek refuge on their estates in Africa. The newcomers knew little of Donatism, and had their own motives for wanting a quiet, conforming peasantry.

The balance of power was shifting. And the Catholics now had, in the person of Bishop Augustine of Hippo, a tireless champion.

Baptismal font from Timgad, with fine geometric mosaic

185

12

THE GREATEST AFRICAN

St Augustine belongs to the world. His teaching on free will and pre-destination, on original sin and the operation of God's grace – largely inspired by his attack on the heresy of the Welsh monk Pelagius, who believed that Christians could earn salvation by virtuous living – was enshrined in countless pamphlets and, above all, in *The City of God*. This book, which he began to write at the age of fifty-eight and finished in his seventies, rapidly became one of the most influential of all theological works. It helped to turn the talents of the most gifted men of his own and succeeding generations away from secular affairs and towards mon-asticism and the organization of the Church; even a millennium later, it served to inspire the most extreme heretics of the Reformation. It earned St Augustine the title of one of the Four Doctors of the Church. Yet during his life much of his energy was absorbed in combating the comparatively unimportant provincial heresy of Donatism at home in Africa.

He was the son of a Christian mother and a pagan father, Patricius, who belonged to the class of *curiales*, or minor gentry, which suffered most from the depredations of fourth-century tax-gatherers. The family was never well-off; Patricius was obliged to borrow money from a richer friend in order to send his son to university in Carthage. But by upbringing and association – although his native town, Thagaste, was thoroughly Libyan in its origins – St Augustine belonged to the official classes which, however much they themselves hated the imperial administration, nevertheless could not afford to sympathize with the peasantry off whose backs they lived. It never occurred to St Augustine to condemn slavery. He had only a smattering of the local dialect – or *lingua punica*, a Semitic language related to Hebrew still widely spoken in the countryside – which served further to distance him from the rural population. And his education, his position and his great intellectual gifts enabled him to satisfy a natural taste for the company of other educated men, not only ecclesiastics but rich landowners, proconsuls and *comites* who belonged to the great world of Africa's Roman masters. Since his Christianity was the approved variety, they in turn could safely give him their friendship.

It might have been otherwise. His birthplace, Thagaste (Souk Ahras) in Numidia, had formerly been – as far as its Christian community was concerned – wholly Donatist. Catholicism probably made its first converts there during the *tempora Macariana*, in the decade before his birth in AD 354. Thus his mother, who bore the un-Roman name of Monica, was a Catholic, and not a Donatist like some other members of her family. Had she been a Donatist, the course of her son's career might well have been very different – and with it perhaps the history of the western Church. Yet African Church history would probably have been much the same: though St Augustine spent half a lifetime fighting Donatism he died believing that he had failed – as indeed, in any but the most technical sense, he had. Donatism survived alongside Catholicism until both were vanquished together by the soldiers of Islam two hundred years after his death. He was to deprive it finally of its intellectual respectability, but he never broke its emotional hold. The name of its founder remained one to conjure with in Africa – more so than his own.

PROGRESS OF A SOUL

The young Augustine was imaginative, shrewd and ardent. He was as African as Tertullian had been – as far removed from Roman *gravitas* as he was from the cosmopolitan sophistication of Constantinople. His spiritual progress in childhood and early manhood is the best documented of antiquity; his *Confessions*, written when he was in his late forties as a kind of open letter to his many friends, ranks as one of the three or four most honest self-exposures ever written. If the later chapters, with their profound and penetrating analysis of the nature of time, reveal the author's gifts as a philosopher, the more famous autobiographical chapters show him to have had the psychological perceptiveness, the eye for significant detail and passion for human truth of a great artist. He was also well aware – fifteen hundred years before Freud – of the existence of the subconscious. In middle age, the ascetic in him finally suppressed the artist; but the great imaginative structure of *The City of God* owes a debt to that other, younger Augustine.

His autobiography makes plain that he had a genius for loving and being loved. His relationship with his mother was possessive to a degree that would raise eyebrows today (his father and any brother and sister he scarcely mentions), yet it never prevented him from loving others – the childhood friend whose death caused him to hate 'all the places we had known together, because he was not in them'; the concubine with whom he lived faithfully for fifteen years, and whom he took with him to Italy; the son she bore him, in whom he felt such fatherly pride and whose death as a young man he could scarcely bear to mention. His grief for his lost friend and his concubine was such that he could not even bring himself to record their names. St Monica's own death, on the eve of their return home after several years in Italy, forms one of the most moving passages in the *Confessions*.

Few have written more passionately of the joys of the flesh than Augustine – even though, having turned his back on them, he harps on their sinfulness with all the over-enthusiasm of the reformed rake; or more eloquently of the pleasures of having like-minded companions with whom to share the study of philosophy.

The capacity to give and inspire affection must make up for the absence in St Augustine's life of the kind of incident or behaviour which the hagiographer can set up as a pattern of Christian living. For even as a Christian and a bishop he could behave extremely badly. Though never much of a scholar in the austerest sense of the word, he had dared to offer criticism to the far more distinguished St Jerome on a point of scholarship; yet was forgiven. He dared to make military suggestions to Count Boniface, the most eminent general of the day, and utter abusive reproaches about the widowed Count's remarriage; yet remained a friend. Without shame he allowed his richest friends, the Roman St Melania and her husband Pinianus, to be forcibly enrolled as parishioners of Hippo, where the congregation had their eyes on their wealth, and then made no attempt to apologize when the visitors remonstrated; yet they soon restored Augustine to their favour. It has been suggested that this undoubted charm had not a little to do with his adopting the doctrine of salvation by grace and predestination. In his own life he received much love that in justice he deserved to lose.

AUGUSTINE'S EARLY LIFE

Augustine started his school career in his home town in the wooded hills of central Numidia; but Thagaste was a small, unimportant place, and at the age of eleven or so he was sent to school in Madauros, some twenty or thirty miles distant, where Apuleius had been born and brought up. Augustine's hatred of school is well known. He detested 'one and one make two, two and two make four', and he failed to acquire any competence in Greek. At the age of sixteen he spent a year at home – the year of the celebrated theft of a neighbour's pears which looms so large in the *Confessions* – while his father struggled to raise money to send him on to Carthage. There he won prizes, more friends and mistresses, and indulged a passion for the theatre and the circus.

Clever boys of his day became teachers, or went into the Church. Augustine – who to his mother's anger had been converted to the Manichaean heresy[1] – became a teacher of rhetoric, first in Thagaste for a year, and then

---

1 Augustine was to be a Manichaean 'hearer' for nine years.

for the next six or seven in Carthage. He was not a very successful one. He could not keep order in the unruly schools of the capital, and his lack of Greek was a handicap. Then, at the age of twenty-nine, he decided to try his luck in Rome. Accompanied by his concubine and their son, Adeodatus, he gave his protesting mother the slip and embarked for Italy.

Once in Rome, he had a struggle to make ends meet. He acquired some private pupils, but he was fortunate after a year to be recommended for a post as professor of rhetoric in Milan. There, he fell under the influence of St Ambrose, the princely bishop of Milan, and one day in a garden, in August 386, when he was thirty-two, after a 'deluge of tears' and a providential reading from the Epistles of St Paul, he experienced his famous conversion. 'It was as though the light of confidence flooded into my heart and all the darkness of doubt was dispelled.'

By now his mother had joined him in Milan – where almost her first action had been to find her son an heiress for a wife. Augustine's concubine was sent home to Africa: such a double standard was entirely acceptable in the educated Roman world, but it was 'a blow which crushed my heart to bleeding,' he wrote later.

There was a brief period living in a borrowed country house near Lake Como with his mother, son and a few friends – the heiress by now given up – while he began to write the first of his philosophical works, before he was baptized by Bishop Ambrose in 387.

He returned to Thagaste in AD 388 – St Monica died at Ostia on the way back – and there founded a celibate community. The monastic movement had started in Egypt a century earlier; Augustine introduced it to Africa. It was a long-held dream. Even before his conversion he and his friends in Italy had discussed the possibility of pooling their possessions and living a communal life 'away from the crowd'. They wanted their womenfolk to share it, however; but 'when we began to ask ourselves whether the women would agree to the plan, all our carefully made arrangements collapsed and broke to pieces in our hands and were discarded. Once more we turned to our sighs and groans.' But celibacy, once accepted, enabled the dream to be fulfilled. For the rest of his life, Augustine lived as a member of a monastic community.

But the life of withdrawal from the world did not last long. By AD 391 Augustine's anti-heretical writings had already brought him a certain fame, and at the instance of a high official who wished to meet him in the expectation of being converted, he went to Hippo Regius (Annaba), on the north coast. Unhappily for him, the bishop of Hippo was an aged Greek, with little Latin and less local *patois*, whose congregation felt the need for a younger, livelier priest who spoke Latin. Seeing in Augustine the man they wanted, they ordained him by force. Augustine was deeply distressed; but a sacrament, however given, had to be accepted as the Will of God. He must have remembered that beloved pagan friend of his youth, who, baptized during a coma, nevertheless rebuked the young Augustine's mockery and died a believing Christian.

Thereafter Augustine preached daily at Hippo in the bishop's place; and he became bishop himself in AD 395. It was just the time when the Donatists, with the backing of the *comes* Gildo, were at the zenith of their power and influence. In the same year, the Catholics suffered a serious loss: the Donatists kidnapped an able young Catholic lawyer of Constantine called Petilian, and submitted him to forcible re-baptism. Like Augustine, Petilian felt there was no appeal against what appeared to be God's Will, and thenceforth his considerable gifts were devoted to the schism which he now believed to be the true Church. As the Donatist bishop of Constantine, Petilian was to be Augustine's principal adversary.

THE CRUSADE AGAINST THE DONATISTS

Augustine's prodigious energies could no longer be devoted solely to the things of the spirit. The role of bishop required a man of action; and though he managed to write hundreds of sermons and pamphlets, and hundreds of private letters, the things of the world demanded his attention. He turned out to be a natural administrator, with a flair for leadership and negotiation. Hippo was not an important diocese, but Augustine became the closest adviser of the primate of Africa, Bishop Aurelius of Carthage, and, in effect, the principal advocate of the Catholic cause. Together he and Aurelius strove to take advantage of the failure of the revolt of Gildo against the Roman administration, and the confusion into which the Donatist party, which had been implicated in the revolt, had been thrown. The re-conversion of the Donatists became a major part of Augustine's life's work. That he failed to achieve this after a decade of vigorous propaganda – debates, a stream of tracts, correspondence with individual Donatist clergy – led him to advocate the strengthening of right with might. Like the Emperor Constantine, he came, with less and less reluctance, to believe in the physical oppression of heretics, taking as his text 'compel them to come in'.

At first, he believed that 'we must act only by words, fight only by arguments, and prevail by force of reason'. It was his experience of the world which changed that opinion; for instance, 'my own town, which although it was once wholly on the side of Donatus was brought over to the Catholic unity by the fear of the imperial edicts ... There were so many others which were mentioned to me by name, that from the facts themselves, I was made to own that to this matter the word of Scripture might be understood as applying, "Give opportunity to a wise man and he will become wiser."' As W.H.C. Frend has pointed out, that 'opportunity' was coercion, 'and this was not so mild as Augustine would lead his readers to think'. It included torture. Although Donatism was an obscure provincial sect, with no progeny, its effects, by changing St Augustine's opinion on this one point, were incalculable. A thousand years later, the perpetrators of the Inquisition could lean on the authority of this Doctor of the Church.

After the death of Gildo the Catholic party did all it could to get the Donatists – so far still only schismatics – declared heretics, so that anti-heresy legislation already on the statute books could be enforced against them. They also tried to set their own house in order. Aurelius of Carthage inaugurated annual episcopal councils to invigorate the hierarchy (it was at the first of these that Augustine had made his name in debate), and bishops from outlying parts spent almost as much time on the road and in Carthage as in their dioceses. A council of AD 401 appointed missionaries to be sent out into the field to re-convert Donatists and other non-Catholic Christians. Where possible, bishoprics were filled by monks from the Augustinian monastery which Augustine had by now founded at Hippo; and Augustine began to recommend Catholic landowners to convert their Donatist peasantry by force.

The Donatists, although on the defensive, were not yet beaten and the scandals on the Catholic side, where embezzlement, simony, quarrels and even sex scandals were rife, fortified their belief in the rightness of their cause. Harassment and persecution were only what they expected; and had not Tyconius written, 'In proportion as the just are persecuted, the unjust feast and rejoice'? Persecution was the proof of virtue. They fought back. One Donatist bishop boldly re-baptized eighty families on an estate virtually on the border of Bishop Augustine's diocese. There was much violence, aggravated by gangs of *circumcelliones* who attacked the villas of Augustine's rich friends. Petilian accused the Catholics of being butchers; to Bishop Augustine's chagrin, members of his own congregation could reel off his rival's words from memory. Petilian also took pleasure in reminding the world of Augustine's Manichee past. The Catholic bishop Possidius of Calama (Guelma), later St Augustine's biographer, was actually captured by *circumcelliones*; and when Augustine tried to get the rival Donatist bishop of Calama (Guelma) to pay a fine of 10 lb in gold, prescribed by law, he failed – even when he had the sentence confirmed by the proconsul himself.

In AD 405, the Emperor Honorius proclaimed an Edict of Unity, whereby Donatism was at long last declared a heresy. All Donatist property belonged to the Catholics; their meetings were forbidden, those who permitted them were to be flogged; Donatists were not allowed to make wills, receive legacies or enter into contracts. But the Donatists still did not give in. Indeed, one Catholic bishop took his entire flock over to Donatism, and two towns in Byzacena turned Donatist. Even in Hippo, their pamphlets continued to appear, and the exiled Primian and Petilian, undaunted, took their side of the story to the western imperial court at Ravenna. The

Emperor gave them permission to return to Africa, and when Stilicho was murdered in AD 408, Donatist hopes revived – and with them their efforts. The unfortunate Augustine stood by helpless while a gang of *circumcelliones* introduced a Donatist bishop into Hippo; some of his own clergy defected.

Typically, however, the indefatigable Augustine was already in touch with Stilicho's murderer, from whom he obtained promises of aid; and fortunately for him the new proconsul – another Donatus, himself an African – was an ardent Catholic, having been converted from Donatism. But when the proconsul, ready to suppress Donatism by any means, introduced the death penalty, Augustine protested: 'You will help us greatly ... if you were to repress this vain and proud sect in a manner which does not let it feel that it is suffering for truth and justice.'

That is the key to Augustine's policy. Throughout these years, though he had come round to advocating the use of force, he believed that it should be seen to be legal – one reason he was so keen to have the Donatists defined as heretics. But, though he wanted the Donatists to be legally in the wrong, he was very anxious not to make martyrs of them. The death sentence was the last thing he wanted. Nor did he always want other penalties exacted: although he took the case against the Donatist bishop of Calama to the proconsul, it was primarily to get a *legal* verdict against him.

It is also why he was determined to get the Donatists to a conference, so that the Catholics might meet them in debate and prove, to their faces, that they were both legally and morally in the wrong. He wanted the world to know it; he also wanted the Donatists to know it, and be seen to know it. The Edict of Unity of AD 405 had been a legal victory, which as usual had been enforced half-heartedly; what the Catholics needed now was a moral and psychological victory. In AD 410, Possidius of Calama and another Catholic bishop were sent to Ravenna to plead with the Emperor for a last effort against the Donatists.

THE SACK OF ROME

Honorius meanwhile had serious troubles on his hands. Alaric, king of the Goths, had been defeated at the time of Gildo's revolt, but had reformed his armies and invaded Italy itself at the opening of the new century. Alaric had been followed within a few years by another barbarian chieftain, whom Stilicho had also beaten back. But the barbarians were not to be held off for long, for they were being pressed on by the Huns at their backs; and at the end of AD 406 the Rhine frontier had been breached for ever by a great horde of Alans, Vandals, Suevians and Burgundians, who had poured into Gaul. By AD 409 the Vandals, among others, were in Spain.

192

Eventually Alaric seized another chance: in August AD 410 he took and looted Rome.

The sack of the Eternal City was the most traumatic event in the history of the later Roman Empire, and haunted the imagination of generations far in the future, as a symbol of kingdoms come to dust; it also provoked *The City of God*, St Augustine's majestic defence of Christians against the charge of being responsible for the disaster. Yet it lasted only three days. Before the end of the month, Alaric turned his attention to southern Italy – and the prospect of invading Africa to seize territory for his people there. A severe storm sank or scattered most of Alaric's fleet, and he died almost immediately afterwards. But it was a portent; in twenty years Africa was to succumb to another, and greater, barbarian army.

Bishop Possidius and his companion were too set on their own concerns to worry about the implications of what was happening in Italy. And in spite of the danger from the Goths, Honorius found time to listen to the two African churchmen. The very day after Alaric entered Rome, the Emperor sent a message to the *comes Africae* Heraclian: heresy was to be put down in 'blood and proscription'. He also sent Count Marcellinus to preside at a conference which was to settle the issues between the two sides once and for all. The result was not in much doubt: Marcellinus was a friend to whom St Augustine had already dedicated one work, and to whom he was to dedicate *The City of God*.

A CATHOLIC VICTORY

The council which met at Carthage in June AD 411 was the decisive encounter between the Catholics and Donatists. It was the only occasion on which Augustine and Petilian met face to face. Bishops of both parties were summoned to attend from all over North Africa. The lengthy roll-call was punctuated by acrimonious accusations: Donatists frequently acknowledged their Catholic opposite numbers with the words, 'I recognize my persecutor'; once there was an accusation of murder; and one signature was alleged to be that of a corpse. Finally, however, the Catholics mustered two hundred and eighty-six names, the Donatists two fewer.

The vital session lasted from dawn to dusk on 8th June; the Donatists remained standing the whole day long, having refused at a previous session to sit down with sinners. Petilian strove to keep the debate on the identity of the true Church, but was driven by Augustine to discussing the momentous events of a century before, when the Donatists had failed to prove that Caecilian was wrongly consecrated bishop of Carthage. The verdict both of the Emperor and of two episcopal councils had gone against them then; they had failed to abide by it, thus becoming the authors of disunity. They had no new evidence which would invalidate Caecilian's consecration; and Count Marcellinus's decision, given by candlelight that very night, went against them now. The Catholic party considered itself vindicated.

Six months later, Honorius made Donatism a criminal offence. But as usual it was one thing to announce proscription and punishment, another to carry it out. Although Augustine had the satisfaction of driving his rival bishop, Macrobius, out of Hippo, Macrobius found alternative employment as leader of a gang of *circumcelliones*. Donatist bishops remained in charge of distant Numidian and Mauretanian dioceses; Petilian, though exiled from Constantine, continued to call Donatist councils; new Donatist priests were ordained. Yet the enforcement was firmer this time; the Roman authorities gave the Catholics better support. Count Marcellinus seems to have visited Numidia where he held trials of refractory Donatists – although, following Bishop Augustine's advice, he commuted the extreme penalty to hard labour. Augustine himself at once published a digest of the proceedings of the conference for the instruction of laymen, and backed it up by preaching in Constantine and other places.

Augustine's personal intervention failed to dislodge the tough incumbents in distant cities such as Caesarea and Thamugadi (Timgad), but Donatism seems gradually to have weakened its hold on the cities of Africa Proconsularis where it was easier for officialdom to enforce its decrees. Augustine hardly mentions it in the last decade of his life. But the future did not lie with the cities: and Donatism remained strong in the countryside, where its roots were nourished by the fundamental antipathy of the rural African to the ordered values of the classical world of the Mediterranean.

THE VANDAL INVASION

The province faced other perils. Certain mountain tribes of the interior and other tribes in the south were now a constant source of anxiety. In a Constitution of AD 409, the Emperor had addressed the vicar of Africa: 'We have learnt that the lands ceded to *confederates* by the far-seeing humanity of our ancestors, in order to assure the upkeep and protection of the *limes* and the *fossatum*, are sometimes occupied by ordinary tenants. If these satisfy their greedy desires by occupying such lands, let them know that they must dedicate their devoted services to the upkeep of the ditch and the guarding of the *limes*, like those that our ancestors proposed for this duty. If this condition is not fulfilled, let them know that the most elementary justice will be to transfer these concessions [to others] so that these precautions may continue to be observed ...' It was one of a stream of orders and decrees intended to prevent the North African provinces from falling apart at the seams. But although the bureaucracy kept its eye on everything, it was with less and less effect.

However, it was not from the desert or the mountains that the conquerors came. In AD 416, the king of the Visigoths, who had finally reached Spain after their long journey from the Danube through Greece and Italy, cast speculative eyes on North Africa as a final home for his people. Though he did not come – his fleet, like Alaric's six years earlier, was destroyed in a storm – it was to be another Arian people settled in Spain, the Vandals, who crossed the straits of Gibraltar. The Vandals invaded Africa thirteen years later – not merely an army, but tens of thousands of men, women and children – perhaps eighty thousand, if Victor of Vita is to be believed, or even more if the figure did not include women and children. Once landed, in August, AD 429, they marched virtually unchecked, their ships keeping them company along the coast, to the frontier of Africa Proconsularis. Here the *comes* Boniface (one of 'the last of the Romans' according to the sixth-century historian Procopius) turned to face them with his army, but it was like commanding a rising tide to ebb. He retreated, after a resounding defeat, to Hippo. He held out there as long as fourteen months only because the Vandals were not used to siege warfare. The Empress Regent, Galla Placidia, eventually arranged for reinforcements to be sent to Count Boniface from Italy and the east; but his new army was beaten even more decisively, and Boniface retired to seek other laurels in Italy.

The Vandal king Gaiseric made Hippo his first capital, settled his people in Numidia, and negotiated a treaty with the Emperor, whom he allowed to keep the western provinces of Mauretania. Technically a *foederatus*, he was actually king in all but name. In AD 439, he seized Carthage: the citizens were cheering at the circus as he approached. North Africa was not ruled from Italy again, until the Italian victory over the Turks in 1911–12.

The refugees who had fled to Africa during Alaric's invasions of Italy had turned tail and fled back to Italy, or to the provinces of the east. They were joined by thousands of citizens of Roman Africa, those who had most to fear from a change of masters. One rich senator of Carthage was reduced to beggary in exile before finding a modest post in the imperial service in another province; his daughter was sold into slavery in Syria by merchants who had bought her from the Vandals. Her story is known from a letter written by a bishop in Syria, entrusting another bishop to return her to her father's care. Hundreds of exiles were not so fortunate. Nor were those who failed to get away.

* * *

During the siege of Hippo, in the August of AD 430, St Augustine had died, less concerned over the dismemberment of Roman Africa than over the conversion to Christianity of one obscure physician, and the penitential psalms which he had had inscribed in huge letters on the walls of his cell, so that he might read them as he lay dying. The City of God awaited him.

13

THE VANDAL INTERREGNUM

At the beginning of the fifth century, before the Vandal invasion, north-west Africa was the only Roman territory in the west which had not yet suffered barbarian incursions from eastern or northern Europe. In spite of the miseries of so many of its inhabitants, its fields continued to yield their generous harvests, its olive trees produced huge quantities of oil, its vineyards and orchards were heavy with fruit, and its pastures still supported horses and sheep and cattle. It is true that a survey of Honorius in AD 422 suggests that the acreage under cultivation had shrunk, perhaps considerably; but if some land had been deserted it was only the most unproductive, and what remained under cultivation was still splendidly fruitful. The unfailing African sun and the scrupulous upkeep by a hard-working peasantry of the irrigation works which utilized every drop of water combined to sustain the province's reputation for fertility. No wonder Alaric the Goth in ravaged Italy, and the Visigoths and Vandals in disputed Spain, had seen it as a promised land.

The Vandals did not come to destroy, but to settle. The atrocity stories spread by alarmed ecclesiastics tell of some of the unavoidable horrors of invasion, the consequences of thousands of newcomers living off the land. And like other conquerors the Vandals were greedy for loot. The Church was rich: like the secular landlords, it was dispossessed of its finest estates, and had to give up its plate, its gold, and treasures of all kinds. But the Vandals had no wish to cut down the olive trees or burn down the vines that were the basis of the prosperity they had every intention of enjoying themselves. In fact, vineyards and olive groves survived to amaze the army of Count Belisarius a hundred years later just as, a millennium before, other crops and orchards had amazed the army of Agathocles. The worst excesses against the civilian population were, no doubt, the private revenges wreaked by Donatists on their hated oppressors under cover of the invasion.

The union of the Roman Empire was dissolved; its genius was humbled in the dust; and armies of unknown barbarians, issuing from the frozen regions of the north, had established their victorious reign over the fairest provinces of Europe and Africa.' That was how it struck Gibbon; and certainly very large parts of the western Empire were now occupied by Germanic tribes under their own kings – Vandals in Africa, Ostrogoths in Italy, Visigoths in Spain and southern France, Burgundians in the Rhône valley, Suevi in Galicia, Franks in northern Gaul and Anglo-Saxons in Britain. But it was not quite how it seemed at the time, at least to the barbarians. Except in Britain, the forms of Roman life remained; the invaders were simply an occupying military caste, who took over the administration. With the exception of the Anglo-Saxons, they had all felt for generations the power and presence of the Mediterranean world symbolized by Rome, an immensely more sophisticated civilization whose benefits they were anxious to share. Contact had been sufficiently close for them all to be converted to Christianity during their journey to the west; a heretical, Arian Christianity, but nonetheless they were as ready as any Roman to render unto Caesar the things that were Caesar's. That included acknowledgement of the Emperor's suzerainty. Even when the last Emperor of Rome was deposed in AD 476, the barbarian kings of Europe continued to acknowledge the Roman Emperor in the east; they thought of themselves as his allies and ruled in his name. All, on entering the Roman Empire, adopted the Latin language: no Germanic words, except those borrowed later, survive in the Romance languages. All used Roman coins, and employed Roman senatorial families in the task of government. Only on the Rhine and towards the Seine and the Danube did the barbarians 'germanize' the local populations.

The Vandals in Africa were the one people who broke completely with the Empire, and that may be credited to the particular energy and ambition of their first king. Yet even Gaiseric was only a partial exception. If he dispossessed the Roman landlords in favour of his own people on a scale unknown in Gaul (where a plutocrat like Symmachus continued to run and profit from his estates), he continued to make use of the *conductores*; he persecuted the Roman Church, but installed an Arian priesthood in its place; he minted Roman coins, made Latin the official language, employed Roman engineers and architects. He and his successors built baths at Tunis and patronized Roman African rhetoricians and poets and grammarians, whose work, though much inferior to that of the great writers of the past, was Roman nonetheless. (The best poet of the Vandal period, however, spent much of his life in prison for a treasonable work in praise of the Emperor; this was Dracontius, whose *Laudes Dei* was admired in the Middle Ages and later inspired Milton's description of Paradise.) Even more interesting, Gaiseric suppressed the tribal organization of his nobles in favour of an autocracy based on the Roman model.

The romanization of the conquerors of the western Empire is not surprising, for they can be counted in tens of thousands, or at most hundreds of thousands, in populations of several millions. In Roman Africa too, the

Vandals cannot have formed more than five per cent of the total. It is true that the Romans themselves, like the Arabs later, managed to transform the people they conquered with numerically tiny forces; but the Vandals were anxious to be transformed themselves.

The Vandals took to the delights of civilization, whether as *grands seigneurs* on their new domains or as urban notables, with Teutonic enthusiasm. The Greek historian Procopius, writing after their downfall, considered them the most luxurious of all known peoples. 'The Vandals, since the time when they gained possession of Libya, used to indulge in baths, all of them, every day, and enjoyed a table abounding in all things, the sweetest and best that the earth and sea produce. And they wore gold very generally, and clothed themselves in garments [of silk], and passed their time, thus dressed, in theatres and hippodromes and in other pleasurable pursuits, and above all else in hunting. And they had dancers and mimes and all other things to hear and see which are of a musical nature or otherwise merit attention among men. And most of them dwelt in parks, which were well supplied with water and trees; and they had great numbers of banquets, and all manner of sexual pleasures were in great vogue among them.'

So the Vandals lived, as far as they could, the life of Roman grandees. They were certainly very rich: they paid no taxes on their own lands, either to their kings or to a foreign overlord, and they acquired loot not only from their new subjects, but by piracy overseas. Their new wealth, however, sapped their barbarian virtues, or so it seemed, and the fleshpots of Carthage – as seductive as they had been in St Augustine's youth – proved as enervating to their energies as King Gaiseric had feared, when he tried to close down the most notorious district of the great seaport.

A PIRATE KING

Gaiseric had kept only the most fertile parts of north-west Africa – roughly the area of modern Tunisia and eastern Algeria. No doubt the Vandals, if only from the Spanish side, also controlled the straits of Gibraltar. In theory, most of Mauretania was ruled from Constantinople, a poor exchange for the rich heartlands of the old Africa Proconsularis; and in fact the western Maghreb was soon re-occupied by the Vandals, or fell to independent Moorish kings. So the Vandal conquest cost Italy the free supplies of corn which she had enjoyed for five hundred years. 'The very soul of the Republic,' said Salvian, 'was destroyed by the capture of Africa.'

But Italy's deprivations, from the point of view of the Empire as a whole, were a comparatively minor matter. Much more serious was the threat to control of the Mediterranean by the Roman Emperors based in Constantinople. Gaiseric was not content with the enjoyment of his new kingdom. He wanted a maritime empire.

Carthage remained an extremely important port in the commercial life of the Mediterranean. Syrians, Jews, Greeks and no doubt the sharper-witted of the Carthaginian *navicularii* continued to operate fleets of merchant ships there, carrying wheat and other foodstuffs. Shipments of olive oil from north-west Africa, now the greatest oil-producing region, still found their way northwards across the Mediterranean, where it was wanted not only for cooking and cleaning but for lamps to light the interiors of the new churches of Gaul. But there was certainly a general fall-off in trade to Rome and Italy. In any case, a commercial empire was not what interested the Vandal king. He wanted quicker rewards, and found another use for Carthage's merchant marine. He became a pirate, and for the first time since the Punic Wars the straits of Sicily were no longer safe for the imperial navy.

The Empire gained a temporary respite by offering the Emperor Valentinian's daughter Eudoxia as a child-bride for Gaiseric's son Huneric. Huneric in fact already had a wife, the daughter of the king of the Visigoths; she was conveniently found 'guilty' of treason and returned to her father with her nose and ears cut off. The various barbarian kings never found it easy to form alliances among themselves; but this was an unforeseen triumph for Roman diplomacy.

Unfortunately his son's new betrothal failed to outweigh the temptations of Gaiseric's position of strength and his huge fleet. The king's thoughts turned to fresh conquest. 'Every year,' wrote Procopius, 'at the beginning of spring, Gaiseric invaded Sicily and Italy, enslaving some of the cities and razing others to the ground, and plundering everything.' Even Illyricum and the Peloponnese were not safe from his raids, and at one point he appears to have harassed his fellow barbarians in north-west Spain. He also seized, and this time occupied, the Balearic islands, Sardinia and Corsica. The western Mediterranean was soon a Vandal lake.

Gaiseric's greatest coup was something the Carthaginians had never brought off: the looting of Rome. In the summer of AD 455 he invaded Italy with an army of Vandals and Moors, and spent fourteen days in the capital collecting as much booty as he could. The authority of Pope Leo, whose personal intervention had three years earlier saved Rome from being attacked by Attila the Hun, was such that he extracted a promise from Gaiseric not to massacre the inhabitants or set the city on fire; though not enough to prevent the Vandal king carrying off the Empress and her two daughters – one of them, Eudoxia, now of age, the fiancée of Huneric. The Vandal booty included the famous seven-branched candlestick of the Jews, brought to Rome by the Emperor Titus four centuries earlier. Half the magnificent roof of gilded bronze tiles was taken from the temple of Jupiter

---

1 It was later retrieved by Count Belisarius and restored to Jerusalem, from where, ironically, it vanished for good in the Persian sack of AD 614.

on the Capitol. Gaiseric's fleet returned to Carthage loaded with treasure and slaves, except for one ship which, weighted down with statues, sank. The spoils were divided between the Vandals and the Moors. Gaiseric had discovered an admirable method of keeping the latter quiet, although by giving them a taste for gold he laid up trouble for the future.

The Empire was too weak, or too incompetent, to avenge this humiliation. In the 460s Gaiseric adroitly destroyed two vast fleets which were sent against him using the new invention 'Greek fire'. Even when he was succeeded after his death in 477 by incompetent relatives, his kingdom seemed impregnable.

THE *TABLETTES ALBERTINI*

In September AD 493, some sixty years after the Vandal conquest, a young woman called Geminia Januarilla became engaged to a man called Julianus. She lived on the *fundus Tuletianos*, an estate which was part of a larger domain in an obscure corner of Numidia, somewhere on the modern border of Algeria and Tunisia between Négrine and Gafsa; its exact location is unknown. She was a daughter of the Geminius family, whose forebear Flavius Geminius Catullinus had once owned the domain; they were the most considerable people on the *fundus*, and at the time of Geminia Januarilla's engagement were busy buying up a quantity of modest leaseholds and freeholds in the area. They were rich enough to give her a trousseau worth several hundred olive trees. It included linen and woollen clothing, sheepskin slippers and jewellery. They were also provincial enough, in spite of great-grandfather Flavius's thoroughly Roman *trinomina* (three names), for Geminia Januarilla to have a wholly Berber taste in clothing.

Her *tabella dotis*, or dowry list, from which these last details are known, is written on one of fifty-six tablets dating from the 490s known as the *tablettes Albertini*, after the distinguished historian who devoted the last decade of his life to deciphering and interpreting them. They were written with a reed quill in ink, possibly of burnt wood or dried carob, direct on to unpolished wood. Most are cedarwood; others are almond, poplar, willow or maple.

The circumstances in which they were discovered in 1928 remain mysterious. They were found by some peasants hidden in a wall or a bank, probably sixty miles south of Tébessa; they appear to have been in a sealed jar, which accounts for their remarkable state of preservation. By devious means and several hands, a few at a time, they reached a government official in Tébessa, and are now in the Musée Stéphane Gsell in Algiers.

---

1 A mixture of nitre, sulphur and naphtha set alight and fired into the air by a pump.

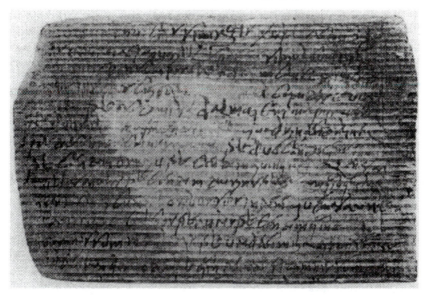

Dowry list of Geminia Januarilla – one of the *tablettes Albertini* of the
Vandal period. Now in the Stéphane Gsell Museum, Algiers

Forty-five have proved more or less legible, with the aid of photography,
and together they form some thirty-four separate documents or fragments
of documents. Most, but not all, relate to affairs on the *fundus Tuletianos*;
most, but not all, are legal documents; a large number relate to the Geminius family. Apart from Geminia Januarilla's dowry list, a table of cal-
culation and a financial account and the bill of sale of a young slave, they
are concerned with the sales of very small parcels of land or numbers of
trees; the largest sale is of thirty-seven trees only. They are, in fact, concerned with matters which could be of no interest except to the participants;
yet for some reason, though there is no obvious common subject linking
them, such as one family or one *fundus*, they were gathered together and
put, not merely into safe-keeping, but apparently into hiding. On several
counts they are among the most important documents ever found in North
Africa.

On these forty-five tablets writing from some thirty different hands
appears. Half of them contribute only an X in place of a signature; the
other fifteen write either the text or their names. Some documents were
written out by a priest or by *magistri* – leaders of the community; but others
were written by the peasant vendors. There is no sign of the work of a
professional scribe. It looks as if the *fundus Tuletianos* and its immediate
surroundings had at least fifteen people, all of whom could write their
letters and some of whom were fully literate. Since the documents are so

few, and cover such a short space of time and such a modest amount of property, these fifteen may have been only a fraction of the literate population of the domain. The language of the document is, admittedly, a debased Latin; but if the writers' schooling was rusty, it was not absent.

Here, in a remote *fundus* on the fringe of the desert in an Africa under Vandal occupation, were fifteen unimportant men who wrote lower-case cursive which can be read today. That points to something that was already a firm tradition. The parties to the documents may, of course, have been the sons of formerly prosperous people dispossessed by the Vandals, and making what shift they could on land the Vandals did not want; in which case their education is perhaps readily explained. But they may not have been; they may have learnt that writing at some small village school. Or had the priest learnt it at some city grammar school long ago, in his youth, and taught his parishioners himself? There is, alas, no evidence to show whether he was a Donatist, or a Catholic, or an Arian; it had certainly been a Donatist neighbourhood, but it is tempting to hope that here was someone trained as a novice in one of St Augustine's monasteries, keeping alive the spirit of learning that was to be the glory of mediaeval monasticism.

The documents reveal a remarkably ready familiarity with the proper forms of legal transactions: signatures were witnessed, guarantees were provided. They are vital evidence for any study of how Roman law worked at grass roots level, for they are the only conveyances of their kind to survive from antiquity. And in the sphere of economic history, they prove that the system of Roman land tenure survived well into Vandal times: many of the transactions were undertaken explicitly under the *lex Manciana* which had governed certain relationships between landlord and tenant (perhaps only in relation to olive-groves and vineyards, and perhaps only in relation to one large tribal grouping) on imperial *saltus* in northern Tunisia nearly four centuries before. Nothing could show more clearly how little difference a change of masters had made to the mass of the population, at least as long as they were left in peace; the Vandals had simply taken over the Roman province, kept it Roman, and would leave it Roman.

The *tablettes* also yield much incidental information, about comparative prices, about irrigation, about the existence of ruins in the neighbourhood, about local trade (the various woods of the tablets were not local trees: they must have come from the Aurès mountains a hundred miles away) and about the position of women: widows were clearly regarded as heads of families, and wives were closely associated with their husbands in transactions of land. They also show that the wealth of this now-desolate region was still based on sedentary dry farming.

Eugène Albertini had already noted that the only sign of the Vandal

Prosperous Vandal leaving his villa: late fifth- or early sixth-century
North African mosaic, now in the British Museum

occupation in these documents was the dating by the year of the reign;
neither they nor the increasing danger from nomadic tribes (though
perhaps they had made those ruins on one of their sudden raids) had yet
disturbed the economy. Apart from their debased Latin, the *tablettes* might
have been inscribed two centuries earlier. Another interesting suggestion,
made by the editors of the *tablettes* who took over after Albertini's death,
was that the Geminius family had fled abroad during the Vandal invasion;
but that the sons and grandsons now felt safe enough to return and buy
up their ancestral property. Justinian's political re-conquest in AD 533 may
have been the spectacular confirmation of a social re-conquest begun half
a century earlier. The editors also see in the low prices of the trees the
possibility of an agricultural slump and consequent forced sales – the
mechanism of the expropriation of the poor by the rich in action.

THE COMING OF THE CAMEL

But more significant for the future is the reference in the *tablettes Albertini*
to a *via de camellos*. It attests to the presence of camels; and reminds us that
this little group of people lived down in the south, on the edge of the
Sahara. It was the camel above all which was to turn the nomads of the
desert and beyond into a dangerous long-distance striking force, because
of its value in transporting supplies.

203

Although it was not indigenous the camel had long been known in North Africa. It was being used as a pack animal from the end of the fourth century BC in the eastern Sahara, and a camel-driver is mentioned in a second-century BC inscription at Dougga in Tunisia. Julius Caesar captured twenty-two of them when he defeated King Juba of Numidia in the first. They are represented occasionally on mosaics (but then so are crocodiles and hippopotami); a fine example of the second century AD was uncovered at Thysdrus (El Djem) in 1959. Third-century sculptures from the frontier farms of Tripolitania show camels being used for ploughing, which suggests that they were not too expensive. There is a possibility that at the end of the third century the Louata (or Levathes), a desert tribe whose raids the Emperor Maximian had had to repel, were camel-borne, and certainly in the 360s Count Romanus was demanding four thousand camels from the city of Leptis Magna.

It is fairly certain that Roman troops from Syria brought camels to Numidia for army use about this time, and that the Roman authorities encouraged the breeding of them in Tripolitania. And there must have been many more beyond the Roman frontier, where they were being increasingly used by the tribes of the desert.

At the beginning of the sixth century, a few years after the *tablettes Albertini* were written, camels appear in just such a context. The Greek historian Procopius describes the battle fought between the Vandals under King Thrasamund and a desert tribe under Cabaon, probably in Byzacena (southern Tunisia): 'Cabaon ... placed his camels turned sideways in a circle as a protection for the camp, making his line fronting the enemy about twelve camels deep. Then he placed the children and the women and all those who were unfit for fighting together with their possessions in the middle, while he commanded the host of fighting men to stand between the feet of those animals, covering themselves with their shields ... The Vandals were at a loss ... for they were all horsemen, and used spears and swords for the most part, so they were unable to do the enemy any harm at a distance; and their horses, annoyed at the sight of the camels, refused absolutely to be driven against the enemy. And since the Moors, by hurling javelins in great numbers among them from their safe position, kept killing both their horses and men without difficulty, because they were a vast throng, they began to flee ...'

These camel-using people were the harbingers of a later, greater race of *grands nomades chameliers* who, with the indispensable help of their strong,

---

1 See footnote on page 181.
2 Richard Bulliet has pointed out that the one-humped camel is difficult to breed away from its original home near the Red Sea, and that the best camel for transport, a cross between the one-humped Arabian camel and the two-humped Bactrian camel, is – like the mule – infertile. Camel-breeding was (and is) a highly specialized tribal craft.

Silenus riding on a camel's back: detail of a mosaic of a Dionysiac
procession, found at El Djem, now in the Bardo Museum, Tunis

undemanding mounts, were to travel inexorably across the thirsty wastes
of the Sahara. But the first Arab invaders had little need of them. They
came along the coast from Egypt, mounted for the most part on horses. It
was only after the Arab conquest, and the foundation of Muslim kingdoms – not only in the Maghreb but also south of the Sahara – and
the resulting development of trans-Saharan trade, that the camel, now
essential, truly colonized North Africa.

THE LAST OF THE VANDALS

Meanwhile the Vandals had had troubles much nearer home. The territory
they ruled was much smaller than the old Roman provinces, and the
withdrawal had led to the gradual development of a number of semi-
independent Berber kingdoms. By the end of the Vandal period their
territory was virtually ringed with them. It is true that King Gaiseric, by
offering bribes and lucrative opportunities for plunder overseas, exercised
considerable authority over them. But after Gaiseric's death in 447 they
grew bolder. Mauretania Caesariensis was lost to a *rex gentium Maurorum*

205

et Romanorum; we hear of a prince of Hodna (the mountain chain south of Sitifis), another kingdom in the Aurès *massif*, and the beginnings of the formation of a tribal principality perhaps centred on Thala and Mactar, right inside the Vandal province. The latter, under its prince Antalas, proved a dangerous enemy not only to the Vandals in the fifth century but to the Byzantines – as the subjects of the Emperor at Constantinople were called – in the sixth.

The fortunately brief reign of Gaiseric's son Huneric was distinguished by the murder of half his family, and the inauguration of a period of persecution for the Catholic clergy who had been tricked into attending a conference at Carthage in AD 484 in order to 'debate' with the Arian ascendancy. It was the Council of AD 411 all over again; but this time the Catholics lost. The edict of persecution was couched in exactly the same words as Honorius's edict against the Donatists. It was carried out with considerably more force. Catholic bishops were flung naked out of their cities, priests were flogged; nearly five thousand clergy were exiled to the prince of Hodna's territory. Hundreds more Catholic Christians fled to Spain. Their martyrdom was written up with edifying improvements (such as the story of the faithful of Tipasa who miraculously continued to enjoy the gift of speech after their tongues were cut out) by Bishop Victor of Vita in exile. The many apostasies, which the bishop omitted to mention, were to create the usual problem when persecution was relaxed in the following reign. In AD 485 there was a serious famine, which the Catholics took to be the appropriate judgement of God, though it seems possible that general unrest aggravated it. Everywhere, wrote Victor of Vita, could be seen, 'like funeral processions, troops of young and old, youths and girls, children of both sexes: these unhappy creatures trailed round fortresses, villages and towns, scattered into the fields and the forests, fighting over dried-up tufts of grass and dead leaves ... Mountains and hills, squares, streets and public highways were no more than an enormous charnel house of the victims of famine.'

Another judgement of God was the death in 484 of Huneric himself, who was succeeded not by his son by Eudoxia, but by his nephews Gunthamund and Thrasamund. The reigns of both were plagued by Moorish invasions (of which the inhabitants of the *fundus Tuletianos* may have been victims).

Thrasamund was the dandy of the Vandal dynasty. He was handsome and cultivated, and his court became something of an intellectual centre. He was an Arian, but enjoyed indulging in theological debate with leading Catholics, although the price of too much persuasiveness, in Fulgentius of Ruspae, for example, was exile in Sardinia; and from time to time the king persecuted them more actively. As an *homme du monde* he felt the allure of

---

1 He, too, used the Latin language, but he called himself king of a people, not a place.

Tomb mosaic showing chapel found at Tabarka, dating from the Vandal occupation

the sophisticated east and was on good terms with the Emperor so long as the independence of Africa was not threatened. Unfortunately a change of Emperor renewed intrigues between Byzantium and the Catholic Church in Carthage: Thrasamund, who was at this time trying to ward off both the horse-borne tribesmen of Numidia and Mauretania, and the camel-supported cavalry of the desert who were menacing Byzacena, sought the support of his fellow Arian Theodoric of the Ostrogoths, and cemented the alliance by marrying Theodoric's sister, Amalafrida.

Shortly afterwards, however, in 523, he died, and was succeeded by his cousin Hilderic. Vandal policy was reversed, for Hilderic was half Roman himself, through his mother Eudoxia (who had been part of the booty captured by his grandfather Gaiseric during the sack of Rome). He may have spent many years in Constantinople – he was now an old man – and he had known the Emperor Justin well and, more important, his nephew Justinian, who was shortly to become Emperor himself. In any case, all his tastes were Roman rather than Vandal. He at once extended not only tolerance but approval to the Catholics. The exiled clergy returned: Fulgentius, whose eloquent sermons they remembered, received an ovation from the Carthaginian crowd. Barbarian instincts survived in Hilderic (though it must be admitted that few Roman rulers were free of them either), old as he was: when his late cousin's Arian brother-in-law Theodoric protested at this apparent treachery, at a time when persecution of the Arians had been renewed in the Empire, Hilderic retaliated by murdering Amalafrida, Thrasamund's widow, and the Gothic bodyguard she had brought as a dowry. The Vandal kingdom was only spared an Ostrogothic expedition of revenge because Theodoric died.

---

1 Byzacena comprised, roughly, southern Tunisia.

Hilderic was totally incompetent as a ruler. He had come to the throne by a law of succession laid down by Gaiseric, whereby the eldest of his descendants surviving at the death of the king should succeed, and not the eldest son. This was designed to spare the Vandal kingdom the hazards of long minorities; in practice, it was a law which 'tended to favour princes who were more remarkable for their longevity than for the soundness of their wits,' in Robert Graves's words. None of the Vandal kings illustrated this stricture better than Hilderic. He divided his kingdom against itself, Catholic against Arian, he turned his Arian subjects against himself, and his treatment of Amalafrida and his close ties with his old friend Justinian, with whom he would exchange expensive presents, gave his own family the excuse to call him traitor. This opportunity was seized by his cousin Gelimer, when an army commanded by Hilderic's nephew – Hilderic himself was quite uninterested in military affairs – was soundly beaten by the powerful tribe which, under Antalas, had formed a virtually independent kingdom in the mountainous plateau round Thala, within striking distance of Carthage.

Gelimer deposed Hilderic in May of AD 530 with the help of what remained of the army, and imprisoned him with his two nephews. He had assumed the throne of an embattled kingdom, but at least his policy was unambiguous: Africa for the Vandals. Unfortunately a century of luxury had softened this once-hard Baltic people. They were no longer the military élite they had been.

Worse, the usurper had given the Emperor Justinian just the excuse he was looking for. An irregularity of succession proved, in the event, as disastrous for the independence of the Vandal kingdom as the treasonable activities of Hilderic might have done. More so, perhaps: had the Vandals recognized the Emperor from the beginning, they might have survived as the Goths and Franks did elsewhere. As it was, they provoked a war of reconquest, and vanished almost at once.

14

AFRICA RETURNS TO THE EAST

The capitol at Sbeïtla – incorporated into Byzantine ramparts. Sbeïtla
bore the brunt of the first Arab attacks

'The Emperor never sleeps,' it was said of Justinian, who succeeded his
uncle on the throne of the eastern Roman Empire – now called Byzantium –
in 527, three years before Gelimer usurped the throne of Vandal Africa. He

ruled for fifty years, and took his duties as a Christian Emperor seriously. The final victory of the Catholic Church, still beset by heresy, and the recovery and glorification of the Roman Empire were his life-long aims at home and abroad.

These two passions inspired two remarkable achievements: the basilica of St Sophia at Constantinople, which was and still is the greatest glory of Byzantine architecture, and the codification of Roman law in the *Corpus Juris Civilis*.[1] They also inspired his recovery of the western Mediterranean provinces from their Arian kings.

Since north-west Africa commanded the straits of Sicily his first object was the conquest of the Vandals. His closest advisers, recalling the disasters that had befallen expeditions sent against the Vandals in the previous century, and unaware of the perilous weakness of their kingdom and of their once-powerful fleet under Gaiseric's successors, counselled against it; but a bishop from Egypt, prompted no doubt by his persecuted brothers in Africa or in exile, proclaimed to Justinian that Christ had appeared to him in a vision instructing the Emperor to reconquer Africa. Justinian accepted this as an omen of success, and in AD 533 five hundred ships, manned by thirty thousand sailors, set sail from Constantinople with an army of sixteen thousand men under the command of Count Belisarius.

Six thousand horses also accompanied the expedition. For a generation, the armies of Constantinople had been fighting the Persians, whose mailed warriors mounted on 'cataphracts', or 'great horses', had given the latter a decisive advantage in the field. More than a third of Belisarius's army was similarly mailed and mounted, and armed with bows and arrows: they could not only strike from a distance, but also had an advantage in weight at close quarters.

The invaders, depleted on the voyage by five hundred deaths caused by cheap bread which had gone mouldy, landed on the flat coast of the gulf of Syrte. The success of Belisarius's African campaign owed more to good fortune and his own common sense than to good generalship. The Vandals were caught unawares. King Gelimer had sent his fleet on an expedition to Sardinia, and he himself was four days' journey inland. Belisarius moved north, unopposed, keeping a tight rein on his troops in order not to antagonize the inhabitants. Soldiers caught stealing the local inhabitants' fruit were flogged, more for 'bringing their hostility' upon the Byzantine army than for the sin. The fleet kept them company along the coast. The local population, pleasantly surprised by an army prepared to pay for provisions, handed over their cities, and supplied food and horses. Only when his army reached the beautiful royal property on the coast at Grassa

---

1 Justinian's greatest talent was for spotting talent in others, whether architects, lawyers, generals, theologians, a historian like Procopius – or his own wife Theodora, an even more astute politician than he was.

(probably Hammamet) did Belisarius allow them to plunder. The scene was described by Procopius, who had accompanied the count to Africa to act as his secretary:

'In that place was a palace of the ruler of the Vandals and a park the most beautiful of all we know. For it is excellently watered by springs and has a great wealth of woods. And all the trees were full of fruit; so that each one of the soldiers pitched his tent among fruit-trees, and though all of them ate their fill of the fruit, which was then ripe, there was practically no diminution to be seen in the fruit.' The soldiers of Belisarius were as amazed and delighted by the fertility of this corner of Cape Bon as the Greek and Roman invaders had been a thousand years before.

VICTORY OVER THE VANDALS

Gelimer, to whom news of the invasion had at last been brought at Bulla Regia, had no intention of yielding his kingdom. When Belisarius offered him surrender terms he promptly had the imprisoned Hilderic murdered and marched to meet the Byzantine army. In spite of their numerical superiority, however, the Vandals were routed ten miles from Carthage, and on St Cyprian's day, 15 September, Belisarius sat down to eat in Gelimer's palace in the capital. 'It happened that the lunch made for Gelimer on the preceding day was in readiness. And we feasted on that very food and the domestics of Gelimer served it and poured the wine and waited upon us in every way.' Procopius points the moral: Fortune was making quite clear 'that all things are hers and that nothing is the private possession of any man'.

The Vandals had lost their kingdom after a hundred years. But the remnants of their army were gathering at Bulla Regia, and Gelimer was soon besieging Carthage, whose walls Belisarius had hastily had repaired. Gelimer cut the great aqueduct ('a structure well worth seeing,' notes Procopius), and tried to bribe Belisarius's Hun mercenaries; but when, in December, the Byzantines emerged to do battle the Vandals were routed once more. Gelimer himself, without a word to his officers, leapt on a horse and fled from his stockaded camp, followed by his relatives and servants. His army, not unnaturally, followed his example. When the Byzantine soldiers moved into the camp, there was not a man in it; only the women and children whom they had deserted and 'a quantity of wealth such as has never before been found, at least in one place. For the Vandals had plundered the Roman domain for a long time . . . and the revenue collected from the commodities produced there was not paid out to any other country in the purchase of a food supply; but those who possessed the land always kept for themselves the income from it . . . And from this it resulted that their wealth, amounting to an extraordinary sum, returned once more on that day into the hands of the Romans [Byzantines].' Belisarius, who was afraid the Vandals might return, had considerable difficulty in restraining his soldiers, 'becoming all of a sudden masters of very great wealth and of women both young and extremely comely'.

Procopius describes King Gelimer's downfall. Gelimer and his party found refuge in a Moorish fastness on a mountain overlooking Hippo.[1] It was winter; accustomed to luxury, they were soon cold and hungry. Procopius gives a vivid account of the wretchedness of the deposed king and his followers in the 'stuffy huts' of the Moors. There was a touching exchange of letters between King Gelimer and Pharas, the Hun soldier whom Belisarius had put in charge of the small company guarding the mountain, which Procopius quotes. 'What in the world has happened to you, my dear Gelimer, that you have cast, not yourself alone, but your whole family besides, into this pit?' wrote Pharas, delicately urging him to surrender. 'They say that it is the wish of the Emperor Justinian to have you enrolled in the senate ... and to present you with lands both spacious and good and with great sums of money, and that Belisarius is willing to make himself responsible for your having all these things ...' Was it that Gelimer dreaded becoming a slave? 'As though liberty were worth possessing at the price of all this misery!' Gelimer, weeping, could not but agree. He did not give himself up at once, but wrote back gratefully to Pharas, begging to be sent 'a lyre and one loaf of bread and a sponge'. Sick of the unleavened barley bread of his hosts, he longed for a taste of freshly-baked wheat bread; the sponge he needed for an inflamed eye, the lyre to accompany an ode he had composed on his misfortunes. Pharas, deeply moved, sent them to him – 'but kept watch more closely than before'.

What finally weakened the king's resolution, even more than the worms the Vandal children were suffering from, was the sight of his small nephew and a Moorish child fighting over a tiny corn cake. The Moor struck the young Vandal over the temple 'and thus compelled him with great violence to cast out the cake which was already in his throat'.

In three months the kingdom had fallen to a few thousand cavalry. 'One would justly marvel at it,' said Procopius. Nothing could better illustrate the weakness of Vandal rule. The local tribes, waiting to see who would be the victors, had not come to their assistance. Once Belisarius was the master of Carthage, they hastened to declare their allegiance to him, asking only that they should receive recognition from the Emperor. King Gelimer and other Vandals were taken to Constantinople, where they formed part of Belisarius's triumph; Gelimer, as promised, received large estates in Galatia in Asia Minor. But the Vandal people simply disappeared, either fleeing to Spain or being absorbed into the population of North Africa, a

---

1 A settlement, perhaps, such as that where St Augustine could not speak the local language.

tiny fraction of the whole: no 'Vandal type' survives there, and the modern Berber vocabulary contains no Vandal words.

They would hardly have been heard of by most people today had not their name been resurrected at the end of the eighteenth century by a bishop of Blois to form the French word *vandalisme*. They had been execrated by churchmen of St Augustine's day and those who suffered under their persecution, and 'Vandal' was a pejorative term to Voltaire; but the bishop's coinage gave it a wider currency, and saddled the Vandals with a reputation for whole-sale destructiveness which they hardly deserved – it was the Byzantines who used many of the most splendid monuments of Roman North Africa as quarries for the building of defensive walls and forts. They were not vandals in the modern sense. Their principal desire had been to enter into and enjoy the Roman inheritance, not to destroy it.

RESISTANCE AND REBELLION

In spite of the welcome the other inhabitants of north-west Africa extended to the Byzantine army, the rule of the eastern Roman Empire proved, to begin with, scarcely more secure than that of the Vandals. Almost as soon as Count Belisarius had sailed for Constantinople with his captives, leaving in charge the able Armenian general Solomon, there were two serious uprisings in the south. Iabdas, king of the Aurès, descended from the mountains to ravage Numidia, and the Moorish chieftain Cutzinas came north-west from Tripolitania with the camels which had already made his fighting men a deadly threat and invaded Byzacena. Solomon, with an army far better able to fight such mobile nomads than that of the Vandals, marched south to deal with Cutzinas, who was defeated after two hard-fought battles (and later became a valuable ally). But Solomon had no time to deal properly with Iabdas before a dangerous insurrection broke out in the Byzantine army. Many of the soldiers had married the Vandal women they had acquired on the battlefield. These latter, having no wish to be worse off than before, considered that their new husbands should be allowed to enjoy their former husbands' properties, instead of seeing them confiscated by the State or returned to the families of their former owners, as Justinian had decreed. Their new husbands were equally eager to settle down to the enjoyment of the prizes of war, rather than embark on a disagreeable campaign in the hot south. In addition, the Hun mercenaries, who were Arians, deeply resented the proscription of their religion which had been a consequence of the Catholic Justinian's victory. There was a plot against Solomon, who barely escaped with his life in time to flee overseas to seek the assistance of Belisarius.

The rebels were under the command of Stotzas, a former member of the guard and a gifted demagogue, who soon attracted to his banner some two thirds of the Byzantine army and the remnants of the Vandals. The situation was grave, though fortunately the return of Count Belisarius prevented the capture of Carthage – more from fear inspired by his reputation than from the reinforcements he brought. But the province was saved for Byzantium by Justinian's cousin, Germanos, whose lavish promises caused a sufficient number of defections from Stotzas, and by the providential failure of Iabdas and his ally Ortaias, the prince of Hodna, to support the rebels. At Cellas Vatari in Numidia, Germanos defeated Stotzas, who fled to Mauretania. There Stotzas married a Moorish princess and waited for a chance of revenge.

Iabdas might have helped put an end to Byzantine domination before it had properly begun. Instead, he preferred to wait and see which way the battle went, and join in the subsequent looting. He was soon punished for his greed. Although Solomon had been a harsh and unpopular general, Justinian rightly recognized his quality, and sent him back to Africa in 539. He was given both the civilian position of praetorian prefect and the military rank of *magister militum Africae*, powers which Justinian normally divided between two men. Solomon was determined to take his revenge for the trouble Iabdas had caused him. This time he took the precaution of severely disciplining and reforming his army (and exiling their Vandal wives); and when he invaded the Aurès he defeated Iabdas who, like Stotzas, fled to Mauretania.

THE NEW AFRICA

There followed five years of peace, which Solomon used to complete the remarkable defensive structure of the province he had begun on Justinian's orders immediately after the defeat of the Vandals, and whose ruins still survive in profusion.

Justinian had ordered the old Roman *limites* of Hadrian's day to be restored, but Solomon recognized that Byzantine Africa's enemies were not only beyond the frontier, but within. Belisarius had arrived to conquer the Vandals, but thereafter it was the threat from the Moors which dictated the Byzantines' defensive policy. It meant the construction of forts, fortifications and citadels not only down on the southern frontier but throughout the Byzantine province, wherever fertile farmlands or city populations needed protection from the tribes now so strongly established in mountainous areas in the north as well as the south. Eighty sites of official military construction have been identified; there are forty more possible sites; and that does not include the unofficial constructions, the thousands and thousands of minor, piecemeal defensive works. Soon, there were forts for garrison troops not only at Timgad, but at Dougga, Mactar, Madauros – to mention only a handful of places which had once had no need of fortification, and certainly no need of a garrison. Other cities were provided with formidable walls, or at least a fortified area to protect the civilian population as well as to house troops – Haïdra, Leptis Magna, Sabratha, Tébessa, Sétif among them. Carthage's walls were repaired. Soon, it seems, scarcely a village was without its look-out post or a secure place of refuge for the local inhabitants.

Prodigious labour was involved. It has been calculated that the fortification of Tébessa alone, where the enormous walls still seal off the heart of the town from its suburbs, and where one gate still bears the name *Porte de Solomon*, must have taken nearly three hundred and thirty-six thousand working days, or the employment of more than eight hundred workmen for two years.

The work was urgent, since the province was all too plainly at the mercy of tribes from both desert and mountain, grown audacious during the Vandal occupation. For this reason it was quicker to use the masonry of neglected monuments in the new walls; it was the Byzantines who were guilty of dismantling much of old Roman Africa. In some places Roman monuments formed part of the fortifications: a church at Haïdra, the great triumphal arch of Caracalla and perhaps a theatre at Tébessa, baths at Guelma, the capitol at Sbeïtla, even a simple classical gateway, complete with columns, at Teboursouk. The new constructions showed every sign of improvisation: the blocks of stone varied greatly in size, dressed masonry was mixed up with roughly cut stone or even rubble and brick. Yet these huge crenellated walls, which were usually between eight and twelve feet thick, well over twenty-five feet in height and punctuated with towers, were properly provided with stables and large reservoirs for the collection of rainwater; and it is also clear that the Byzantine engineers, for all their lack of time, chose the most strategic positions for their fortresses.

Of Justinian's policy in Africa, Procopius wrote in his *Secret History*: 'Justinian, after the defeat of the Vandals, took no trouble to ensure the complete occupation of the country. He failed to realize that the best guarantee of authority resides in the goodwill of the subject ... but administering the African provinces from a distance, pillaged and sucked them dry at his pleasure. He sent agents to estimate the value of the soil, instituted new and heavy taxes, himself claimed all the best lands, forbade the Arians to practise their religion, and ruled the army very harshly, continually putting off the despatch of reinforcements.' This was less than fair to the Emperor, who had received the news of Belisarius's success with joy, and had already, in the confident expectation of victory, prepared elaborate plans to expunge all Vandal influence and reorganize the administration. Justinian took the closest personal interest in the province whose recovery enabled him eventually to win back all those in the west except Britain. Few details of defence or administration were too small for his concern; the hierarchy, both civilian and military, was reformed; the province was honoured (not always to its advantage) with a succession of governors who were either his favourites or members of his family; and he celebrated the conquest with a civic building programme which reflected, though it could not match, the military constructions undertaken by his lieutenants. Several new towns were expressly founded by Justinian; at Carthage, the port was developed, baths were erected in honour of his Empress, a great basilica was built, higher education was encouraged; Leptis Magna, half-ruined and virtually deserted, was in part rebuilt, on his orders, and the rebuilt area near the harbour defended with a new wall. Throughout the richer part of the province, learning and art, particularly the art of mosaic, enjoyed a minor renaissance, which was enthusiastically fostered in dozens of new monasteries and churches. Mundane concerns were not forgotten: everywhere, waterworks were repaired and improved, and the Emperor took pains to encourage agriculture: once more, corn and oil were exported, this time to the east. A stream of instructions issued from Constantinople, and, if many were not obeyed, it was not for want of effort on the part of Justinian. His principal ambition was that north-west Africa should be once more worthy of its inheritance.

A PRECARIOUS PEACE

The cost of Justinian's ambitions was heavy, and the Africans paid the price. Now, not only did the army and the administration have to be supported; the Church, too, was an increasing non-productive burden on the backs of the poor. Many must have been worse off than they had been under the Vandals, when any food exported was actually paid for, and Vandal revenues – lavishly augmented by the fruits of piracy – were spent within the country, on buildings and artefacts and entertainments and services of all kinds, so that money gradually percolated downwards; and when there was probably less pressure to raise large taxes in kind, since (as Procopius pointed out) there was no mother country to feed.

Byzantine Africa had to raise money for her own army and fortifications; she was also called on to raise money and men for Justinian's campaigns elsewhere in the Empire. His reign was long and in many ways glorious, but he bled the provinces white, even if it seemed to him to be for their own good. Shortage of money in North Africa's public treasury was chronic throughout the sixth century, and the army was frequently owed huge arrears of pay.

Military discontent was compounded by civilian misery. The restoration of Catholic supremacy led to the proscription not only of Donatists and Arians but of Jews, pagans and heretics of all kinds: many suffered forcible conversion, and hundreds more fled from the territory ruled by the Byzantines to swell the ranks of the tribes. Changes in the ownership of land also led to confusion and discontent. Even the heirs of the old Roman owners who were now reinstated were dissatisfied, since they felt that not enough was done for them. For Justinian refused to allow them to bring back into serfdom the descendants of the original tenants who had been tied to the land by the decrees of Diocletian and Constantine, if they or their fathers had escaped their bondage during the Vandal interregnum by fleeing to another estate or to the cities.

Matters were made worse by corrupt administration. Favours were bought and sold, the poor were sometimes taxed twice in a year, those converted to Catholicism continued, contrary to the law, to be taxed as pagans or heretics. Many of Justinian's rescripts were exhortations, or even pleas, that his subjects in north-west Africa should be dealt with justly and gently. All too often his instructions fell on deaf ears, and the Emperor was too far away to ensure obedience.

However, the reign of Solomon was a comparatively prosperous one; the African poet Corippus was to look back to it as a golden age. Count Belisarius had discovered that the ambitions of the tribal chieftains hardly went further than the recognition by the Emperor of their individual sovereignty; and Solomon made use of this to cement a number of alliances, including one with Cutzinas, which safeguarded the peace. By paying the chieftains pensions, and flattering their dignity with titles and honours – such, still, was the Empire's magnetism – he ensured that at least they would not readily unite in rebellion. But it was a precarious peace, dependent almost entirely on the tact and diplomacy of the Byzantine commander towards the tribal chieftains and his popularity with his own army, whose loyalty was constantly strained by delays in payment. In these circumstances, a bad appointment was an invitation to disaster.

THE RETURN OF CIVIL WAR

Disaster was not slow in coming. Anxious to reward his *magister militum*, Justinian agreed to the appointment of Solomon's nephew Sergius as duke of Tripolitania. In 543 Sergius appears to have allowed his troops to plunder the territory of the powerful Louata tribe in Tripolitania, and then killed seventy-nine of the eighty deputies who came to Leptis Magna to complain. This massacre led to a general insurrection of the tribes of Tripolitania, and they were joined by Antalas of Byzacena, who had a private score to settle with Solomon. The alliance of Cutzinas was not enough to save Solomon. He won a battle near Tébessa, but half his army refused to join in a second near Cillium (Kasserine) because he had not let them plunder the battlefield. Solomon himself, fighting to the last with a few faithful guards, was killed.

Yet the insurrection would have died down – Antalas grandly declaring that he had no quarrel with the Emperor, and the Louata being eager to regain their tribal encampments in Tripolitania with their booty – had not Justinian decided to honour the memory of Solomon by appointing Sergius *magister militum* in his uncle's place, with, as *co-magister*, his own nephew by marriage, Areobindus. Sergius alone had little hope of restoring peace, since he was hated by officers and men alike for his brutality and arrogance, and the tribes had sworn undying vengeance for the massacre of Leptis Magna. But the divided command made matters worse, since the two men were jealous of each other and refused to go to each other's assistance.

In the confused civil war which followed, Stotzas – Solomon's rebel officer – arrived from Mauretania to give his support to Antalas; the Byzantine army suffered a heavy defeat at the hands of the Louata tribe near Sicca Veneria (El Kef, in northern Tunisia); Cutzinas and Iabdas joined the rebels, who at one point threatened Carthage itself; and Areobindus, at long last left in sole command by the recall of Sergius, was murdered by the ambitious duke of Numidia, Guntarith. Duke Guntarith, who had been treating secretly with the tribes, intended to make himself ruler of Africa and, at the same time, the husband of Areobindus's widow Prejecta, who was a niece of Justinian. Africa seemed lost to Byzantium; Procopius wrote that the victories of Belisarius might never have been. Fortunately Africa found a temporary saviour – and Prejecta a protector – in the person of a talented and handsome regimental commander called Artabanes. Guntarith's hold on the army and on his barbarian allies was as precarious as Sergius's had been, and Artabanes became the leader of a conspiracy against him. In May of AD 546 Guntarith was murdered at a military banquet, and his reign of terror – there had been innumerable summary executions of possible enemies during his thirty-six days in power – was over. But if control of Africa had been technically restored to the Emperor, this was by no means true in fact. The tribes had undeniably demonstrated their power to strike right at the heart of the old Roman territory, and they were still unconquered. Now the province lost the one man who might have achieved a stable peace.

Artabanes had fallen in love with Prejecta, and she, overjoyed to be spared a forced marriage with Guntarith, had agreed to marry him. He pursued her back to Byzantium. In vain: he already had a wife and, although Prejecta's grateful uncle Justinian loaded him with honours, he could not prevail against the implacable hostility of the Empress Theodora. Prejecta was married off to a member of the imperial court, and Artabanes' career was effectively over.

Africa was left in misery and uncertainty. For two years rival armies had marched back and forth between Carthage and Numidia, between Byzacena and Tripolitania: *fumans perit Africa flammis*, wrote Corippus, 'smouldering Africa perished in flames'. Many people sought refuge in the towns and cities fortified just in time by Solomon. Yet the tribes did not take advantage of the weakness of their enemy to seize the empty farmlands once and for all. For their aims were always short-term – an annual expedition from their mountain or desert fastnesses in search of booty, or a 'pension' from the Byzantines in return for a temporary truce.

Their chieftains were inspired solely by the interests of their own tribe; they were as ready to take up arms against their fellows as against the Byzantines. Indeed, they regarded the Byzantines as useful allies in tribal warfare rather than as the common enemy. Nationalism was entirely foreign to them. This was the weakness which the Byzantines were able to exploit.

Artabanes' successor in Africa was John Troglita, the hero whom Corippus celebrated in his epic poem the *Johannides*. At long last Justinian had sent out one of his ablest generals; a man already experienced in African warfare, who had enough authority to restore discipline to the army, the diplomatic skill to win first Iabdas, king of the Aurès, and then Cutzinas (with his thirty thousand cavalry) to the imperial standard, and

Byzantine fort at Ksar Lemsa, near Mactar

finally the decisiveness and confidence to carry the war into the desert. Even so, it took him two years of alternate fighting and negotiation, during which he himself suffered serious losses both in battle and from an epidemic (probably the plague). His enemies actually reached the walls of Carthage once more, before a great victory in the south, in the year 548, defeated the tribes of Byzacena and Tripolitania; seventeen of their chieftains were killed, and Antalas became 'as if a slave' to John Troglita.

Fifteen years of intermittent warfare, since the arrival of the Byzantines, were followed by fifteen years of peace. Within four years of the battle the province was sufficiently peaceful for John Troglita to send both troops and a fleet to help Justinian abroad.

Peace remained precarious, however. In AD 563, at the end of Justinian's reign, a disastrous new governor murdered Cutzinas, who had been a faithful ally for fifteen years. An army had to be sent from Constantinople to suppress the rising which the murder provoked, and the province was ravaged anew. In the years that followed, three Byzantine generals appear to have met their deaths in battle with the Moorish king Garmul, until Garmul was killed in AD 579 by the *magister militum* Gennadius. Many of the well-off fled abroad to Spain and elsewhere, and those who were obliged to remain seem for the first time to have built fortifications on their own initiative.

In the 580s the Emperor Maurice instituted administrative reforms whereby provincial governors were given more power, amounting virtually to that of vice-regency. But the exarchate (as a group of provinces was now called) of Africa was very restricted. Tripolitania was joined to the new exarchate of Egypt. The modest territory round Septem (Ceuta), immediately south of the straits of Gibraltar, continued to be part of Spain. Almost all the rest of Mauretania west of Sitifis and the Chott El Hodna had long since been lost to any semblance of imperial authority.

Maurice was an able Emperor, and Gennadius, whom he appointed his exarch in Africa, was at least militarily extremely successful. There were tribal uprisings in AD 587, and a tribal attack on Carthage as late as AD 595–6, but thereafter the tribal incursions that had been endemic since the Vandal period seem to have ceased. In AD 543 an outbreak of plague in the province had been a signal for tribal invasion; but in AD 599 a similar epidemic seems not to have been exploited at all. Little is known of this period of North African history, from the death of Justinian to the Arab conquest; but whether by warfare or diplomacy Gennadius appears to have done his work well.

A CHURCH MILITANT

The Church, too, was sufficiently free of the stresses of warfare to engage in the middle of the century in what came to be known, erroneously, as the Three Chapters controversy. For eight years it was in combat with its benefactor Justinian, leading the resistance in the western Church against the Emperor's condemnation of three points of doctrine which the Church itself had not condemned. It was a period at once distinguished and desperate in the history of the African Church, distinguished because its leaders were men of intellectual authority and moral courage, and desperate because Justinian did not hesitate to use force in his determination to win: bishops were imprisoned, banished, sentenced to corporal punishment. Unfortunately the papacy was on Justinian's side, and henceforth the African Church lost, this time for good, the theological ascendancy it had enjoyed in the days of St Cyprian and St Augustine. But during that time bishops from all parts of the province were constantly meeting in council at Carthage, and their leaders went on deputations to Constantinople; there appears to have been no trouble or threat of trouble in their dioceses to prevent them leaving home for weeks or even months at a stretch.

In the wake of secular victory came Christian conquest. From this time onwards populations hitherto untouched by either Catholic or Donatist influence were converted to Christianity – the tribes of the Aurès and the Chott Djerid and the northern oases, and even the people of the Fezzan far south of Leptis Magna, for Arab historians were later to report that the new masters of north-west Africa found Christian inhabitants there. In Mauretania, too, powerful tribes near Pomaria (Tlemcen), in the mountains of Zab and around Tiaret became Catholic Christians. Almost nothing is known of the cultural and commercial links which these developments reflect. But the times were sufficiently peaceful for bishops from even these distant communities to attend councils in Carthage.

The property of the Church was restored to her, and many new churches built – five, Procopius reports, at Leptis Magna alone. Many of the columns in the mosques of modern North Africa clearly date from the Byzantine period, and must have come from the naves of Christian basilicas, or the cloisters of the many monasteries which, from literary evidence, are known to have been built at this time.

Mauretania was effectively left to the tribal kingdoms: the Bavares, the Quinquegentiani, the Baquates emerge once more. For them, too, it was a prosperous time – at least to judge by the remains of magnificent royal tombs of the sixth and seventh centuries near Tiaret in Algeria, some of which must have been as imposing as those built by their ancestors nearly a millennium earlier.

Towards the end of the sixth century the Church enjoyed another kind of triumph, but one which again brought credit mostly to the papacy. The Emperor Maurice was no more successful than Justinian had been in stamping out corruption and exploitation; the expenses of the province were heavy and, as usual, paid for by those who could least afford it. In desperation, people appealed to the Church to help them fight their secular oppressors. In turn, the leaders of the African Church appealed to the bishop of Rome. It gave Pope Gregory[1] a chance he welcomed to establish his authority over the African bishops. Innumerable letters and instructions from Gregory reached Africa, and shed some light on an otherwise obscure period; we know, for instance, that Gregory was greatly exercised by the re-emergence of Donatism, and that he considered its suppression a prime duty of his correspondents.

But such was the impact of his personality that he also established his

---

1 The Pope Gregory in question was the same Gregory the Great (c. 540–604) who sent a mission to the Anglo-Saxons.

authority over civilian administration, and even the military. He mediated between the exarch Gennadius and the bishops; he did not hesitate to complain to the Emperor about the conduct of the exarch's officials; he made suggestions to Gennadius about the defence of the province. Soon one prefect was confiding in him details of the shortcomings of the civil authorities; and Gennadius himself went out of his way to please the Pope and earn his approval, although to be sure – as Gregory pointed out – it was a way of pleasing not only the kings of the world but the King of Heaven.

Imperial authority grew weaker; the Pope and the exarch grew stronger. And the Church in Africa clearly became, what had been unthinkable in St Cyprian's day, a daughter Church of Rome.

THE HOUSE OF HERACLIUS

In 595 Heraclius, one of Maurice's most brilliant generals, was appointed exarch of Africa. When Maurice was murdered by a usurper, Phocas, in 602, Heraclius took the lead in opposing him. However, he was an honourable and prudent man, and hesitated to commit the Empire to what might have been a long and bloody civil war, at a time when the armies of the Persian king Chosroes had reached Chalcedon and were threatening Byzantium. But once more an insult to womanhood provided the goad: Heraclius's niece Eudocia, the fiancée of his son, and her mother were taken as hostages by Phocas.

In AD 608 Heraclius withheld corn supplies destined for Constantinople, and the rest of the Empire turned to him as to a saviour. Feeling himself to be too old, Heraclius sent his son, also Heraclius, and his nephew Nicetas in his place to avenge the murder of Maurice.

In the event the mere approach of the fleet commanded by the young Heraclius provoked a revolution in Constantinople. Phocas was killed; young Heraclius was acclaimed in his place and Eudocia, rescued, became the bride of an Emperor.

The links between Africa and Constantinople were closer than they had ever been. The elder Heraclius died in office a year or so after his son had assumed the purple; and the exarchate of Africa was shortly entrusted to the new Emperor's friend and cousin Nicetas. Africa now regularly supplied Constantinople with corn and olive oil; even the tribal chieftains were devoted to the Heraclian dynasty, lending them troops for military expeditions and perhaps also paying them taxes instead of, as for so long, receiving pensions; agriculture flourished, and the towns on the northern flanks of the Aurès *massif* were prosperous once more. So peaceful does the province seem to have been that in AD 620, at a time when the east was particularly hard-pressed by the Persians, Heraclius seriously considered moving the seat of imperial government to Carthage. That he was dissuaded, and that he and his successors remained in Constantinople, saved the eastern capital for a future, as Byzantium, even more glorious than its past.

Heraclius ruled for thirty years, and proved himself one of the noblest of Roman Emperors. His most important achievement was saving the Eastern Empire from the Persians.

But an even more dangerous enemy was at hand. In AD 632, the Prophet Muhammad died at Medina, and within a few years the holy armies of his successors, the caliphs Abubaker and Omar, had made of Palestine and Syria a province of Arabia. Egypt soon followed.

Meanwhile the temptation for Africa to secede from the Empire remained – even after the exarch Nicetas's daughter Gregoria was married to Heraclius's son and heir Constantine. The temptation was strengthened towards the end of Heraclius's life by the passionate opposition of the African Church (now restored to its role as the most energetic champion of orthodoxy) to the monothelite heresy, which Heraclius had adopted.

The Arab invasion of Egypt had also brought a flood of refugees to north-west Africa, among whom were a large number of priests, monks and nuns. They were welcomed indiscriminately by the praetorian prefect of Africa, the devout and hospitable George, who arranged for them to be given monasteries and convents. Many of them, however, turned out to be ardent monophysites (another eastern heresy), eager to make converts of the orthodox Catholics.

At this point, in 641, Heraclius died. He was succeeded briefly by his son Constantine, who was an orthodox Emperor, and orders soon came from Constantinople that heresy was to be suppressed. George, who had been caught unawares, tried to confiscate the monasteries and convents he had given in good faith to the refugees, only to be faced, on Constantine's death, with another change of policy and another set of instructions: 'heresy' was to be permitted once more. Tempers were now so high, however, and religious clashes so likely, that George was driven to pretend that the new imperial instructions were a forgery. He even produced 'witnesses' that the Empress dowager Martina, who was responsible for this latest switch, was free of the taint of heresy. When, inevitably, he was summoned to the court to explain himself, the Africans mourned his going with a fervour which boded ill for their continuing loyalty to the Empire.

The refugees were not all heretics, however. The African Church found its most effective defendant, and the house of Heraclius its most formidable critic, in the celebrated abbot Maximus, of whom after his death his biographer wrote: 'Not only clerics and bishops but also magistrates and people alike hung on his words, and clung to the saint like iron filings to the magnet, or sailors to the songs of the sirens.' As long as the race of Heraclius ruled, so long would God be hostile to the Roman Empire, was Maximus's inflammatory theme. In AD 645 he scored a notable triumph in a public debate over the monothelite leader Pyrrhus, who confessed the error of his beliefs and did penance. The African bishops, while giving lip-service to their loyalty to the Emperor, castigated the heresies which emanated from Constantinople with renewed confidence.

The lip-service did not last long. The debate between Maximus and Pyrrhus had taken place in the presence of the exarch Gregory, perhaps another member of the house of Heraclius, who had ambitions of another kind, and in AD 646 proclaimed himself Emperor. The abbot Maximus had a useful dream, of choirs of angels chanting 'Victory to Gregory Augustus' sufficiently loudly to drown rival choirs of angels chanting 'Victory to Constantine Augustus'. There were rumours, too, that the Pope was a party to the usurpation, even giving the exarch Gregory his blessing, and although the African Church welcomed it with some caution, in view of their recent protestations, Gregory's move was accepted in the province without open demur. He made no attempt, however, to try conclusions with the Emperor in Constantinople; he remained in Africa. His action was a declaration of independence, the better to be able to face a new and deadly enemy.

THE COMING OF THE ARABS

The countries bordering the Mediterranean basin had been brought under the Roman standard in the first and second centuries BC, and welded into an Empire. That unity had been broken by the northern barbarians in the fifth century AD, but was patched up by the armies of Justinian in the sixth. Under his successors the Empire began to disintegrate once more; but the Mediterranean basin was still unified in one important respect: in spite of heresy, schism and other disputes, it was a Christian lake.

Islam exploded out of the Arabian peninsula in the 630s, and within a couple of generations of Muhammad's death the Mediterranean was a Christian lake no longer. North Africa, Egypt and the Middle East were lost to Christendom for good, and most of Spain for seven hundred years. In the early eighth century Islam was even threatening the heart of France, and had overrun central Asia as far as the borders of India and China.

The Arabs took half a century to swallow up North Africa, a half century for which there are almost no contemporary records. Arabs themselves are the main source of our information, but they are Arab historians of succeeding centuries: in the interval the stories of the conquest have been embellished, fantasized and improved upon after countless re-tellings. As one French historian has put it, 'they obligingly supply the heroes of Islam with adventures worthy of *The Thousand and One Nights'*. But it is significant that, after Gregory, the Byzantines scarcely figure in the legends of the conquest of Africa. To the newcomers, the Berbers – and it was the Arabs

224

who gave the native Africans their modern name – were their real opponents.

After seizing Syria and Palestine in the space of a few years, and conquering the Persians who had been weakened by the long wars with Byzantium, the Arabs had captured Egypt in AD 641. In AD 642 they occupied Cyrenaica, and the following year besieged Tripoli, laid waste Sabratha and penetrated the eastern Fezzan. Their progress was only halted on the orders of the Caliph Omar to leave 'the distant and treacherous far west' alone. Constantinople, preoccupied with the Arab threat nearer home, had made no effort to prevent the losses in Africa.

These were the circumstances in which the exarch Gregory declared his independence from Constantinople. He appears to have had no difficulty in keeping the loyalty of the tribal chieftains, and in order to prepare the defence of the province he moved his capital from Carthage to Sufetula (Sbeïtla). The expected attack was not long in coming. The Caliph Omar had died in AD 644, and in AD 647 his successor, Othman, authorized the governor of Egypt, Abdallah ibn Saad, to invade the Maghreb. The subsequent annihilation of Gregory's army and the Berber reinforcements at the hands of an Arab force, perhaps only twenty thousand strong, sent a shudder of fear round the Empire; the defeat was reported even by obscure local chroniclers in Gaul and Spain.

Gregory died with the courage of despair in the defence of Sufetula, and the warrior who killed him received the honour, it was said, of taking the good news back to Medina. Legend had it that Gregory's daughter fought at his side, and that her hand in marriage had been promised by her father to whoever killed Abdallah ibn Saad, and by the latter to whoever killed her father. But she did not live to be humiliated by her enemies. She committed suicide by throwing herself off the camel on which she was being carried away captive.

The survivors retired to the fortified towns and fortresses of their second line of defence, leaving Sufetula and southern Byzacena to the Arabs. But like the Vandals, the Arabs had no inclination for siege warfare, and prepared to ride back to Egypt with their considerable booty. It had been an exceptionally profitable long-distance raid. It was made more so by an enormous bribe which the frightened Byzantine administration offered the Arabs in return for their departure. No one knows how much was paid, save that the amount astonished the invaders and gave them a very good idea of the possible wealth of the Maghreb.

The tale was told of a significant exchange between the Arab general and a party of Africans: 'Seeing the coins put in front of him, Abdallah ibn Saad asked the Africans where their money came from. One of them looked about him, as if he were searching for something; then, having found an olive, he brought it to Abdallah. "The Greeks," (meaning the Byzantines) he said, "have no olive trees in their country, and they come to us to buy oil with this money." ' A country which commanded such an income would be worth making into a permanent conquest.

Meanwhile, a huge exodus of the inhabitants began, inspired by the fear of the invaders' imminent return. But the internal troubles of the Arab empire gave Africa fifteen years' respite, though the attempted invasion of Sicily and another, smaller, raid on Byzacena in the 650s made it quite clear that the Arabs had not forgotten the west. During this period the Emperor in Constantinople re-established his authority over his north-west African territory, but it seems to have been a pitifully restricted authority: the southern part was permanently abandoned, and the Berber chieftains became more independent than ever. As usual, money was lacking and taxation was cripplingly heavy; Arab historians record a revolt at Carthage. By the time the real struggle took place, the Byzantines had lost the initiative in the defence of north-west Africa.

A series of raids in the 660s, against which imperial reinforcements were as helpless as the Africans themselves, was a prelude to the great campaign of Okba in AD 669. With a force, it was said, of only ten thousand cavalry, Okba subdued the desert south of Tripolitania, conquered the island of Djerba, and took possession of Byzacena. This time, conquest was intended to be permanent, and to this end he founded the city of Kairouan, both as an arsenal (*kairouan* means place of arms) and, equally important, as an outpost of Islam: 'When an *imam*,' wrote En Noveiri, 'invades Africa, the inhabitants save their lives and their property by professing Islam; but as soon as the *imam* leaves the country, they revert to their pagan beliefs.[1] . . . So it is essential to found a city which can serve both as a camp and as a foothold for Islam until the end of time.'

Kairouan took five years to build, yet the Byzantines, still entrenched in their line of mountain fortresses overlooking the site from the north, made no attempt to oust the invaders. To the south, the forces – and the religion – of Islam had a free run. The surviving Christian population faced massacre or enslavement; many, no doubt, suffered forcible conversion. But Okba's most notable triumphs appear to have been among the Berber tribesmen. Representing himself as a prophet and miracle-worker, he played on their natural superstitions, and prepared the way for the mass conversion to Islam of almost the whole population of the Maghreb which was to follow in the wake of conquest.

There was an unexpected setback. It was caused partly by a truce between the Arabs and Byzantium in the Near East which released Byzantine troops for the defence of Africa, and partly by the rise of a really powerful Moorish kingdom in Mauretania under the chieftain Koseila; but mostly by Okba's own recklessness. In AD 683, confident of his strength –

---

1 The Arabs later asserted that some of the inhabitants of north-west Africa changed their religion thirteen times in all.

though not strong enough to attack the Byzantine fortresses to the north – Okba turned westward through southern Numidia and Mauretania. He intended to carry Islam to the Atlantic. In so doing, he was trespassing on the territories of the tribal chieftains, and he seriously miscalculated the strength of the opposition. There were hard-fought battles near Bagai (north-east of Timgad) and Lambaesis, and further west at Tiaret; Okba's army, though victorious, was severely mauled. Yet without a thought for his lines of communication or the hazards of the return journey, Okba pursued his course to the Atlantic. It was, indeed, a notable expedition, much celebrated in the chronicles of the Arabs; but on his way back Koseila was waiting for him, with substantial Byzantine forces at his side. Okba rode into an ambush near Thabudeos (just east of Biskra), and was killed with most of his army.

Byzantine fortress at Aïn Tounga (Thignica), in the valley of the oued Siliana near Dougga

His death meant, for the moment, the end of the Arab occupation: Kairouan was abandoned. Yet the weaknesses of Islam's enemies were not cured by their victory. The Byzantines made no attempt to re-occupy Byzacena; the great tribal alliance shortly disintegrated, as was the usual fate of tribal alliances, when Koseila died. A large part of his prestige, however, accrued to the queen of the Aurès. This remarkable woman had already taken an important part in the defeat of Okba; now she was to lead the final, unavailing resistance to the Arabs. They called her 'Al-Kahena', 'the prophetess' – which suggests the kind of authority she wielded over her people.

At the time of Hassan's invasion a decade later, in AD 695, the strongest prince in North Africa, according to En Noveiri, was 'the commander of Karthadjinna': the Byzantines had recovered some of their lost supremacy, but not enough to impress the exarch's name on their enemies – or to keep the Arabs at bay. Hassan and his forty thousand men moved straight up the coast of Byzacena and captured Carthage. Then Hassan turned against the Kahena, only to be defeated by her enormous army which had been augmented by large numbers of Christians. The news of Carthage's fall had led to the sending of an imperial army, which recaptured the city in AD 697. Defeated on two fronts, Hassan retreated to Cyrenaica.

Here African resistance to the Arab invasions was long believed to have ended: the amphitheatre at Thysdrus (El Djem)

But in AD 698 Hassan returned. This time Carthage was permanently taken. Only a few Byzantine garrisons in the old Africa Proconsularis survived; one by one they were invested and destroyed.

There remained Al-Kahena in the Aurès mountains. She summoned her fellow Africans to resistance, ready to fight to the death. Unfortunately she attempted to persuade her compatriots not only to die, but to destroy their livelihood – to burn their crops and their settlements, and to cut down their trees, so that the enemy would no longer want their country. This intransigent scorched earth policy had little appeal for people who had already suffered enough; many defected to Hassan. Somewhere between the Aurès and the sea – a dozen localities dispute the honour – the prophetess met her death after a long and bloody battle. Centuries later, the inhabitants of El Djem still firmly believed that their great Roman amphitheatre was her last citadel.

The Emperor, struggling to save face, continued to record the exarchate of Africa on the imperial lists: it consisted of Sardinia, Majorca and Minorca, a few places on the coast of Spain and, in Africa, Septem on the straits of Gibraltar. Septem, under Count Julian, outlasted the loss of Carthage by ten years. By then it had ceased to have even notional importance. Its occupation by the Arabs was mentioned only by western annalists. It was the last surviving vestige of Byzantine Africa, which in truth had expired long before.

The Emperor Justinian has been reproached with undertaking an impossibly heavy burden in attempting to resuscitate an imperial Africa well past its prime, which had been dying a long slow death under the Vandals. In fact, the province revived remarkably under the Byzantines, so much so that, although much of its new administration was Greek, north-west Africa itself remained resolutely Latin in its language, its literature and its religion; its Church attached itself more firmly than ever to the Roman half of Christendom. Both the Latin language and Christianity survived the Arab conquest, though in a necessarily tenuous form; epitaphs were inscribed in recognizable Latin in the tenth and eleventh centuries, money was minted in Latin, the inhabitants of Gafsa still spoke it in the twelfth century (according to El Idrisi). The Latin words for yoke, plough, various trees and cultivated plants and the months of the year survived, debased but recognizable, in the Berber dialects of farming communities, even beyond the Roman frontier; and if most of the population adopted Islam, Christian communities survived, here and there, until the persecutions of the twelfth century – corresponding with Rome, disputing the primacy of Carthage, going into schism until the bitter end. Rome's ghost still walked.

Yet it was doomed: the Byzantine revival could not avert the disappearance of Roman Africa. The Byzantines, however, provided the bridge which linked one civilization with another. The Arabs conquered not barbarians, but a generation of Africans who were still accustomed to the usages of civilization, to reading and writing, to building and carving, to the upkeep of water supply and extensive agriculture, to the habit of learning and to universal religion; who had not, in short, forgotten what the Romans had brought them.

The Arabs found much to admire in their new conquest: 'its continuous succession of villages, from Tripoli to Tangiers', the fertility of its fields, the magnificence of its olive groves, the splendid efficiency of its aqueducts. They, like the Vandals, were delighted to enter into the Roman inheritance. Unlike the Vandals, they brought gifts of their own. Under them, Africa was to flourish anew, but not in the Roman way.

Appendix of Site Plans

This Appendix of site plans has been derived from a number of sources. The publishers are particularly grateful to the following for making available copyright material as reference:

Swan Hellenic Cruises (Carthage, Dougga, Thuburbo Maius, Sabratha)

Pneu Michelin (Volubilis)

North Carolina Press (Volubilis)

Philippe Leveau and J.L. Paillet (Volubilis)

Librairie Hachette (Caesarea/Cherchel)

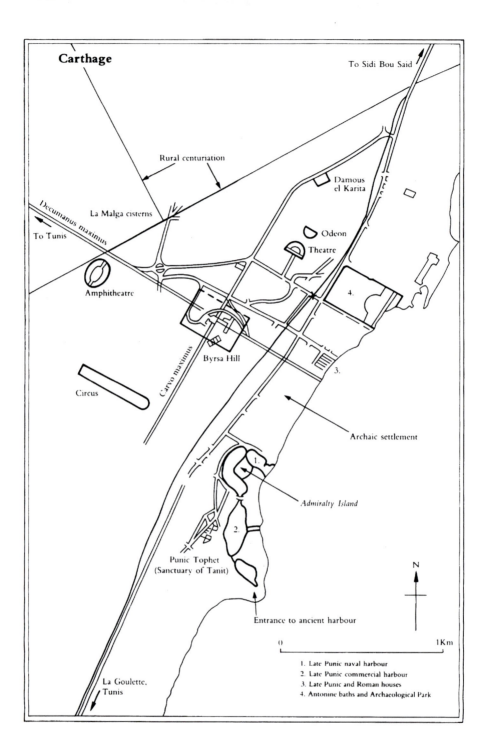

Carthage

To Sidi Bou Said

Rural centuriation

Damous
el Karita

Decumanus maximus

La Malga cisterns

To Tunis

Odeon

Theatre

Amphitheatre

4.

Cardo maximus

Byrsa Hill

3.

Circus

Archaic settlement

1.

Admiralty Island

2.

Punic Tophet
(Sanctuary of Tanit)

Entrance to ancient harbour

N

La Goulette.
Tunis

0   1 Km

1. Late Punic naval harbour
2. Late Punic commercial harbour
3. Late Punic and Roman houses
4. Antonine baths and Archaeological Park

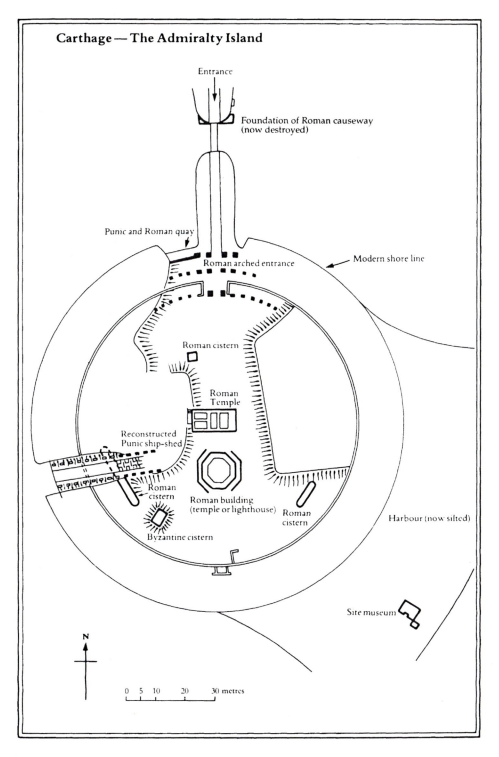

Carthage — The Admiralty Island

Entrance

Foundation of Roman causeway
(now destroyed)

Punic and Roman quay

Roman arched entrance

Modern shore line

Roman cistern

Roman
Temple

Reconstructed
Punic ship-shed

Roman
cistern

Roman building
(temple or lighthouse)

Roman
cistern

Byzantine cistern

Harbour (now silted)

Site museum

N

0 5 10   20   30 metres

233

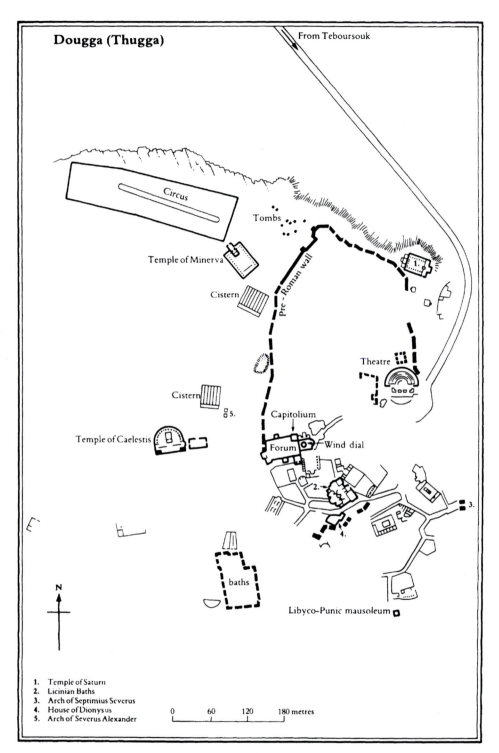

Dougga (Thugga)

From Teboursouk

Circus

Tombs

Temple of Minerva

Cistern

Pre – Roman wall

1.

Theatre

Cistern

5.

Capitolium

Temple of Caelestis

Forum

Wind dial

2.

3.

4.

N

baths

Libyco–Punic mausoleum

1. Temple of Saturn
2. Licinian Baths
3. Arch of Septimius Severus
4. House of Dionysus
5. Arch of Severus Alexander

0   60   120   180 metres

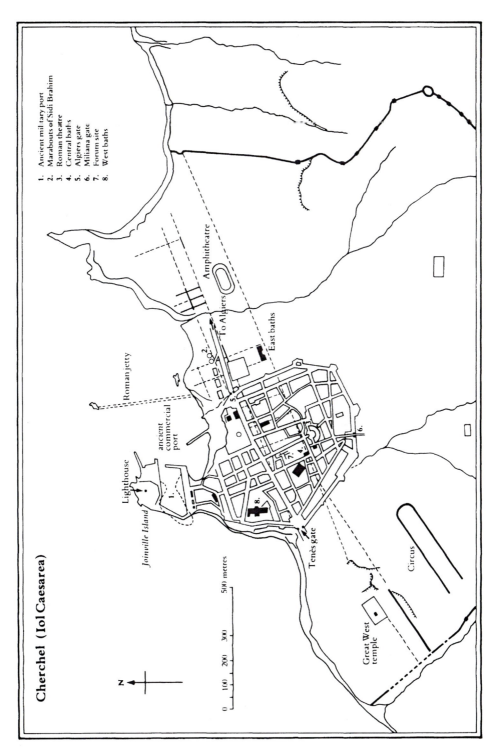

Cherchel (Iol Caesarea)

1. Ancient military port
2. Marabouts of Sidi Brahim
3. Roman theatre
4. Central baths
5. Algiers gate
6. Miliana gate
7. Forum site
8. West baths

Lighthouse

Joinville Island

Roman jetty

ancient commercial port

Amphitheatre

To Algiers

East baths

Tenès gate

Great West temple

Circus

N

0 100 200 300 500 metres

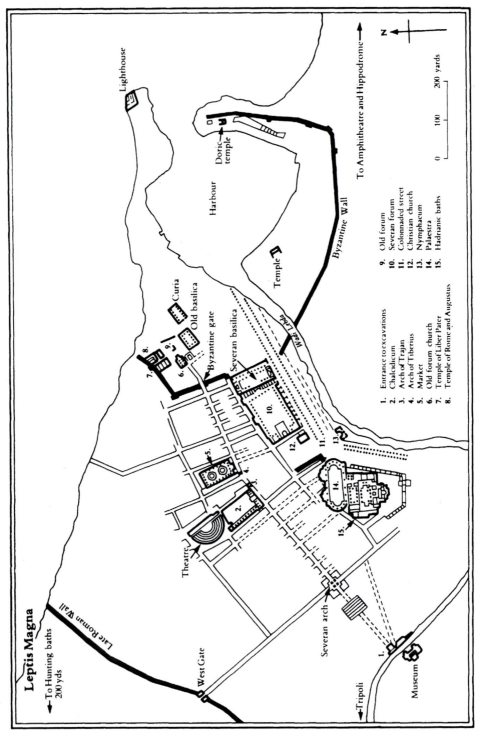

Leptis Magna

→ To Hunting baths
200 yds

Late Roman Wall

West Gate

Theatre

Curia

Old basilica

Byzantine gate

Severan basilica

Severan arch

Museum

→ Tripoli

Harbour

Lighthouse

Doric temple

Temple II

Byzantine Wall

Wadi Lebda

N

0   100   200 yards

To Amphitheatre and Hippodrome

1. Entrance to excavations
2. Chalcidicum
3. Arch of Trajan
4. Arch of Tiberius
5. Market
6. Old forum church
7. Temple of Liber Pater
8. Temple of Rome and Augustus
9. Old forum
10. Severan forum
11. Colonnaded street
12. Christian church
13. Nymphaeum
14. Palaestra
15. Hadrianic baths

236

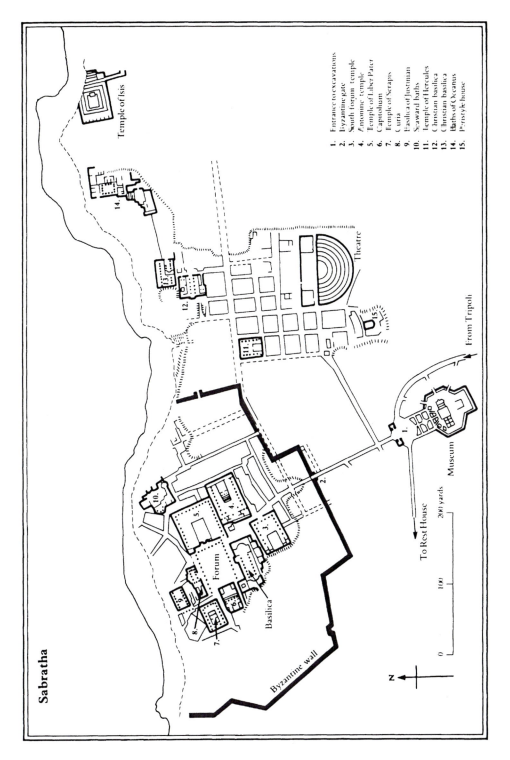

Sabratha

1. Entrance to excavations
2. Byzantine gate
3. South forum temple
4. Antonine temple
5. Temple of Liber Pater
6. Capitolium
7. Temple of Serapis
8. Curia
9. Basilica of Justinian
10. Seaward baths
11. Temple of Hercules
12. Christian basilica
13. Christian basilica
14. Baths of Oceanus
15. Peristyle-house

Temple of Isis

Theatre

From Tripoli

To Rest House

Museum

Forum

Basilica

Byzantine wall

N

0   100   200 yards

237

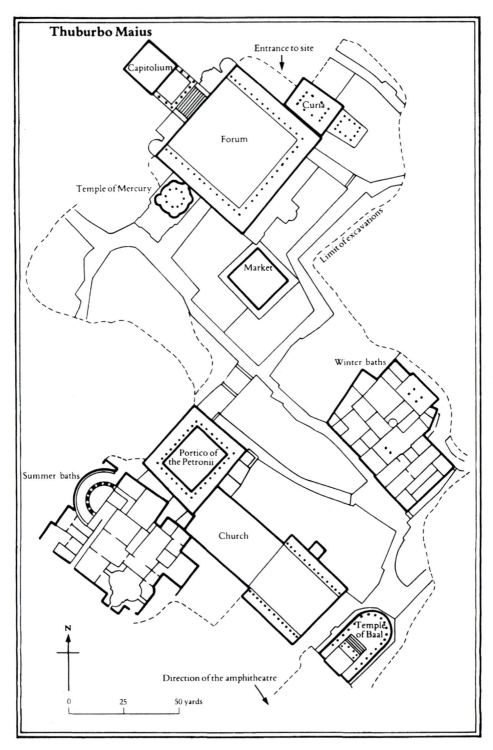

Thuburbo Maius

Capitolium

Entrance to site

Curia

Forum

Temple of Mercury

Limit of excavations

Market

Winter baths

Portico of the Petronii

Summer baths

Church

Temple of Baal

N

Direction of the amphitheatre

0   25   50 yards

Tipasa

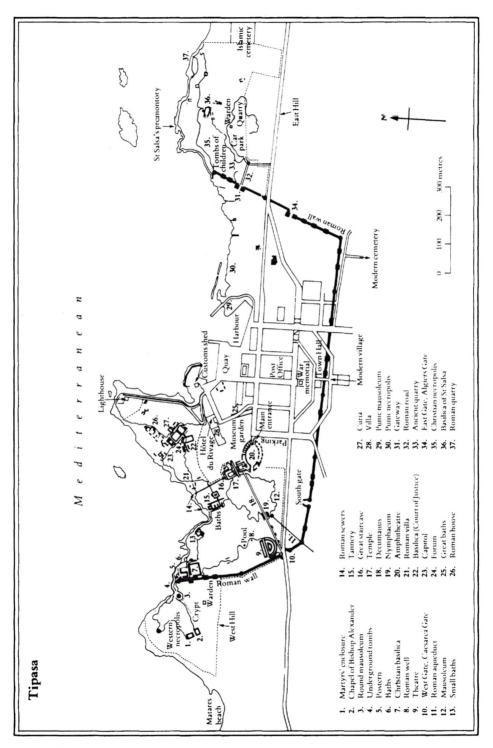

1. Martyrs' enclosure
2. Chapel of Bishop Alexander
3. Round mausoleum
4. Underground tombs
5. Postern
6. Baths
7. Christian basilica
8. Roman well
9. Theatre
10. West Gate, Caesarea Gate
11. Roman aqueduct
12. Mausoleum
13. Small baths
14. Roman sewers
15. Tannery
16. Great staircase
17. Temple
18. Decumanus
19. Nymphaeum
20. Amphitheatre
21. Roman villa
22. Basilica (Court of Justice)
23. Capitol
24. Forum
25. Great baths
26. Roman house
27. Curia
28. Villa
29. Punic mausoleum
30. Punic necropolis
31. Gateway
32. Roman road
33. Ancient quarry
34. East Gate, Algiers Gate
35. Christian necropolis
36. Basilica of St Salsa
37. Roman quarry

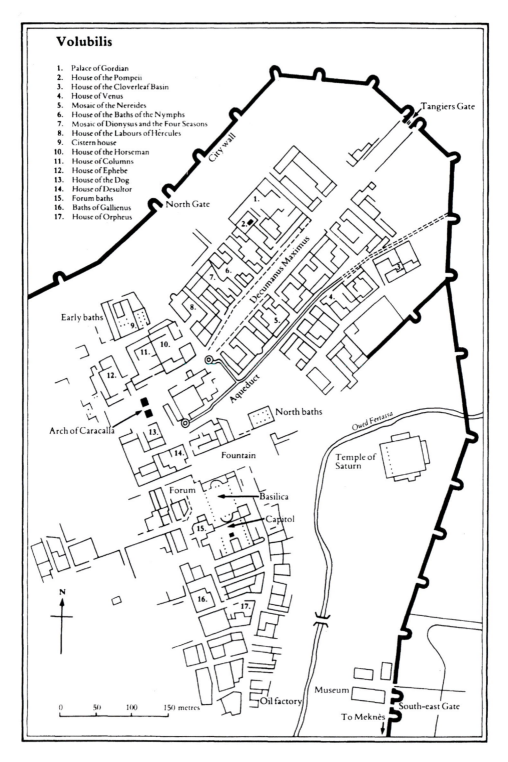

Volubilis

1. Palace of Gordian
2. House of the Pompeii
3. House of the Cloverleaf Basin
4. House of Venus
5. Mosaic of the Nereides
6. House of the Baths of the Nymphs
7. Mosaic of Dionysus and the Four Seasons
8. House of the Labours of Hercules
9. Cistern house
10. House of the Horseman
11. House of Columns
12. House of Ephebe
13. House of the Dog
14. House of Desultor
15. Forum baths
16. Baths of Gallienus
17. House of Orpheus

Tangiers Gate

City wall

North Gate

Decumanus Maximus

Early baths

Aqueduct

North baths

Arch of Caracalla

Oued Fertassa

Fountain

Temple of Saturn

Forum

Basilica

Capitol

N

0   50   100   150 metres

Oil factory

Museum

South-east Gate

To Meknès

BIBLIOGRAPHY

ALBERTINI, Eugène, *L'Afrique romaine*, Algiers, 1932.

AUDOLLENT, Auguste, *Carthage romaine, 146 avant Jésus-Christ – 698 après Jésus-Christ*, Paris, 1901.

BARADEZ, Jean, *Fossatum Africae*, Paris, 1949.

BARKER, G.W.W. and JONES, G.D.B., 'The UNESCO Libyan Valleys Survey III, Palaeoeconomy and Environmental Archaeology in the Pre-desert', *Libyan Studies* 13, 1982.

BARKER, G.W.W., GILBERTSON, D., JONES, G.D.B. and MATTINGLY, D., *Farming the Desert: The UNESCO Libyan Valleys Archaeological Survey*, Vols I and II, Tripoli, 1996 (available from the Society for Libyan Studies, London).

BARNES, T.D., *Tertullian, A Historical and Literary Study*, Oxford, 1971, reissued with corrections and postscript, 1985.

BARTON, I.M., *Africa in the Roman Empire*, Accra, 1972.

BÉNABOU, Marcel, *La résistance africaine à la romanisation*, Paris, 1975.

BIRLEY, Anthony, *Septimius Severus: the African Emperor*, London, 1971, 2nd edition, 1988.

BIRLEY, Anthony, 'Some Notes on the Donatist Schism', *Libyan Studies* 18, 1987.

BLANCHARD, Michele, SLIM, Hedi, SLIM, Latifa and ENNAFER, Mongi, *Roman Mosaics of Tunisia*, London, 1996.

BONNER, Gerald, *St Augustine of Hippo: Life and Controversies*, revised edition Norwich, 1986.

BRETT, M. and FENTRESS, E., *The Berbers*, Oxford, 1996.

BROUGHTON, T.R.S., *The Romanisation of Africa Proconsularis*, Baltimore, 1929, reprint New York, 1968.

BROWN, Peter, *Augustine of Hippo*, London, 1967.

BROWN, Peter, *Religion and Society in the Age of St Augustine*, London, 1972.

BROWN, Shelby, *Late Carthaginian Child Sacrifice and Sacrificial Monuments in their Mediterranean Context*, Sheffield, 1991.

BULLIET, Richard, *The Camel and the Wheel*, Cambridge, Mass., 1975.

Cambridge History of Africa, Volume II, Cambridge, 1975.

CAMPS, Gabriel, 'Massinissa ou les débuts de l'histoire', *Libyca* VIII (i), 1960.

CAMPS, Gabriel, *Berbères: aux marges de l'histoire*, Paris, 1980.

CAPUTO, G., and CAFFARELLI, V., *The Buried City: Excavations of Leptis Magna*, London, 1966.

CARY, M., and WARMINGTON, B.H., *The Ancient Explorers*, London, 1929, revised edition, 1963.

CHARLES-PICARD, Gilbert, *La civilisation de l'Afrique romaine*, Paris, 1959.

CHARLES-PICARD, Gilbert, *Le monde de Carthage*, Paris, 1956, trans. as *Carthage* by Gilbert Picard, London, 1964.

241

CHARLES-PICARD, Gilbert and Colette, *La vie quotidienne à Carthage au temps d'Hannibal*, Paris, 1958, trans. as *Daily Life in Carthage at the Time of Hannibal*, London, 1961.

COURTOIS, C., LESCHI, L., PERRAT, C.H. and SAUMAGNE, C.H., *Les Tablettes Albertini*, Paris, 1952.

COURTOIS, Christian, *Les Vandales et l'Afrique*, Paris, 1955.

DANIELS, Charles, *The Garamantes of Southern Libya*, Cambridge, 1970.

DANIELS, Charles, 'The Frontiers: Africa', in *The Roman World*, edited by John Wacher, London, 1987.

DANIELS, Charles, 'Excavation and fieldwork among the Garamantes', *Libyan Studies* 20, 1989.

DIEHL, Charles, *L'Afrique byzantine*, Paris, 1896.

DUNBABIN, Katherine M.D., *The Mosaics of Roman North Africa*, Oxford, 1978.

ENNABLI, A. (ed.), *Pour sauver Carthage: exploration et conservation de la cité punique, romaine et byzantine*, Paris and Tunis, 1992.

FENTRESS, Elizabeth W.B., *Numidia and the Roman Army*, British Archaeological Reports International Series 53, Oxford, 1979.

FÉVRIER, Paul-Albert, *Approches du Maghreb romaine*, 2 vols, Aix-en-Provence, 1989, 1990.

FÉVRIER, Paul-Albert, *Art de l'Algérie antique*, Paris, 1971.

FREND, W.H.C., *The Rise of Christianity*, London, 1984.

FREND, W.H.C., *The Donatist Church: a movement of protest in Roman North Africa*, Oxford, 1952, 3rd impression, 1985.

FREND, W.H.C., *The Archaeology of Early Christianity*, London, 1996.

GAUTIER, E., *Le passé de l'Afrique du Nord: les siècles obscurs*, Paris, 1937.

GSELL, Stéphane, *Histoire ancienne de l'Afrique du Nord*, 8 vols, Paris, 1913–28.

HAMMAN, A.-G., *La vie quotidienne en Afrique du Nord au temps de Saint Augustin*, revised edition Paris, 1985.

HARDEN, Donald, *The Phoenicians*, London, 1962.

HAYNES, D.E.L., *Antiquities of Tripolitania*, Antiquities Department of Tripolitania, Libya, 1956.

HORN, Heinz Gunter, and RÜGER, Christoph B., *Die Numider: Reiter und Könige nördlich der Sahara*, Köln-Bonn, 1979.

HURST, Henry, 'Carthage: the Punic city', in *Origins*, edited by Barry Cunliffe, London, 1987.

JONES, A.H.M., *Constantine and the Conversion of Europe*, London, 1948.

JONES, A.H.M., *The Later Roman Empire*, 3 vols, Oxford, 1964, also published in 2 vols, Oklahoma City, 1964.

JOUFFROY, Hélène, *La construction publique en Italie et dans l'Afrique romaine*, Strasbourg, 1986.

JULIEN, Charles-André, *Histoire de l'Afrique du Nord*, Volume I, *Des origines à la conquête arabe*, Paris, 1931, second edition revised and edited by Christian Courtois, Paris, 1951.

KEHOE, Dennis P., *The Economics of Agriculture on Roman Imperial Estates in North Africa*, Göttingen, 1988.

LANCEL, Serge, *Carthage, A History*, trans. Antonia Nevill, Oxford, 1995.

LASSÈRE, Jean-Marie, *Ubique populus: peuplement et mouvements de population dans l'Afrique romaine de la chute de Carthage à la fin de la dynastie des Sévères (146 a.C.–235 p.C)*, Paris, 1977.

LE BOHEC, Yann, *La Troisième Légion Auguste*, Paris, 1989.

LEPELLEY, Claude, *Les cités de l'Afrique romaine au bas empire*, Paris, 1979.

LEVEAU, Philippe, *Caesarea de Maurétanie: une ville romaine et ses campagnes*, Rome, 1984.

MCBURNEY, C.B.M., *The Stone Age of Northern Africa*, London, 1960.

MACKENDRICK, Paul, *The North African Stones Speak*, London and Chapel Hill, NC, 1980.

MACMULLEN, Ramsay, *Changes in the Roman Empire: Essays in the Ordinary*, Princeton, NJ, 1990.

MANTON, E. Lennox, *Roman North Africa*, London, 1988.

MATTINGLY, D.J., *Roman Tripolitania*, London, 1995.

MUSURILLO, Herbert, *The Acts of the Christian Martyrs*, Oxford, 1972.

OWEN, E.C.E., *Some Authentic Acts of the Early Martyrs*, Oxford, 1927.

PEDLEY, John Griffiths (ed.), *New Light on Ancient Carthage*, Ann Arbor, 1980.

POTTER, T.W., *Towns in Late Antiquity: Iol Caesarea and Its Context*, Oxford, 1995.

PRINGLE, Denys, *The Defence of Byzantine Africa from Justinian to the Arab Conquest*, British Archaeological Reports International Series 99, i and ii, Oxford, 1982.

PROCTOR, Dennis, *Hannibal's March in History*, Oxford, 1971.

SAGE, M.M., *Cyprian*, Cambridge, Mass., 1975.

SHAW, Brent, *Environment and Society in Roman North Africa*, Aldershot, 1995.

SHAW, Brent, *Rulers, Nomads and Christians in Roman North Africa*, Aldershot, 1995.

SOREN, David, BEN ABED BEN KHADER, Aicha, and SLIM, Hedi, *Carthage: Uncovering the Mysteries and Splendours of Ancient Tunisia*, New York and London, 1990.

TLATLI, Salah-Eddine, *La Carthage punique: étude urbaine*, Paris, 1978.

WARD-PERKINS, J.B., *Roman Imperial Architecture*, London, 1981.

WARMINGTON, B.H., *Carthage*, London, 1960.

WARMINGTON, B.H., *The North African Provinces from Diocletian to the Vandal Conquest*, Cambridge, 1954.

WELLS, Colin, *The Roman Empire*, London and Stanford, Calif., 1984.

WELLS, C.M. (ed.), *L'Afrique romaine/Roman Africa: Les Conférences Vanier/The Vanier Lectures 1980*, Ottawa, 1982.

WEST, Rebecca, *St Augustine*, London, 1933.

WHEELER, Sir Mortimer, and WOOD, Roger, *Roman Africa in Colour*, London, 1966.

WHITTAKER, C.R., 'Land and Labour in North Africa', *Klio* lx, Berlin, 1978.

A much fuller bibliography can be found in David J. Mattingly and R. Bruce Hitchner, 'Roman Africa: An Archaeological Review', *The Journal of Roman Studies* 85, 1995, pp. 165–213.

ANCIENT SOURCES

Ancient historians referred to or quoted from in the text are available in translation in Penguin paperback and/or the Loeb Classical Library. Apuleius' *The Golden Ass* and St Augustine's *Confessions* are also available in Penguin. *The Decline and Fall of the Roman Empire*, by Edward Gibbon, was published between 1776 and 1788; an abridged version was published by Penguin in 1963.

MODERN AND ANCIENT PLACE NAMES

Annaba, Bône   Hippo Regius
Announa   Thibilis
Besseriani   Ad Majores
Biskra   Vescera
Bizerta   Hippo Diarrhytus
Bou Grara   Gigthis
Bougie   Saldae
Cartagena   Kart Hadasht (New Carthage)
Ceuta   Septem
Chad, Lake   Agisymba (?)
Chemtou   Simitthu
Cherchel   Iol Caesarea – Caesarea
Chullu   Collo
Constantine   Cirta
Djemila   Cuicul
Dougga   Thugga
El Djem   Thysdrus
El Kasbat   Gemellae
El Kef   Sicca Veneria
El Khadra   Oppidum Novum
El Kherba   Tigava
Essaouira   Mogador
Fériana   Thelepte
Gabès   Tacapae
Gafsa   Capsa
Germa   Garama
Ghadames   Cydamae
Guelma   Calama
Haïdra   Ammaedara
Jijil, Djiljelli   Igilgili
Kasserine   Cillium
Khémissa   Thubursicu Numidarum
Korba   Corubis
Lemta   Leptis Minor
Medjerda river   Bagradas river
Messaad   Castellum Dimmidi
Oudna   Uthina
Philippeville   Rusicade
Ras Botria   Acholla
Ras Salakta   Sullectum
Sbeïtla   Sufetula
Sétif   Sitifis
Souk El Ghoziane   Auzia
Sousse   Hadrumetum
Tabarka   Thabraca
Tangiers   Tingis
Tébessa   Theveste
Tebourba   Thuburbo Minor
Ténès   Cartennas
Timgad   Thamugadi
Tripoli   Oea

244

INDEX

For locations in NW Africa the ancient names are used; modern names are shown on page 244. Reference to a footnote is shown by 'n'. Illustrations are not indexed; a list is given on pages x–xii.

Printed in the United States
119919LV00001B/1-39/A